OTHER BOOKS BY JENNIFER JILL SCHWIRZER

Dying to Be Beautiful

Finding My Way in Milwaukee

A Deep but Dazzling Darkness: Exploring God's "Dark Side" in the Light of His Love

(with Leslie Kay)

I Want It All

A Most Precious Message: My Personal Discovery of Liberating Joy in the Gospel of Jesus

Testimony of a Seeker: A Young Woman's Journey to Grace

13 Weeks to Peace

*Allowing Jesus to
Heal Your Heart
and Mind*

JENNIFER JILL SCHWIRZER

Pacific Press® Publishing Association
Nampa, Idaho
Oshawa, Ontario, Canada
www.pacificpress.com

Cover design by Steve Lanto

Cover illustration resources from dreamstime.com

Inside design by Michelle C. Petz

Unless otherwise noted, all scriptures quoted are from The New King James Version, copyright © 1979, 1980, 1982, Thomas Nelson, Inc., Publishers.

Scripture quotations marked ESV are from The Holy Bible, English Standard Version® (ESV®), copyright © 2001 by Crossway, a publishing ministry of Good News Publishers. Used by permission. All rights reserved.

Scripture quotations marked NASB are from *The New American Standard Bible*®, Copyright © 1960, 1962, 1963, 1968, 1971, 1972, 1973, 1975, 1977, 1995 by The Lockman Foundation. Used by permission.

Scripture quotations marked NIV are from the HOLY BIBLE, NEW INTERNATIONAL VERSION®. Copyright © 1973, 1978, 1984 by International Bible Society. Used by permission of Zondervan Publishing House. All rights reserved.

Scripture quotations marked KJV are from the King James Version of the Bible.

Additional copies of this book are available by calling toll-free 1-800-765-6955 or by visiting http://www.adventistbookcenter.com.

The author assumes full responsibility for the accuracy of all facts and quotations as cited in this book.

Library of Congress Cataloging-in-Publication Data
Schwirzer, Jennifer Jill, 1957-
13 weeks to peace : allowing Jesus to heal your heart and mind / Jennifer Jill Schwirzer.
    p. cm.
Includes bibliographical references.
ISBN-13: 978-0-8163-2494-1 (pbk.)
ISBN-10: 0-8163-2494-8 (pbk.)
1. Christianity—Psychology—Textbooks 2. Counseling—Religious aspects—Christianity. I. Title. II. Title: Thirteen weeks to peace.
BR110.S365 2011
253.5—dc22

2011007739

11 12 13 14 15 • 5 4 3 2 1

Dedication

I dedicate this book to the people who walk through my door seeking for peace within. Your honesty and courage inspire me.

I wish to thank:

Michael Schwirzer for loving a nerd (me).

Pat Arrabito for being an unfailing friend and a counselor's counselor.

Tara VinCross for her beaming countenance and for "getting" me.

Kristin McGuire for a predictable-but-ever-fresh good character.

Kimmy Schwirzer for proof that people can change and for making me laugh.

Alison Schwirzer for singing constantly.

Nancy Adams for encouraging my ambitions and helping me fulfill them.

Cindy Calcagno for pushing for biblical psychology.

My church family in Chestnut Hill, Philadelphia, for a weekly dose of joy.

Jill Wilson for her generosity and motherly pride.

All the seminar attendees over the years who wanted this book to exist.

The illustrations in this book represent true stories.
The details have been changed to protect the privacy of the individuals involved.

Contents

Introduction

After twenty years of teaching on the subject of biblical inner healing, I'm just now writing this book. I'm passionate about the subject and have spoken at countless churches, retreats, schools, and conferences all over the world. Several years ago, I "made it official" by obtaining a master's degree in mental health, a state license, and a private practice in counseling.

What I've shared over the past twenty years is now packaged in this book for a three-month healing journey to be used either by an individual or a group. Ideally, it works like this: Read one chapter a week during your devotional time, complete all the assigned worksheets, and answer the thought questions at the end of the chapters. Then, after you have finished reading the book and gained a blessing, gather a group of people and form a small group. Have each group member obtain a copy of the book and work through the book again. Meet each week and use the discussion questions as the basis for sharing. You, being the "graduate" of the group, should facilitate. Then each "graduate" of your group should start a new group, and the wave of healing will continue until Jesus comes.

I believe if you do this, you'll see positive fruit. I'm not bragging about my book because the book conveys the truths of God's Word. True, it does so imperfectly. I'm admittedly a weak vessel. But He works through such things, doesn't He? Take this book and use it. Decades of my experience and, more important, an eternity of God's wisdom fill its pages.

Purpose Is Everything

Raul had always been uncannily close to perfect. In spite of his parents' divorce and a difficult childhood, he thrived academically, making his family proud when he attended Johns Hopkins University on a scholarship. He specialized in otolaryngology, with a concentration in facial reconstruction. A high achiever religiously as well, Raul trained as a lay pastor and planted a church. As far as the dazzled onlookers were concerned, this exemplary young man painted a picture of leadership, poise, and spirituality. Then, at the height of his professional success and youthful drive, he proceeded to have a breakdown that forced him into a medical leave from the hospital; he spent days languishing in his bed, and finally booked an appointment with me.

In spite of his acute condition, sessions with Raul unfolded almost effortlessly. At times, I felt like saying, "You know, I really should be paying *you*." We discovered that Raul questioned his life's purpose. Although the occasional burn victim or deviated septum gave him the chance to use his training altruistically, most of his patients were models and socialites striving for the perfect face. He hated that his skills fed the vanity and excesses of the rich. As we talked, Raul discovered his disdain for the narcissism of both the patients and the physicians he saw on a daily basis.

Then, in the midst of the rubble of his crumbling "perfect" career, a tiny seed of new purpose began to grow. Raul resolved to use his training in facial reconstruction in third-world countries. He laid plans for a nonprofit corporation that would airlift victims of facial trauma to his hospital, where he would perform their surgeries. He envisioned eventually relocating to a developing country; founding a charity called "Save Face"; and living out his life in the obscure places of the world, ministering to broken, marginalized people. As these dreams and plans developed, Raul transitioned out of depression as naturally as one wakes from sleep.

Purpose is everything.

For a worksheet on finding your life's purpose, see "God's Plan Life Purpose" in the toolbox.

Any good theory of psychology must answer three questions:

1. What is our ideal state?
2. How have we deviated from it?
3. How are we brought back to the ideal?

These questions could be summarized in three words: (1) purpose, (2) problem, and (3) solution.

I'll address the first question, our purpose, in this chapter, and the second question, our problem, in the next. I'll spend the rest of the book exploring the glorious answer to the third. I want to dwell most heavily upon Jesus, our blessed Solution.

A sense of purpose can determine whether someone keeps his sanity or loses it. Friedrich Nietzsche said, "He who has a why to live for can bear with almost any how."[1] Embattled soldiers, outnumbered revolutionaries, and persecuted believers all testify that a firm purpose braces the human spirit against the odds. Conversely, purposelessness makes us into wet noodles. As the scent of a lost child on a path keeps rescue dogs on the trail, purpose motivates us and guides us through the tangled dark forest of life.

We function properly when we respect the Designer's specifications. If I use my husband's electric shaver to mow the lawn, it will soon break down. Using a blow-dryer as a bathtub toy will harm everyone involved and destroy the blow-dryer. Likewise, if we attempt to live at cross-purposes with our Creator, damage ensues. As we search for a specific life purpose, it then becomes essential to know the Designer's objective in bringing us into existence. What was God thinking when He fashioned Adam from the dust of the ground and Eve from the rib of Adam? What were His plans? What were His dreams? In short, what is our *raison d'être,* humanity's God-given purpose in life?

In order to answer these questions, let's observe the historical context of planet Earth. Rewind to the eons of time before the creation of humankind. Lucifer, God's "anointed cherub" who walked "on the holy mountain of God" fell into sin. Perhaps the word *fell,* with its descending motion, isn't the best description of Lucifer's sin—for his heart was "lifted up" (Ezekiel 28:14, 17). Selected phrases from his speech recorded in Isaiah 14 reveal a brooding megalomaniac: "I will ascend . . . I will exalt . . . I will also sit on the mount of the congregation . . . I will ascend . . . I will be like the Most High" (verses 13, 14). These words drip with narcissism. Lucifer wanted nothing less than God's throne.

Obsessed with this unholy purpose, Lucifer propagandized heaven, projecting his own tyrannical character onto God through sophistry and political sleight of hand. He succeeded in seducing a sizable portion of heaven's electorate. "There was war in heaven" (Revelation 12:7, NASB). John's revelation features a dragon swiping a third of heaven's stars to the earth, symbolizing this mass apostasy (see verses 3, 4). We don't know how many years passed while this struggle wore on. We do know that planet Earth inherited the fallout in the form of this fallen angel, "called the Devil and Satan" (verse 9).

Imagine heaven, post Lucifer. The smoke of battle still hangs in the hallowed air. Buried deep in God's heart is unspeakable pain and loss; yet He has no time to nurse the wounds, for the exigencies of war demand immediate action. He's been accused of power mongering, of maintaining supremacy for its own sake. He knows that the very existence of the universe hangs on His governance, but even this can't compel Him to use force to tame the political landscape. He must win back estranged and doubting hearts. Only the worship of love will do. Piecing together the pre-earth story, we see that God created humankind in response to this emergency, with a very important purpose in mind.

According to Genesis, the "book of beginnings," which is the interpretive key for the rest of Scripture, God determined that He would create a uniquely Godlike order of beings. He would form the human race, stand back, and say, "Look at them, and you'll see Me." And so, "God created man in His own image . . . male and female He created them" (Genesis 1:27). The word image is translated from the Hebrew *tselem* and means "a representative figure."

This theme weaves itself throughout the Bible. For instance, Isaiah 43:6, 7 says, "Bring My sons from afar, and My daughters from the ends of the earth—everyone who is called by *My name, whom I created for My glory*" (emphasis added). Made in God's image, called by His name, created for His glory—these are purpose statements. Image, glory, and name all allude to the more contemporary word *character.* The only hint of the word *character* in the Bible is the Greek *charakter,* translated in Hebrews 1:3, "the express image of his person," speaking of Jesus reflecting the character of God (KJV). But the *concept* of character, and specifically humanity's call to reflect the character of God, saturates Scripture. God clearly created us to showcase, manifest, display, exhibit—to *reveal* His character; *character* is defined as "main or essential nature especially as strongly marked and serving to distinguish."[2] The essence, or character, of a being pervades and permeates that being. It also defines that being. It is the inner life of that being, flowing out expressively through actions the way perfume flows from a rose. Ellen White wrote, "Thoughts and feelings combined make up the moral character."[3]

In his letter to Ephesus, Paul speaks of "the mystery which for ages has been hidden in God who created all things; so that the manifold wisdom of God might now be made known through the church to the rulers and the authorities in the heavenly places" (Ephesians 3:9, 10, NASB). Scrutinizing his words carefully, we notice that the wisdom of God is made known *through* the church *to* the powers in heaven. In other words, heaven learns from earthlings—church members, no less! Holy, perfect, heavenly angels are watching sinful, flawed humans for a knowledge of God's love.

Try as we might, we can't fool them. Character amounts to much more than mere outward actions. Character is "who you are in the dark." The Lord said to the prophet Samuel, who was examining the sons of Jesse to anoint one to be the future king of Israel: "Man looks at the outward appearance, but the Lord looks at the heart" (1 Samuel 16:7). We could paraphrase this as "people see the actions, but God sees the character."

When traveling in the South, I was bitten by chiggers. Being a Yankee, I'd never felt anything like those huge, hot, itchy bites. Someone told me to try peppermint essence, and praise Jesus, it worked. The incident made me think about how our character essence must be pressed out like peppermint essence. Only pressure could squeeze from those leaves the healing extract that soothed my itchy skin.

Character has been likened to a soup tureen carried on a waiter's head, which spills out only when the waiter is tripped, or rats in the basement are only seen when the basement is entered suddenly. Self-conscious restraint for the purpose of human approval can drive us to act well, but the shocks, accidents, pressures, and pains of life reveal our characters. The word *hypocrisy,* from the Greek *hypokrisis* means "playacting." Very clever actors convince their audiences, but let the theater catch fire and the façades disappear. The inner life comes spilling out.

To a degree, we're all acting. As a teenager, I attended wilderness camps and spent many hours surviving rough conditions. On one particular trip the tent leaked. When it poured rain, several of us had to beg to be let into other people's tents! Cold, wet, hungry at times, portaging canoes, and carrying heavy backpacks, we strained every fiber of our bodies, returning to base camp exhausted. All our worst traits of character had long before spilled out. But this was a good thing. God desires authenticity. He wants us to know ourselves. When convinced of our depravity, we learn to depend upon Him.

Think about the loftiness of our purpose. If we were created to be like God in character, and if thoughts and feelings make up the moral character, then we're called to *think* like God and *feel* like God. Merely acting like God won't fulfill His purpose for us. We were created to have inner lives like the inner life of God! This is amazing! Perhaps "in His image" alludes to certain physical features. Perhaps our eyelashes, noses, and fingers are somehow more like God's than the inhabitants of other planets. But much more, our inner lives are uniquely fashioned in the shape of God's psyche, with the capacity for divine love, kindness, compassion, and all the qualities that comprise His goodness.

With this in mind, let's visualize the inner lives of human beings. We'll see which capacities God created in human beings, and see how those capacities find their highest use.

For more information on physical wellness, see "The Eight Doctors" in the toolbox.

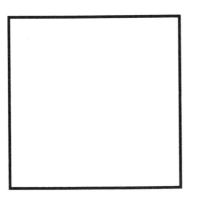

First of all, we might draw a large square to represent the body, the "house we live in." Human nature is integrated, meaning that the parts interrelate and coordinate into the whole. The human mind exists in the context of a physical organ—the brain. The brain exists in the context of the body. Incidentally, this fact provides a compelling reason to care for our bodies: they house our characters, which are to reflect God's character.

A circle within the square represents the mind—the thoughts and feelings mentioned previously. The two bear an intimate relationship to one another (the

mind-body relationship is further developed later
in this book). Here we find the imagination, drives,
desires, appetites, passions, tastes, affections, and the
complex range of emotions that we humans experience.
This might be called the soul. The Greek word
translated as "soul" is *psuche,* as in our word *psyche*. It
simply means "the immaterial part of human beings."

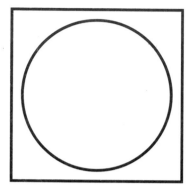

Finally, a triangle in the center of the circle
represents something that places human beings in
contradistinction to all other animals—the spirit, or
the spiritual aspect of human nature.

The spirit is the part of us that connects with the
supernatural. God created us with this unique capacity
above other animals. The spiritual impacts the soul very
intimately, for good or for evil. A connection with God
will sanctify and purify thoughts and feelings. But the
influences of "the prince of the power of the air, of the
spirit that is now working in the sons of disobedience"
(Ephesians 2:2) will taint the thoughts and emotions.

Unlike the mental or emotional aspect of human
nature, the spiritual aspect can't be accounted for in
purely naturalistic terms. In other words, there's more
to the spirit than meets the eye—even the technically
advanced "eye" of brain function imaging devices, such
as functional magnetic resonance imaging (fMRI),

*For a study of mental illness
versus demonic activity,
see "Diseases or Devils?"
in the toolbox.*

magnetoencephalography (MEG), and electroencephalogram (EEG). This doesn't mean
that the human spirit has life apart from God—quite the opposite. It simply means that
the spirit derives from a spiritual Being—God Himself—and *transcends* physical life.

The words *soul* and *spirit* each have multiple shades of nuanced, subtle meaning.
Often these meanings overlap. Perhaps Hebrews 4:12 alludes to this when it speaks of the
Word of God "piercing even to the division of soul and spirit, and of joints and marrow."
Soul and spirit, joints and marrow intertwine so closely that their untangling requires

something "sharper than any two-edged sword" (verse 12).[4] So, even though the words *soul* and *spirit* are often used interchangeably, for the sake of simplicity, we'll call the mental and emotional aspect of human nature (the circle) *soul* and the spiritual aspect (the triangle) *spirit*.

The spiritual aspect of human nature possesses four important capacities, or what are called governing powers or kingly powers. They are the (1) will, (2) reason, (3) faith, and (4) conscience. I'll give a synopsis here and expand the ideas in later chapters.

Will resides at the center of the spirit. Holocaust survivor Victor Frankl rejoiced in the gift of free will with these words: "Everything can be taken from a man but one thing: the last of the human freedoms—to choose one's attitude in any given set of circumstances, to choose one's own way."[5] The ability to choose is our most secure and valuable gift. It is through this "door" of the will that Jesus offers to enter and transform our inmost lives. Specifically, through the axis of the will, God accesses all other kingly powers of reason, faith, and conscience, enlightening and empowering them to mold to His own image. The will reigns as the king of the kingly powers.

For a more complete explanation of these subjects, see "Biblical Model of Human Nature" and "Spirit and Soul" in the toolbox.

Reason moves from cause to effect, enabling us to think sensibly, truthfully, logically, and soundly. Without reason, human beings quickly regress into infantile states, led by every whim and feeling. Reasoning, contemporarily called higher cognition, functions out of the forebrain, as do the other kingly powers.

Cognitive-behavioral therapy owes its success to the bolstering of reasoning powers. Learning to believe facts as opposed to irrational, automatic, and feeling-based thoughts, patients stabilize, sometimes to a remarkable degree. One client who had suffered a breakup with his girlfriend, cried out to me, "I'm worthless! No one will ever love me!" We were able to talk through that distorted belief and replace it with a more balanced view. He successfully transitioned out of that relationship and is thriving today, simply because he believed the truth rather than his feelings.

I wish to insert a disclaimer here: to exalt reason beyond its proper sphere, to feel that human reason is the final court of appeal on truth, is rationalism, not to mention the height of arrogance. We may stretch our reasoning powers to the breaking point, but they still fall short of grasping the fullness of Truth. Human reason is finite and unable to encompass the infinite depth and riches of God, which are "unsearchable" (Romans 11:33).

But just like our physical muscles, we stretch the "muscles" of our reasoning powers to great benefit.

Faith takes over when reason fails. We may be able to grasp certain aspects of the great truths of the Bible, but, ultimately, they are beyond our ken. Then we must come crashing down at the altar of revelation, grasping by faith the things we don't fully understand. A healthy religious experience balances faith and reason.

But even irreligious, nonreligious, and antireligious people have a God-given "measure of faith" (Romans 12:3). This faith is defined by the King James Version New Testament Greek Lexicon as "conviction of the truth of anything."[6] We all exercise faith in something; if not something true, then something false, because we are, by nature, believers. It's as if God has put one-sided Velcro on our hearts.

Conscience works like a moral meter, the needle flailing when something is wrong and resting when all is well. Leo Tolstoy said, "The antagonism between life and the conscience may be removed in two ways: by a change of life or by a change of conscience."[7] Designed to motivate us to better choices, our conscience can throb with pain in protest of wrongdoing. A mistreated conscience can develop malfunctions, becoming hypoactive or hyperactive. It can grow numb or even seared if long resisted. It can go haywire with pangs of false guilt if not carefully guided by the Spirit and molded by the Word. But a rightly informed and enlivened conscience faithfully provides moral direction and boundaries.

In our original state, these kingly powers governed all other aspects of our being. The spiritual aspect of human nature governed thoughts, feelings, and behaviors. When Adam spied a luscious fruit, he actually *thought* about whether or not to eat it. Eve's emotions aligned with reason and conscience. Passions, drives, desires, all submitted to principle. Human beings walked in dignity and elegance because God created us for self-mastery; for overflowing joy, peace, and fellowship; and for the high and holy purpose of showing the universe His true character of love.

What happened? We're turned upside down now—our physical impulses, our automatic thoughts and feelings, our instincts, appetites, and drives dominate the spiritual aspects of our being until the image of God drags in the dust. The next chapter explains the how and why of our backward, disordered state.

I remember a tense chat I had with my youngest daughter, who at about five years old, became angry and stalked off during dinner, planting herself on the couch with an ugly scowl. I walked over and began to speak softly to her, apologizing for the offense I'd caused. She stolidly refused to forgive. I began to speak of God's forgiveness, reminding her that Jesus had prayed, "Father forgive them."

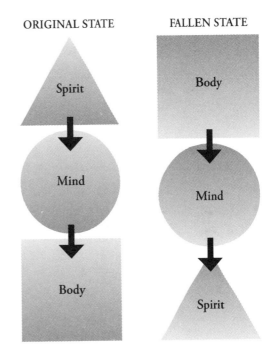

ORIGINAL STATE   FALLEN STATE

Spirit → Mind → Body

Body → Mind → Spirit

"Do you think God forgave them?" I asked.

"Yes!" she scowled.

"Do you think God forgives me?"

"Yes!"

"Then why don't you forgive me?" I asked.

She leaned toward me, her blue eyes in spiteful slits, and hissed, "I'm not God!"

No, you're not God, I thought, *but you're created in His image. You're created with the purpose of revealing Him. You've just temporarily lost sight of that fact.*

DISCUSSION QUESTIONS

1. What was God's purpose in creating human beings?

2. How does an understanding of the controversy between Christ and Satan affect your view of yourself?

3. How does it affect my view of other people?

4. What do you think it was like for God to be accused of tyranny?

5. What are some of your own personal character issues?

6. In what ways are your thoughts and feelings in harmony with God's thoughts and feelings?

7. In what way are your thoughts and feelings out of harmony with God's thoughts and feelings?

8. In what ways has the upside-down state of humanity—living by emotion and physical drives rather than reason and conscience—affected your life?

9. How has God helped you learn to use your governing powers, and how has it improved your life?

10. What insights did you gain from completing the "God's Plan Life Purpose" worksheet?

---

1. Friedrich Nietzsche, quoted in Viktor E. Frankl, *Man's Search for Meaning* (New York: Washington Square Press, 1959), 97; emphasis in original.

2. Merriam-Webster's Online Dictionary, s.v. "character," accessed February 22, 2011, http://www.merriam-webster.com/dictionary/character.

3. Ellen G. White, *Mind, Character, and Personality* (Nashville, Tenn.: Southern Publishing Association, 1977), 2:593.

4. The Greek for "sharper," *tomoteros,* implies a decisive and exacting blow as opposed to repeated hacking. God has perfect aim!

5. Frankl, *Man's Search for Meaning,* 86.

6. KJV New Testament Greek Lexicon, s.v. "pistis," accessed February 22, 2011, http://www.biblestudytools.com/lexicons/greek/kjv/pistis.html.

7. Leo Tolstoy, *The Kingdom of God Is Within You,* trans. Constance Garnett (Stilwell, Kans.: Digireads.com Publishing, 2005), 72.

You and Me in Genesis 3

I'm going to depress you now—just a little. Sorry, but I have to tell the truth. We are going to probe the deep, dark, dank, defiled recesses of the human condition—the carnal heart and the fallen mind. We are going to investigate the inspired account of the original sin in such a way that I hope you feel down to your cells how the web of iniquity is tangled around your very nature. Sickened by this, you'll appreciate the chapter that follows on the gospel—God's solution to the sin problem. Don't worry. You'll recover. Ultimately, the bad news will serve to heighten your appreciation of the good news.

Before my conversion, God coordinated events in my life so that I violently collided with the fact of human depravity. The college campus I attended idealized freedom, which resulted in revolting licentiousness. Anything went. When I found out a boyfriend had cheated on me and I confronted him, he responded, "I never said I was monogamous." I soon learned promiscuity was the order of the day. Students hopped from bed to bed—even into teachers' beds. At a school retreat, an orgy erupted in the middle of the cafeteria.[1] Students explored sexual alternatives I'd rather not put into print. I had initially longed for and idealized freedom from societal constraints but exposure to moral anarchy finally broke me. I began to long for innocence.

I finally found my innocence again in Jesus, but my naivety would never return.

Like cancer patients, we need an understanding of our condition in order to begin treatment. Recall that any good psychological theory will first identify our ideal state, how we've deviated from it, and the means of returning to the ideal—purpose, problem, and solution. In the previous chapter, we identified our ideal state—made in God's image; governed by spiritual powers; and living in joyful, loving worship of Him and in fellowship with one another. Now we need an explanation of how we've deviated from that ideal state. In medical terminology, what's our diagnosis? The most brilliant minds of psychology address this question, often voluminously. Sigmund Freud wrote at least fifteen books, Carl Rogers wrote nine, and the Alfred Adler Institute published a twelve-volume set of his collected writings. From a human perspective, explaining the human condition isn't an easy task.

In contrast, the Bible does it in one chapter. Actually, it does it in one word: *sin*. Let's take a walk through the genesis of sin in Genesis 3 to see if we don't test positive for the sin diagnosis.

The opening scene finds Eve and the serpent locked in dialogue. Adam was either absent or silent. This fact, in and of itself, sheds light on the problem. Apparently, Eve's curiosity drove her away from good sense and loyalty to her Creator and to her husband. She placed herself in temptation's way, and the weakened connections made her even more vulnerable. Isolation breeds spiritual weakness, which is why God places us in a community of believers. Volumes of research correlate church attendance with better physical, mental, financial, and relational health. The service of love and concern about others that actuated heaven filled the "church" in Eden. Any idle self-interest constituted a break from the established order. Suddenly, seeing herself as an isolate, out of the context of her social network, Eve started down the path of perdition.

Basically, Eve left the church.

The situation quickly regressed. The serpent's first word, recorded in Genesis 3:1, implies that the conversation had flowed for some time. In Hebrew, he says *aph*, which means "moreover," "therefore," or "even." Here is the entire sentence as it flows in the original language (the Hebrews didn't waste their time with wordiness): "Moreover, God said eat tree Garden?" He essentially said, "Besides, didn't God say you could eat from the trees of the Garden? It's OK! God said so!"

Eve demurred but ineffectively. She put words in God's mouth by adding the word *touch* to the prohibition list. Polemics often cause such distortions; reactivity, rather than reality, drives the debate. By adding to God's law, Eve set herself up for failure (as thousands of legalists have since done). The serpent quickly took advantage of her misstatement and placed the fruit in her hands.[2] Observing her still-intact state, she assumed eating the fruit would cause no further harm. As we all know, it did.

"You won't die!" the serpent cooed. Read, "God lied." Then he attached a motive to the "lie," insinuating that God was a jealous, stingy, insecure power-monger, subordinating His children through empty threats. In actuality, the serpent described himself. We call this phenomenon *projection* because we project our own attributes upon another. For someone who projects, others are effectively blank screens. It's a very self-absorbed way to live! A girl I know who has struggled with drug addiction became convinced that I—a clean-living abstainer—regularly tripped on psilocybin mushrooms. This was projection at its most hallucinatory.

According to Genesis 3:6, the temptation appealed on three levels: appetite, beauty, and pride. This three-part temptation correlates with 1 John 2:16: "For all that is in the world—the lust of the flesh, the lust of the eyes, and the pride of life—is not of the Father but is of the world." In the temptations of Jesus as well, Satan began with the physical and proceeded to the spiritual. Lust, vanity, and pride share the essential principle of *selfishness*. In a supreme act of self-serving, Eve partook of the fruit; she then gave it to her husband, who partook as well.

Humanity fell.

Several dramas unfolded in rapid succession. In this we see broad categories of traits that have plagued the human race ever since. It is my observation and belief that all the dysfunctions and disturbances from which we suffer fall under these broad categories. See if the shoe doesn't fit, and if the Bible isn't the most concise and precise of all psychology books.

Guilt and shame

First, "the eyes of both of them were opened, and they knew that they were naked" (Genesis 3:7). How would you feel if you were suddenly naked in a public place? Obviously embarrassed, ashamed, and exposed. This statement sums up the guilt and shame that ride on the tail of sin, which, however dim in comparison to our true guilt and shame, attests to our condemned state before a Holy God. Like thunder clouds darkening the sky, a sense of foreboding rolled over the fallen pair. The air chilled, the first plant cells died, the verdure faded slightly, and a strange unrest crept over their childlike hearts. It was a deep fear, like horror, but muted by incomprehension.

Guilt and shame are similar but distinct. Guilt pertains to specific actions, while shame is more pervasive and nonspecific. In other words, guilt is for something I did; shame is for who I am. While these two things should be distinguished, they do fuse somewhat, especially in the wake of a fall. As I ponder this, I recall many, many clients whose losing battle with addiction led to deep depression as they identified with their sin. Guilt for our actions can often trigger feelings of shame for who we are. King David coupled guilt and shame when he said, "I acknowledged my sin [guilty action] to You, and my iniquity [shameful condition] I have not hidden" (Psalm 32:5).

> *For a more comprehensive discussion on guilt and shame, see week 9, "The Care and Feeding of the Conscience."*

These emotions can kill. Jesus' life expired on the cross, not solely because of physical trauma, but because of secondary physical trauma—physical conditions caused by emotional trauma. God "made Him who knew no sin to be sin for us" (2 Corinthians 5:21). Holy (knew no sin) but sin-laden, Jesus carried in His breast the two most mutually reactive elements in the universe—sin and righteousness. React they did. Under divine displeasure, enduring massive internal stress, Jesus probably suffered from pericardial effusion, a condition in which the stressed heart develops edema and could literally explode. The water and blood that flowed from His side when pierced by a Roman sword speak to the fact that Jesus' heart burst from grief: "My heart is like wax; it has melted within Me" (Psalm 22:14). Ellen White states that Jesus' "heart was broken by mental anguish."[3]

Self-justification

Self-preservation drove Adam and Eve to repel the experience of guilt as a man flees from a flaming car. Quickly, they "sewed fig leaves together and made themselves coverings" (Genesis 3:7). Ah, temporary relief from the burning shame. But "the fig-leaves represent the arguments used to cover disobedience."[4] These arguments are essentially self-justification, as flimsy as a layer of plant tissue.

In a sense, self-justification is the original sin. Yes, in their innocence, the pair partook of the fruit—the first sin ever committed by humans. But self-justification was humanity's first sinful response to the sin problem and is therefore the first sin committed by fallen humans. The two stand worlds apart. The sin of eating the fruit was inconceivable. The pair had no internal impetus and no proclivity, penchant, or propensity to sin. No great threat loomed over them to compel them to action. Yet they sinned tragically. The fig leaves, on the other hand, sprung compulsively out of a depraved nature and a fearful sense of condemnation. Wearing fig leaves seemed like the only escape from death. In our fallen state, we sin the way a coyote howls and a bird chirps—instinctively, naturally, and normally. Sin shocked a perfect world but not a fallen one.

Self-justification seems so right, doesn't it? But this attempt to cover sin actually constitutes it. In other words, our attempts to fix ourselves make us worse. Listen to Isaiah 64:6,

> But we are all like an unclean thing,
> And all our righteousnesses are like filthy rags;
> We all fade as a leaf,
> And our iniquities, like the wind,
> Have taken us away.

Our "righteousnesses" plural, it says! In other words, our multiplied attempts to cover our sins—they are themselves sinful, filthy rags.

Self-justification is the ultimate pride in that we blasphemously usurp God's role. When humankind fell, we created a God-sized problem. Through self-fixing attempts, we deny this, taking on God's prerogatives and His position of "the justifier" (Romans 3:26). In addition, we lower God's standard in order to make this self-fixing possible. Like little antichrists, we "speak pompous words against the Most High" and "intend to change . . . law" (Daniel 7:25). After all, one meaning of *antichrist* is "in the place of Christ." We apply self-righteousness "in the place of" Christ's righteousness. The greatest moral and spiritual dilemma humans face is what we will do with the innate guilt and shame of our fallen condition. Will we self-fix, adding sin to sin, or surrender to the Savior?

Self-justification comes in a myriad of forms. Countless mutations of the original fig leaves flimsily drape our naked souls. All stem from our desire to fix ourselves, to right what's wrong, and to make ourselves worthy. And all fail. Here are a few types of fig leaves I've observed (but remember the list is endless):

- Legalism—trying to save ourselves by obedience and works of the law.

- Rationalism—making excuses for sin through argument and false reasoning.
- Hedonism—pursuing pleasure to avoid pain and drown the conscience.
- Materialism—acquiring riches as a means of feeling worthy and building pride.
- Narcissism—exhibiting vanity and pride; exaltation over others as a means of feeling worthy.
- Emotionalism—seeking the ultimate relationship or emotional state.
- Achievism[5]—setting and fulfilling goals as a means of achieving worthiness.
- Egotism—replacing the desire for God's approval with the approval of others.
- Perfectionism—doing things precisely and perfectly to alleviate a sense of dissonance.
- Nihilism—obsessing with death and self-destruction; atonement through self-punishment.

Most of us have garments comprised of a patchwork of these leaves. A skirt of legalism, a few feet of materialism, threads of narcissism—all are woven together into our personal blend of self-fixes.

To identify your own fig leaves, see the "What Are Your Favorite Fig Leaves?" worksheet in the toolbox.

There are two sides to a leaf—the bright, shiny side and the paler underside. There are two sides to fig leaves as well. Some are more prone to bright, shiny self-justification in the form of entitlement, that is, "I'm so special, so good, I *deserve* to be treated well." Others seem to live life with a chronic sense of unworthiness, as in, "I don't deserve God's love, but I'll keep trying to earn it." Most of us have a mix of both attitudes, zigzagging back and forth between the two extremes. Whether entitlement or unworthiness, these two attitudes operate from the same premise—that it is possible to stand in our own merits. Neither attitude recognizes our complete inability to justify ourselves. Until we fully embrace this truth, we're doomed to act out the dictates of an unforgiven and uncleansed nature.

Denial

Denial is not a river in Egypt. Denial is an essential component of the sin problem. During my internship, group therapy with addicts gave me an unprecedented exposure to this phenomenon. Some had lost everything—friends, marriages, houses, cars, and sanity itself—before being forced into counseling because of a DUI or a furious spouse. One man took an entire package of cold medicine to get high; instead, he became psychotic at his workplace. The event forced him into the psych ward and then rehab. Without exception, these devastated, newly enlightened people remarked, "How did I miss the signs that I had a problem?" The simple answer is denial. The self-soothing fig-leaf wearers are compelled to lie to themselves about their condition.

Conversely, acknowledging one's condition is the first step toward changing it. Step one of Alcoholics Anonymous states, "We admitted we were powerless over alcohol—that our lives had become unmanageable." Addicts typically try to control their use of substances versus abstaining because they deny this powerlessness. "I can handle it!" they say. "I just need to cut back a little." These are some common variations of denial:

- Projection—putting onto others one's own sin, for example, "That skinny guy? He's a meth addict!"
- Rationalization—giving reasons for one's addiction, for example, "I need this for my back pain."
- Minimization—denying the severity of the problem, for example, "I take only a few pills a day."
- Comparison—relating ones' behavior to others' worse addictions, for example, "She takes eight pills!"
- Suppression—ignoring the problem, that is, "What? Me? Alcoholic?"
- Social withdrawal—avoiding people in order to avoid the truth.
- Escapes—using the addiction to avoid the consequences of the addiction.

Tragically, humans possess apparently unlimited capacity for denial, often carrying a near-delusional lie in their breasts right down to their death.

To complicate matters, denial has a legitimate function. God, in His mercy, allows for it as a survival measure. A full revelation of sin overwhelms the blunted faculties with unprocessable information. Witness Judas in his moment of truth; he took his own life. Rather than drive the fallen pair to suicide or psychological meltdown, God allowed the human mind the luxury of a subconscious, a kind of incubator for a soul unprepared to face the onslaught of truth.

I grew up in the seventies when recreational use of lysergic acid diethylamide (LSD) was still popular. A group of neighborhood kids took a little too much one day, stripped off their clothes, and ran naked through the neighborhood's very manicured suburban lawns, screaming psychotically. LSD is known to induce psychosis and will often push a psychologically weak person over the threshold of normalcy. Some never recover; the neighborhood kids never seemed the same after the incident. I believe that these types of drugs reveal secrets of the subconscious mind before the individual is ready to process them. I had the same experience with certain meditation exercises during my teens when I experimented with New Age philosophy and religion. I began to get in touch with certain awarenesses—the stark realities of my depraved, alienated, lost condition—but with no gospel to offer hope, light, or courage. I became depressed, filled with a severe, nameless despair that made my mother wring her hands and wish I would just join the pom-pom squad like other girls my age.

Fear

As valorous as our attempts at covering our nakedness are, they fail. As the chilly air of Eden swirled over the skin of the fallen ones, it heightened their already prickling goose bumps. Fear of condemnation had set in, especially now as God entered the Garden "in the cool of the day" (Genesis 3:8). Terrified, Adam and Eve dove into the trees. Then God called—the Hebrew word indicates loudly—"Where are you?" (verse 9).

Adam volunteered, "I was afraid" (verse 10). He deserves a few points for his honesty.

Since Eden, fear blights human experience. In the United States alone, an anxiety disorder will affect 18 percent of adults in a given year.[6] Take note: this means more than that 18 percent of Americans are afraid; it means that 18 percent of Americans are *pathologically* afraid *for durations of six months or longer*! It's safe to say that many more tremble beneath less-severe symptoms. Truly, people's hearts are "failing them from fear" (Luke 21:26).

Interestingly, Adam and Eve feared God but underestimated Him at the same time. Yes, the fact that they thought it was *necessary* to hide showed an ignorance of God's love. But the fact that they thought it was *possible* to hide showed an ignorance of God's power.

God's words rang in their ears: "For in the day that you eat of it you shall surely die" (Genesis 2:17). If unfallen, they could have drawn from their minds sweet memories of His kindness, hoping for mercy in their undone state. But fear dismantles the more refined cognitive functions, such as reason and reflection. It quickly turns the human brain into an animal brain, which is concerned solely with survival. The fight-or-flight reaction kicks in, adrenaline pumps, the heart rate increases, blood vessels constrict, hearing becomes selective, peripheral vision dims, and digestion slows. These handy mechanisms enable survival in a dangerous world; but the mechanisms themselves become dangerous if sustained for long periods. Stress becomes distress and leads eventually to exhaustion and debility.

The primal, ultimate fear is the fear of death. Speaking of Jesus' vanquishing of the devil, Hebrews 2:15 says that He released "those who through fear of death were all their lifetime subject to bondage." We fear death, and we languish in chains because of it. If allowed to run riot, this fear and its many mutations become irrational, even delusional, as evinced by the self-concealment of Adam and Eve. From the slight altering of their view of God before temptation, they now careened into full-blown misapprehension.

Misapprehension

Eve began her descent into sin when she entertained the serpent's lie about God. Once her teeth sank into the fruit, confusion morphed into delusion. Each human being has a psychological wall on which a portrait of God is meant to hang. In Eden, the enemy swapped pictures. Now his image hangs in the place of God, casting its shadows upon everything else. Since Satan marred God's reputation, the Lord can do no right in our eyes until the Holy Spirit enlightens us.

I once conversed with a coworker who knew of my faith and said, "I can't possibly be a Christian. Here's why. My father molested my sister till she left home at fifteen. I can't serve a God who would stand by and watch that. And I read in the Old Testament that He destroyed entire cities! How can I serve such a mean, vengeful God?" It occurred to me that my coworker faulted God first for passivity and then for action. The heathen peoples that God destroyed engaged in fertility rituals, which produced unwanted children, and those children became the victims of child sacrifice. In other words, they committed the worst form of child abuse, and God finally intervened to stop the momentum of evil in the world. Yet this young man insisted on seeing it as capricious violence rather than heroic intervention. In his distorted thinking, God was damned if

He did and damned if He didn't. Similarly, we incline ourselves toward seeing God in the worst possible light.

Often counseling sessions reveal a tight connection between an emotional disturbance and the God concept. The two form a feedback loop that looks something like this: an ugly picture of God causes ugly emotions, then ugly emotions project an ugly picture of God. Such was the case with Regina. Raised in a strictly religious but guilt-ridden home, she began to experience a panic disorder in her midthirties. Terrified of losing her mind, she would plead and bargain with God, "What did I do that You're punishing me? I'll do anything if You simply take this away!" The more she panicked, the more punished she felt, and the more punished she felt, the more she panicked. I proposed to Regina that we make Bible study, specifically on the character of God, part of our counseling sessions. Fortunately, she agreed, and she began to form a new concept of God. Gradually, her fears melted away into gratitude for His amazing love and forgiveness. "There is no fear in love; but perfect love casts out fear, because fear involves torment" (1 John 4:18).

Blame

God probed Adam. It wasn't information He sought; it was connection. But the connection couldn't be reestablished until the guilty man confessed. Instead, Adam said, "The woman whom You gave to be with me, she gave me of the tree, and I ate" (Genesis 3:12). He might have owned his part, but, instead, he placed the entire burden on his wife who stood silently (for the moment at least) by his side.

Blame must go somewhere. In the package of self-justification comes blaming. Social science has uncovered something called *self-serving bias,* which says that people choose explanations to strategically make themselves appear in a more favorable light. For instance, Joe trips on a rock. He believes the rock made him trip, but Jenny believes he tripped because he was clumsy. Now let Jenny trip. Jenny suddenly believes that the rock was the problem, and Joe suddenly thinks that Jenny is clumsy. Now let Joe do something elegant—ace a test, for example—and he will see it as attributable to his intelligence, whereas Jenny will say it was an easy test. Let Jenny ace the test, and she feels like the smartest one in the room, while Joe will say it was an easy test. Although some of us suffer from a reversal of this so-called low self-esteem (to be addressed later), we all at least *want* to feel good about ourselves and are inclined to bend the facts to accommodate that feeling.

Self-serving bias kicks in especially in a life-and-death situation, in which vindication means life and a guilty verdict means death. Essentially, Adam said, "I sinned because of the woman, not because of me." Eve said, "I sinned because of the serpent, not because of me." Both blamed another directly and God indirectly.

Marriage counseling continually reveals this blame phenomenon. One particular man epitomized it. In response to unemployment and poverty, his wife convinced him to return to college. When he still couldn't find work after graduation, he was forced to search far and wide. He finally found a job in another state but lacked the funds to move his family. Angry and brooding at how his wife "ruined everything," he blamed her thoroughly for his misfortune.

"Then I'll get a job!" she'd say.

"No, it's already too late!" he'd say.

Again and again, she'd humble herself, trying to find something more to apologize for. Again and again, he'd say it was too late, that the family was ruined, and it was all her fault. The woman wondered aloud to me if he had another lover. "I don't think so," I told her. "But he's definitely having an affair with his own righteousness." Some can live contentedly in loneliness, squalor, and pain as long as they have the gratification of blaming someone else for their problems.

Animosity

This blaming takes on greater significance when we consider its intended result. Remember, Adam had lost sight of God's omniscience, as evidenced by his ducking behind the tree. Apparently, he believed he could persuade God of Eve's culpability. To what purpose? Remember that God had said they would die "in the day" that they ate (Genesis 3:5)? Could it be that Adam believed God had come to vindicate justice? That he, Adam, was about to die? Behavioral science says all human behavior is operative, meaning that all behavior is an attempt to acquire or avoid something. Adam, in blaming Eve, attempted to avoid divine retributive justice. He blamed his way out of hell. Or so he thought.

The drama is even more shocking when we recall that Adam, only hours before, partook of the fruit out of deep affection for Eve. While Eve was deceived into sin, Adam was not. (See 1 Timothy 2:14.) He counted the cost and decided that he'd rather die with

Eve than live without her. Worshiping the gift rather than the Giver, he idolized his wife and his marriage. The moment idolatry infused his soul, he acted out in disobedience and sold creation into the hands of the enemy. Only hours later, he faced the consequences of his choice—and oh, what a different attitude. Instead of savior, she now played the role of scapegoat. Through his blaming, he set her up to die in his place (or so he thought). His fondest hope in that moment was that God would say, "Oh, really? It's all her fault? Step aside, Adam, and I'll nuke her." How quickly passion evaporates!

Many a divorced person knows that only a love rooted in divine love survives. Like nutrient-rich loam, it nourishes the plant of human affection that would otherwise wither and die. The initial rush of human love may drive us to idolize a person or relationship; but let that idolatry sever us from God, and soon trouble will come. Let trouble come, and human affection dries up like an abandoned bouquet of roses. Or worse yet, honey turns to bile. Listen to the description of the human heart before conversion, recorded in Titus 3:3: "Serving various lusts and pleasures, living in malice and envy, hateful and hating one another." God's fallen children may fall in love one moment, only to fall out of love the next. With a nearly 50 percent divorce rate in America, the fact emerges that if a few social constraints are lifted, the animosity of the heart charges forth like a wolverine. We have no natural love for one another. Don't fool yourself. All we have is a bit of natural affection (vestiges of God's image perhaps), but affection that is pleasure driven, dysfunctional, and ultimately expendable, dilutable, and destructible.

I have firsthand experience in the expendability of human affection, having lived through a high-school crush. For three years, Rick and I were inseparable. The butterflies moved into my stomach for those years; the feelings remained almost insanely intense, rendering me useless for most other things. But to my shock, they eventually evaporated, and we went our separate ways.

If we'd been locked into a marriage, things may have gotten nasty. Several times in marriage counseling, I've been forced to set boundaries with clients: no screaming, no swearing, and no throwing things. Every time I see a snarly face or hear a hate-laced comment, I think of Eden.

Despair

There's no specific statement in Genesis 3 that suggests despair, but how could there have been anything else? Their forbidden-fruit-fructose-overload high came to a screeching halt with the horrifying realization that all was ruined. Neuroscientists call such an event a *dopamine hangover* because the forenamed neurotransmitter, which mediates pleasure, can produce *anhedonia,* a reactive deficiency that reduces the brain's capacity for any and all enjoyment. Solomon had all the pleasures a man could ask for but lost the ability to enjoy them because of overindulgence. In the bitterness of his aging years, he cried out, "Vanity of vanities, all is vanity!" (Ecclesiastes 1:2). We can be reasonably sure that as the pair watched the first leaf wither and smelled the first dead carcass that their wildly beating, guilty hearts felt that ache in the chest we call clinical depression. One generation later, God would say of their son Cain, "Why are you angry? And why has your countenance fallen?" (Genesis 4:6). Centuries later, David would say,

> When I kept silent, my bones grew old
> Through my groaning all the day long.
> For day and night Your hand was heavy upon me;
> My vitality was turned into the drought of summer (Psalm 32:3, 4).

One in ten Americans are on antidepressant medication, and nearly 7 percent of the population of the United States will be diagnosed with major depression in a given year.[7] Global statistics, though hard to come by, are similar.[8] In his book *Depression: The Way Out,* Neil Nedley shows the relationship between depression and forebrain function, revealing the unmistakable connection between violated conscience and pathological sadness. I experienced this forebrain-despair phenomenon as a teen through drug experimentation. At times I would become hysterical, with unexplained grief and hopelessness. And I was supposed to be having a great time!

Speaking of depression, you're probably depressed after reading all this bad news. Fortunately, I won't leave you here. But while we're on the subject, imagine the crushing depression of the Creator who, while knowing the future, still lives in the present, and still experienced the fall of man with all the consternation of a brokenhearted Parent. Like an artist finding his masterpieces vandalized, God wept that His "images" were tattered! Our emotive Original foreknew the Fall but still experienced it with the shock and dismay of One who didn't. Yet His purpose for the human race—to reveal God's character—was unthwarted. He would send Jesus. Jesus would witness to us of God, and we would then witness of Him to others.

Leaden sorrow in His heart, God pronounced curses upon womankind, then mankind. But not before He promised, in a strangely oblique speech directed toward Satan, to send a Savior. That Savior and the message of His healing grace is the next step in our study of biblical psychology.

DISCUSSION QUESTIONS

1. Isolation from Adam made Eve vulnerable to temptation. Can you think of a personal example of how isolation affected you similarly?

2. How did Eve worsen her situation by arguing? How have you done similarly?

3. Did you see yourself in Genesis 3? Of guilt, shame, self-justification, denial, fear, misapprehension, blame, animosity, and despair, which did you relate to?

4. From the worksheet, what were your favorite fig leaves? Give examples of how you've used them in your life.

5. What experiences in life have caused a sense of guilt? What experiences have caused a sense of shame?

6. In what way have you tried to hide from God out of fear of judgment?

7. In what forms of denial have you engaged and how? (The forms of denial are projection, rationalization, minimization, comparison, suppression, withdrawal, escape.)

8. How have you blamed others in an attempt to avoid condemnation?

9. With what relationships in your life have you experienced the natural animosity in your fallen nature?

10. Have you ever felt despair? How has God helped to dry your tears and encouraged you to keep going?

---

1. Fortunately, it was cold and most people kept their clothes on.
2. See Ellen G. White, *Patriarchs and Prophets* (Mountain View, Calif.: Pacific Press® Publishing Association, 1958), 55.

3. Ellen G. White, *The Desire of Ages* (Mountain View, Calif.: Pacific Press®, 1940), 772.

4. Ellen G. White, "Christ's Attitude Toward the Law," *Advent Review and Sabbath Herald,* November 15, 1898, 2.

5. I admittedly made up this word.

6. "Anxiety Disorders," *National Institute of Mental Health,* accessed January 18, 2010, http://www.nimh.nih.gov/health/publications/anxiety-disorders/complete-index.shtml.

7. See R. C. Kessler et al., "Prevalence, Severity, and Comorbidity of 12-Month DSM-IV Disorders in the National Comorbidity Survey Replication," *Archives of General Psychiatry* 62, no. 6 (June 2005): 617–627.

8. Country living tends to reduce incidence of major depressive disorder: See B. A. Crowell Jr. et al., "Psychosocial Risk Factors and Urban/Rural Differences in the Prevalence of Major Depression," *British Journal of Psychiatry* 149 (1986): 307–314, http://bjp.rcpsych.org/cgi/content/abstract/149/3/307.

Righteousness-by-Faith Therapy

The famous psychiatrist Karl Menninger once said that if he could convince the patients in psychiatric hospitals that their sins were forgiven, 75 percent of them would walk out the next day! He was right. I lose clients on a regular basis because they come to know Jesus, get better, and end counseling. Frankly, I hope I go out of business.

More than three hundred theories of psychology are used today with as many methods of treatment. They tend to be expressed in acronyms: CBT (cognitive behavioral therapy), REBT (rational emotive behavioral therapy), DBT (dialectical behavioral therapy), etc. While these therapies can be helpful, righteousness-by-faith therapy, or RBFT, outstrips them all.

For a "Summary of Current Counseling Models," see the toolbox.

In all seriousness, just as the most fundamental human problem is self-justification, the universal human need is the righteousness of Christ. Many of us understand this need from a judicial standpoint; we know that without His righteousness we'd stand condemned before God. However, what I'm focusing on in this book is how the experience of justification—or forgiveness or grace—changes us internally.

Let's review a case study named Bryan. During my internship, he lumbered into my office, fortyish, towering, and handsome. Extending a massive hand, he boomed a basso profundo greeting; smiled a bright, melting smile; sat down; and proceeded to cry like a small child, tears coursing down his cheeks and dotting his blue work shirt.

"I'm just so . . . *depressed.* I . . . I've . . . been this way for a long time, and I don't know how to shake it," he sobbed.

The story tumbled out easily: Bryan was an ex-cop, a tough guy who had sustained work related disabilities that pushed him into early retirement. His marriage, also to a law enforcement official, had ended bitterly and left him to raise two teen children. The disabilities, the divorce, and the struggles of parenting weren't his presenting problem, however. A deeper wound festered. He had cheated on his girlfriend with the woman whom he ultimately married and with whom he fathered two children. The souring of that relationship and the increasing calamities of his life seemed to validate his core belief: he was unforgiveable.

"I pray every night," Bryan gasped. "But I just can't seem to earn God's forgiveness." There it was—five hundred years after the Protestant Reformation, in spite of countless televised sermons preached on unmerited grace, at least a few of which I'm sure he had heard—the drive to deserve. His words validated my premise that human beings possess an innate urge to justify themselves, an urge that transcends culture, training, education, and era. We want to self-fix. The core belief lurks in all of us.

"So you're trying to earn God's forgiveness?" I asked.

"Yes, and I just *can't*!" Bryan cried.

"Would you be interested in learning what the Bible says about this?"

"Yes," Bryan looked straight at me, bright blue eyes rimmed red.

I said, "The Bible says you *can't* earn God's forgiveness. No one can. 'All have sinned and fall short of the glory of God, being justified freely by His grace' [Romans 3:23, 24]. Grace is unmerited favor, Bryan. If you earned it, it wouldn't be grace any more. Forgiveness is to give *before,* to release from debt. You sinned in cheating on your girlfriend; you caused her pain and brought consequences into your lives, yes, but God extends forgiveness to you through Jesus. Your part is to confess the sin and receive God's forgiveness. The promise is, 'If we confess our sins, He is faithful and just to forgive us our sins and to cleanse us from all unrighteousness [1 John 1:9].' "

It was a kindergarten-simple sermon, but his soft heart received it gladly. Bryan got it. Depression lifted like morning fog. After only eight sessions, he felt ready to end counseling. He said, "I've been coming to this clinic for fifteen years, and not one of the many counselors I've seen has been able to help me with this depression. I come to you, a lowly intern, and in two months, I feel happier than I've felt in years."

Granted, it's a dramatic story. Granted, not all experience such a flight into health. As a counselor, I have my share of frustrating experiences. I don't intend to make myself or any idea or technique appear magical. I do intend to illustrate a simple truth: the gospel heals. When a person really gets it, when the good news of the free gift of righteousness can penetrate the barriers of self-justification, when we gladly and humbly receive an undeserved gift, a powerful psychological release takes place. The compulsion to deserve and all its compounded fig-leaf sin abates. Guilt and shame melt away. Gratitude springs up. Joy overflows. Peace reigns. And last but not least, love wells up and spills out to God and His children.

There's even more. Through receiving this divinely supplied righteousness, we come back into line with our original purpose. Think about the concept of righteousness for a moment: Because we have no righteousness of our own, God gives us His. But what is God's righteousness? Is it not His disposition to do—and even be—entirely right? What is *right* then? It implies adherence to a law, code, or book of rules one must consult. Does God consult an outside source to know what is right? No, for He *wrote* the book, He *originated* the code, and He *authored* the law. For God to be righteous, then, entails Him adhering to Himself, upholding His own glory. When God is righteous, He's just being Himself.

When we receive God's righteousness, we receive Him. When He dwells in us, our lives glorify Him. Conversely, Paul described the "unrighteousness of men" in terms of "they did not glorify Him as God" (Romans 1:18, 21) and said that "all have *sinned* and fall short of the *glory* of God" (Romans 3:23; emphasis added). The essence of sin is not the act but the failure to fulfill our purpose of glorifying our God, the wasting of ourselves for nothing.

Don't do it. Give up your own futile attempts to manage your sin problem without God. Receive without reservation the righteousness of Jesus and live in that righteousness every day.

The symbol of the skins

How did God communicate this simple but profound truth to His newly fallen ones? Let's go back to the Garden for a moment. Can we see any signs of the gospel? Fancy theological terms would have escaped the pair. They knew nothing of atonement, substitution, imputed and imparted righteousness, justification, and sanctification. But a simple, functional, practical symbol made a powerful statement: "For Adam and his wife the Lord God made tunics of skin, and clothed them" (Genesis 3:21).

God replaced the fig leaves with animal skins. A greater Lover of animals than the most passionate People for the Ethical Treatment of Animals (PETA) member, God nonetheless knew it would take extraordinary measures to convey the atonement. Adam and Eve's fruitarian, deathless existence hadn't prepared them for the rivers of blood flowing from the necks of their beloved pets. To connect emotionally to their experience, think of your own pet dying in your arms, then wearing its coat to protect you from the elements. The emotional trauma must have broken Adam and Eve, but in that teachable, tearful moment, God spoke through the metaphor: "This is a symbol of My Son, whom I'll send to die for you." A more effective sermon Jesus Himself didn't preach until He Himself hung on the cross. A bleeding, dying picture is worth a thousand words.

Being denied the dignity of a loving burial, the tragic pair watched the skin being torn from their animal comrades' lifeless bodies, as the skins were turned into vestments that would shield them from shame and from storm. Flimsy fig leaves in tatters on the ground, the tragedy of death covering them, Adam and Eve must have tried desperately to wrap their minds around the symbol of the skins. Let's consider what they represented.

The skins originated with God. Notice that "*they* sewed fig leaves together" versus "*the Lord God* made tunics" (verses 7, 21; emphasis added). The tragic pair's action of sewing fig leaves together sprung from their newly discovered humanism. A twisted blend of denial and self-sufficiency, it minimized the sinfulness of sin while implying that human means sufficed to fix it.

I recall having this response when first confronted with the gospel. A friend came to my house, breathless and agitated, because a woman he knew had become demon possessed. She was burning her own flesh, talking in a low foreign voice, and threatening people. In relating this disturbing situation, my friend shook with fear, crying, "Only the name Jesus makes the demon go away!"

Immediately, pride welled up in my unconverted heart and I said, "We don't have to go *that* far, do we? Can't we take care of this ourselves?" I minimized the problem by minimizing the solution.

A generation after Adam and Eve, God refused Cain's vegetarian offering on the same basis as the fig leaves. Although apparently kinder and gentler, it also denied the problem by creating an easy fix. Sadly, throughout sacred history, animal sacrifices themselves would become a means of self-justification. This was simply because the One symbolized faded away from the minds of the people. A religion that exalts human effort always underestimates sin.

The skins required death. As God's words echoed, "In the day that you eat of it, you shall surely die," the confused couple must have noticed that their innocent animal friends were the ones that died that day (Genesis 2:17). *Hmm,* they mused, *they died; we didn't.* Because of the skins, the concept of substitutionary death could take shape in their minds. At the core of the gospel lies this ugliness—the death of innocent life. It tells us of the heinous nature of sin, but it also stands as a reminder of the value of a soul. As they stretched their minds to comprehend the death that covers, Adam and Eve began to feel *expensive.* In soil watered by blood, a true sense of self-worth thrives.

I'm a survivor of anorexia. Healing came to me when I embraced the fact that I was expensive whether I liked it or not. You see, through self-starvation, I attempted not to cost anything. I essentially, but unconsciously, tried to atone for my sins by lowering my price tag. I finally realized that what I did in the physical realm betrayed a spiritual resistance to the Cross. When the love of Jesus broke through my defenses, I acknowledged my value in His eyes. Ironically, admitting I had value was extremely humbling.

The skins actually covered. "They . . . made themselves aprons," or literally loin coverings (Genesis 3:7, KJV). In contrast, God made them "tunics," which in Hebrew is *kethoneth,* from a root that means "to cover." Like oblivious babies, Adam and Eve pranced around in diapers until God dressed them properly.

I relate to them. Once while in high school, I dressed in very short shorts and a T-shirt. My mother objected, but in typical defiance, I insisted my outfit complied with the (very lenient) dress code of the school. The T-shirt was made of a stretchy fabric, though, and by the end of the day, it covered my shorts. I looked like I was walking around in nothing but a T-shirt. I remember the gradual sense of embarrassment that crept over me. I couldn't wait to get home. Adam and Eve must have felt similar, on one hand, insisting fig leaves provided enough cover, but sensing almost subliminally their nakedness.

R. C. Sproul said, "The first act of God's redemptive grace occurred when He condescended to clothe His embarrassed fallen creatures."[1] The garments symbolized a righteousness that is as much stronger than self-righteousness as leather is stronger than plant tissue. Just as the skins fortified the fallen pair before the wrath of the elements, the righteousness of Jesus shields us from condemnation before God.

Fallen humans grasp after self-fixes compulsively, instinctively, and rashly. The searing guilt of our sinful condition makes our nakedness before God as intolerable as a third-degree burn. Only the aloe of righteousness can ultimately soothe the pain. Self-righteousness works temporarily and shallowly, compounding the problem, adding self to self and sin to sin. The more fig leaves are piled on, the deeper the guilt and the more profound the denial. Self-fixing can escalate out of control until our lives are little more than a cycle of shame, denial, and sin.

The righteousness of Jesus halts this cycle. If we but embrace the message of grace, the drive to justify ourselves drains away. Self-righteousness loses relevance in the face of real righteousness. "There is therefore now no condemnation to those who are in Christ Jesus, who do not walk according to the flesh, but according to the Spirit. For the law of the Spirit of life in Christ Jesus has made me free from the law of sin and death" (Romans 8:1, 2). Why defend against condemnation when there is none?

I want to be clear about something. The skins, like the other metaphors of the robe, breastplate, and blood, had no power to justify—only to teach the reality of true justification. The death of Jesus would postdate Eden by four thousand years, but justification became effective with the inception of sin. That death would *actually* atone for *actual* sin before an *actually* broken law of an *actual* God. Once received, that atonement actually changes our status from condemnation to justification. Symbols have no power if not backed by reality. Faith in Jesus isn't just a mind game, a mere matter of reframing or cognitive restructuring. We don't create reality by believing it. Our faith isn't in faith itself. We didn't simply need a change of heart to be saved; we needed a change of status, a legal release from penalty and a pardon from an offended Sovereign.

But because our study is biblical psychology, I'll focus on how the *experience* of justification by faith changes people. Traditionally, Catholics defined justification as spiritual regeneration, and Protestants, in more legal terms, as a declaration. I can see both aspects of justification. It rights us in the legal sense but also in the ontological or ethical-moral sense. It clears our name and also cleanses our hearts.

What difference do justification, pardon, and grace make in the face of emotional pain, overmastering habit, character deformity, and other psychological ills? A remarkable one, I believe. In no way am I proposing that all mental illness vanishes with a prayer, or that religion excludes appropriate professional intervention. But God forbid that I give short shrift to the power of the gospel as a viable healing force. As I share its message in these pages, I'm wearing my counselor hat, keeping hurting people in mind. The gospel works, I've seen it; or in professional parlance, I've clinically validated it.

But how? How do we incorporate into our lives, on a practical level, the righteousness by faith message? It's one thing to have a cognitive grasp of it. So what? Even the devils believe and tremble. They acknowledge the facts but remain in bondage to fear. How do we manage to imbed these glorious truths deep in our souls? The next several chapters will focus on the answer to these questions.

DISCUSSION QUESTIONS

1. Have you tried to earn God's forgiveness? How?

2. Sin is more than an act. It is a failure to fulfill our purpose in reflecting God's character of love. How could this expanded definition of sin change your way of relating to it?

3. The concept of justification is one of the most dwelt-upon themes of the Bible. Why do you think this is so?

4. How does the teaching of justification by faith relate to the teaching of God's character of love?

5. Imagine how Adam and Eve felt when watching their animals die. Can you think of a similar experience where your sin caused another pain? Share that experience.

6. Can you think of a time when you reacted with pride, wanting to do for yourself what only God could do for you? Share that time.

7. Do you like or dislike the idea that you are extremely expensive? Why?

8. Can you think of a time you felt spiritually naked, exposed, or embarrassed? Share that time.

9. How does it feel to realize that self-fixing, self-justification, is a universal human problem?

10. How does it feel to know that God is the only One who can save us, fix us, and justify us?

---

1. R. C. Sproul, *Faith Alone* (Grand Rapids, Mich.: Baker Books, 1995), 102.

Sad Can Be Good

I clearly remember the scenes of the church campout: paddling a canoe alone on a tranquil stream, swimming in the crystalline waters of Grassy Lake in upstate Wisconsin, and getting a tick burned off my stomach. The pressure to smoke marijuana with my friends felt foreign in the world of natural highs. But peer pressure being what it was, I succumbed. Shortly afterward I found myself sobbing hysterically into my sleeping bag. The revelation of God's love through nature broke my teenage heart.

I want to spend this chapter probing what stands as one of human psychology's most mysterious phenomena. One can't find much about it by searching a database of psychology journals, but it saturates Scripture. We don't talk about it much at parties; popular worship songs never mention it (that I know of). Poetically, it's a clunker. But spiritually, it's a life-or-death need.

I'm talking about repentance.

A quick perusal of the New King James Version yields several facts about it:

- It's called *metanoia* in Greek and means "a change of mind."
- It's barely named, but often demonstrated, in the Old Testament.[1]
- The ministry of repentance prepared the way for the Messiah.[2]
- Today, it prepares us for the forgiveness of sin.
- It bears good fruit.[3]
- It's a gift.[4]
- The goodness of God leads to it.[5]

- There is a godly form and an ungodly form of it.[6]
- It's possible to lose the capacity for it, at least temporarily.[7]
- God wants everybody to have it.[8]

Empathy

To better understand this mystery, we'll probe another mystery—that of empathy. At the heart of repentance lies a focus on others, an unselfish awareness of the far-reaching, social impact of our choices. Our nervous systems stand discrete, disconnected, at least physically. Yet, in empathy, we vicariously partake of another's experience of pain, sorrow, anxiety, or anger. We get untangled from our myopic, narcissistic guilt cycles to freely observe how sin affects those we influence. Ultimately, we see how sin affects God, whose heart broke under its infinite weight, for "the cross is a revelation to our dull senses of the pain that, from its very inception, sin has brought to the heart of God."[9]

Jesus predicted, "Because lawlessness will abound, the love of many will grow cold" (Matthew 24:12). His prophecy finds fulfillment today. A recent study on college students showed a 40 percent decline in empathy over the past thirty years.[10] Researchers postulate that this stems partly from violent mass media, which has been shown to increase aggression and decrease empathy and prosocial behavior.[11] (Sometimes I wonder why researchers even bother to study such things. I've worked with troubled youth who spent their days shooting virtual M1A1 carbines at virtual enemy special ops, with virtual blood splashing on the virtual site. And we wonder if this practice discourages empathy?) Another potential contributor to the loss of empathy may be an addiction to online media versus real face-to-face encounters with actual people. In research, empathy tends to be positively associated with the ability to read and engage in facial expressions.[12] Empathy also correlates with good parenting and negatively correlates with negligent, permissive, or authoritarian parenting styles.[13] Whatever the cause, the enemy of empathy calculatingly effects his plan to circumvent our compassion and deaden us to the voice of conscience, and thus make repentance impossible. Empathy stands between each of us and utter moral ruin. One researcher says, "Psychopaths are characterized by an absence of empathy and poor impulse control, with a total lack of conscience."[14]

Heaven help us all!

How do we get this quality called empathy? How can one person experience the pain of another? Empathy for self-improvement purposes is an oxymoron; the self-centered motive circumvents the goal. So how do we move from self to love and compassion? The gift aspect of repentance enters here. Working up repentance like some kind of spiritual sweat is an exercise in futility. The Holy Spirit must intervene. This is why, if we're ever to change, we must come to Jesus as we are. This is where biblical psychology distinguishes itself from all secular theories—it points to a power Source, an actual external Entity that acts as a life-source for the transformation process.

As a means of building empathy with a loved one, use the "Establishing Empathy With E.A.R." exercise in the toolbox.

So come to Jesus in your weakness. Even if your heart sits like a stone in your chest, unmoved and unwilling, come to Jesus. Even if you're in the throes of addiction and its hideous fallout, come. Even if you feel you don't *want* to come, respond to the part of you that *does* want to come, respond to the Holy Spirit, who passionately desires you.

To come means to come away from the escapes you have used to drown the Spirit's voice and numb your spiritual nerves. This may require rehab if you're an addict; or it may require that you smash your TV or your Xbox with a baseball bat. You may have to cut your credit cards into little pieces or block your lover's cell phone number. You may have to dump your alcohol, cigarettes, and/or chocolate in the toilet. The point is, give Jesus a shot at you. Come to Him. Go down on your knees and say, "I'm here, willing to be made willing to be made willing to be made willing to receive your gift of repentance."

Jesus said, "He who finds his life will lose it, and he who loses his life for My sake will find it" (Matthew 10:39). Paradoxically, when we get outside of ourselves, we ensure our own stability. Isaiah makes a statement to this effect: "By His stripes we are healed" (Isaiah 53:5). This might be expanded and paraphrased as, "When we see what sin did to *Jesus,* we find healing from what sin does to us."

Seeing sin in the context of a relationship, and ultimately our relationship to God, changes our mind and relationship with it. This is the essence of repentance. God may pour out His divine forgiveness upon the world and, indeed, has in Jesus, but this forgiveness completely heals and transforms only those whom it penetrates. Repentance creates a condition in the mind similar to a well-turned garden bed—broken up and ready to receive.

Escaping the guilt cycle

Let's consider an important statement from Scripture about the nature of true repentance: "Godly sorrow produces repentance leading to salvation, not to be regretted; but the sorrow of the world produces death" (2 Corinthians 7:10). Notice that in this contrast and comparison that godly sorrow generates life, whereas worldly sorrow generates death. This identifies two ways we can sorrow over our sin.

Godly Sorrow ➜ Life

Worldly Sorrow ➜ Death

Let's conceptualize these two kinds of sorrow in the experiences of Peter and Judas. Their respective sins weren't all that different—Peter denied Jesus with cursing and swearing; Judas betrayed Him with a kiss. Make note of the fact that Judas never intended for Jesus to die. He simply wanted to shock some "sense" into Him, impelling Him to throw off Roman power, and become the political Messiah they all wanted. He essentially acted out the wishes of all the disciples but more cleverly and calculatingly. Yet when he realized Jesus would submit to the Cross, Judas despaired—not out of empathy with Jesus, not because of harm to others, but over his ravaged reputation. *Look what I did to myself!* he thought and committed suicide. His narcissistic sorrow for sin quite literally led to death.

Peter's response contrasts with this cowardly escape. While the third denial and the cock's crow still vibrated the air, "The Lord turned and looked at Peter" (Luke 22:61). What did that look convey? What did the Lord's eyes hold? Something that produced godly sorrow, for, "Peter went out and wept bitterly" (verse 62). Stumbling out into the night, not knowing where his steps would lead him, he finally threw himself down in Gethsemane, at the very spot where Jesus had prayed.[15] Perhaps Jesus' blood still moistened the rocks and mingled with Peter's tears. Into the night he sobbed, wishing he could die but not daring to take his own life. Something changed in Peter that night, and the great denier went on to become the great proclaimer of the gospel, even suffering a martyr's death.

Repentance is the foundation for lasting change.

To summarize, the distinction between godly and worldly sorrow lies in its focus.

Godly sorrow exercises an others focus and empathizes with the victim. Worldly sorrow indulges a me focus and frets over the consequences of sin to *myself*.

Godly Sorrow → Empathy → Life
Worldly Sorrow → Selfish → Death

Sin tends to produce cycles. Out of it springs guilt, guilt causes pain, pain compels us to escape, escape brings consequences, the consequences remind us of the sin, which brings guilt. Here it is visually:

Cycles propel themselves endlessly, in many cases straight into the grave (which is often an early one). To break a cycle requires an entry point. In this case, the entry point is guilt, which God transforms into repentance.

The topic of repentance has fallen out of fashion in recent years, but I thoroughly endorse it as a clinician. Tears, like little wet evidences that the heart still has "juice" enough to leak, often mark a therapeutic victory. I can't think of anything more emotionally cathartic than admitting one's sin with a sense of connection and shared pain with the victim. In the wake of repentance lies peace and joy. I've both experienced and observed this many times.

The ultimate soul release

Repentance is a soul cathartic. In our fallen state, fig leaves keep us in a state of denial. We repress guilt, forcing it into the unconscious realm. God mercifully allows this, given that apart from an awareness of God's forgiveness, the revelation of our sin would probably trigger a psychotic break. But even unconscious guilt weighs us down and causes us stresses. In contrast, repentance allows unconscious sin to be processed through the conscious mind and released through confession to a sin-bearing Redeemer.

Although He bore the accumulated sin of humanity, Jesus experienced on a macro, cosmic level what sin bearing would cause in our personal microcosm. Under the burden of the world's guilt, His psyche stressed to the point of physical death. As previously mentioned, Jesus' death was caused by multiple stress-triggered conditions such as pericardial effusion, hypovolemic shock, exhaustion, asphyxia, stress-induced arrhythmias, and congestive heart failure.[16] Remember that the Roman soldiers incredulously pierced Jesus' side to validate that He'd actually died. Experts in the death process, they knew that the physical injuries alone, though great, wasn't sufficient to kill Jesus only hours after He was crucified. Staggering under the revelation of sin's true character, Jesus died of a broken heart.

> I am poured out like water,
> And all My bones are out of joint;
> My heart is like wax;
> It has melted within Me (Psalm 22:14).

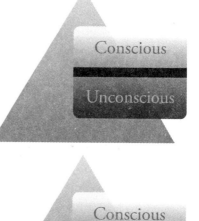

If allowed to face our sin without a Savior, guilt would likewise overwhelm our nervous system to the point of self-destruction. Thank God, He has provided another way to process guilt. Once we become secure in His love and forgiveness, we find the courage to confess our sins, thus releasing it to the Sin Bearer. Through repentance, the unconscious vomits out repressed sin, and the soul frees itself from the burden of guilt long held in the dark recesses of the soul. The catharsis creates space for the healing stream of forgiveness.

This divine-human transaction establishes the process of deep character change. In the safety of Christ's love and righteousness, we thrive and grow. "But for you who revere my name, the sun of righteousness will rise with healing in its wings. And you will go out and leap like calves released from the stall" (Malachi 4:2, NIV).

As a young person searching spiritually, I hated my compulsions and bad habits; yet they clung to me like leeches and sucked away my self-respect. I desperately sought a means of purging myself—meditation, fasting, yoga, and encounter group therapy, to name a few. My self-fixes gave a fleeting illusion of improvement that only made way for more addictive behavior. Christian friends finally shared the gospel with me one lonely night in the kitchen of my rented house. I began to understand that when I did wrong, it was against Someone else. One friend loaned me a little book called *Steps to Christ*, which I read in one day while locked away in my room. It opened my eyes further to a compassionate, merciful Savior. The Spirit revealed to me that my sins separated me from a God of everlasting love. One night I sobbingly told a Jesus I had never seen in person that I wanted to return to Him and to God.

In a very short time, my life was unrecognizable. The unprincipled, impulsive, thrill-seeking party girl became thoughtful, caring, and devotional. My ungodly friends were shocked at the change. They thought I'd lost my mind! One cussed me out on the phone. Another gleefully belittled both me and the Christian faith. Another told me, "This is just another one of your trips, Jennifer. Soon you'll be on to something else." That was thirty-three years ago.

A story is told of a bridge operator who made a brave and self-sacrificing decision. When he saw an unexpected train barreling down the tracks, he quickly prepared to lower the bridge. To his horror, he realized his young son had fallen into the gear shaft. Forced to choose between preserving his son and allowing the train to plunge into the river or preserving the train and crushing his son, he agonizingly lowered the bridge.

As the train rolled by, the hysterical man observed the oblivious passengers gazing out the windows. Not one realized what their lives had just cost him. He thought, *If they knew, would they care?*

God watches humanity roll by like the passenger train, most of us oblivious to what sin cost Him. He looks for some recognition in our eyes, some sign of appreciation, some awareness of the pain caused.

"Is it nothing to you, all you who pass by?

Behold and see
If there is any sorrow like my sorrow,
Which has been brought on me,
Which the LORD has inflicted
In the day of His fierce anger" (Lamentations 1:12).

For most of the human race, the sacrifice of Christ is nothing. God ever strives through His Spirit to change that, to soften our hearts, and bring us to tears of remorse for what our sin cost. With those tears and their attending confessions, we release the pent-up, crushing burden of guilt to Jesus, who already carried it to a lonely cross.

DISCUSSION QUESTIONS

1. Can you think of a time when repentance had a healing, freeing effect on you? Share that time.

2. What are some things you've noticed that have increased your level of empathy?

3. As you come to Jesus to receive the gift of repentance, what distractions might you have to leave behind?

4. Do you listen well when conversing with people? How could you improve in your listening skills?

5. What are some of the reasons you avoid empathy?

6. When you consider the effect of sin on other people and God, how does your view of it change?

7. What hurts in your life have motivated you to engage in escapist behaviors?

8. What escapes did you or do you use to avoid pain?

9. Which unconscious thoughts, feelings, motives, and attitudes has God's Spirit revealed to you?

10. What sinful escapes has God freed you from in the past?

1. For example, see Hosea 13:14, KJV.

2. See Matthew 3:8–11; Mark 1:4; Luke 3:3–8.

3. See Luke 3:8; Acts 26:20.

4. See Acts 5:31; 11:18; 2 Timothy 2:25.

5. See Romans 2:4.

6. See 2 Corinthians 7:10.

7. See Hebrews 6:6; 12:17.

8. See 2 Peter 3:9.

9. Ellen G. White, *Education* (Mountain View, Calif.: Pacific Press®, 1952), 263.

10. This study is reported in several publications. "Generation Me: Study Finds College Students Lack Empathy," Education-Portal.com accessed July 27, 2010, http://education-portal.com/articles/Generation_Me_Study_Finds_College_Students_Lack_Empathy.html.

11. C. A. Anderson et al., "Violent Video Game Effects on Aggression, Empathy, and Prosocial Behaviors in Eastern and Western Countries: A Meta-Analytic Review," *Psychological Bulletin* 136, no. 2 (March 2010): 151–173.

12. See, for instance, L. Carr et al., "Neural Mechanisms of Empathy in Humans: A Relay From Neural Systems for Imitation to Limbic Areas," *Proceedings of the National Academy of Sciences of the United States of America* 100, no. 9 (2003): 5497–5502.

13. Julia Krevans and John C. Gibbs, "Parents' Use of Inductive Discipline: Relations to Children's Empathy and Prosocial Behavior," *Child Development* 67, no. 6 (June 28, 2008): 3263–3277, accessed July 27, 2010, http://www3.interscience.wiley.com/journal/119199368/abstract?CRETRY=1&SRETRY=0.

14. M. C. Craig et al., "Altered Connections on the Road to Psychopathy," *Molecular Psychiatry* 14 (2009): 946–953, doi: 10.1038/mp.2009.40.

15. White, *The Desire of Ages,* 713.

16. William D. Edwards, Wesley J. Gabel, and Floyd E. Hosmer, "On the Physical Death of Jesus Christ," *Journal of the American Medical Association* 255, no. 11 (1986): 1455–1463, doi: 10.1001/jama.1986.03370110077025.

Have You Tried Forgiveness?

The most shocking thing about the 2006 murders of five Amish girls in Nickel Mines, Pennsylvania, weren't the murders themselves, but the forgiveness that followed. After killing the girls, Charles Carl Roberts blew out his own deranged brains, leaving his family horrified and heartbroken. Strangely, preternaturally, compassion flowed more freely than the blood. Only hours after the shooting, an Amish neighbor appeared to comfort the Roberts family. Kind visits were paid to Roberts's widow, parents, and in-laws. One Amish man spent an hour with Roberts's sobbing father in his arms. Finally, about thirty Amish attended the killer's funeral. An Amish man said, "I don't think there's anybody here that wants to do anything but forgive."[1]

Twenty-six years before, a happy blond sixteen-year-old named Debbie Morris sat with her boyfriend, Mark Brewster, on the riverfront in Madisonville, Louisiana, drinking milkshakes. Two strangers burst out of nowhere and kidnapped them at gunpoint. They shot Mark and left him for dead (he survived, but with a permanent disability) and over the next thirty hours repeatedly raped Debbie, threatening her with knives and guns. She overheard her kidnappers' plan to lock her in the trunk of the car and burn it. Miraculously, Debbie escaped. Even more miraculously, she eventually, intentionally, and intelligently chose to forgive Robert Willie, who died by the electric chair four years later.[2] In her words: "I needed to be able to let go of the hate and the anger before he died. I needed to find a way to forgive him."[3]

Scrolling back another thirty-five years to World War II, Japanese soldiers in Thailand forced a group of Scottish prisoners to build a jungle railroad. One day a shovel went missing. The officer in charge raged, demanding that the missing shovel be produced—or else. When the Scottish squadron stood silent, the officer raised his gun, threatening to kill them all. Finally, one man stepped forward. The officer put away his gun, picked up a shovel, and beat the man to death. The survivors picked up the bloody corpse and carried it with them to the second tool check. This time, no shovel was missing—there had been a miscount at the first checkpoint! The word spread like wildfire through the camp—an innocent man had been willing to die to save his comrades! A new spirit overcame the squadron. The men began to treat each other like brothers. When the victorious Allies swept in, the survivors, human skeletons, lined up in front of their once captors. Instead of retaliating, they insisted, "No more hatred. No more killing. Now what we need is forgiveness."

As counterintuitive as it seems, even irrational, forgiveness is ultimately the best response to sin. I've heard X-rated, bloodcurdling, gut-wrenching abuse stories. Even for these victims, forgiveness is best. They may need to "find their anger" first, but the ultimate goal is forgiveness. Without it, the "root of bitterness springing up cause[s] trouble, and by this many become defiled" (Hebrews 12:15). Ruminating on the deeds of their offenders, the victims drive the thorns deeper into their wounds.

Forgiveness of others becomes possible when we realize God's forgiveness of us. What follows in this chapter is a study of biblical forgiveness, shared with the objective of helping us become channels of God's forgiveness. I pray that we can receive—and give—this precious commodity. As the rain swells the brook so it can smooth the stones in its bed, the forgiveness of God fills us and gives us spiritual momentum to smooth over the hard places in our lives.

Justice + Mercy = Forgiveness

On the surface, forgiveness seems like a denial of justice. The same Book that says, "Eye for eye, tooth for tooth, hand for hand, foot for foot, burn for burn, wound for wound, stripe for stripe," also says, "Turn the other" cheek (Exodus 21:24, 25; Matthew 5:39). In actuality, forgiveness builds upon the foundation of justice. This is why the first step in the forgiveness process entails admitting that someone sinned against us. We gain nothing by denying the extent of the damage.

Abuse victims especially tend to excuse sin; they were well trained to do so. But without a foundation of justice, forgiveness becomes cheap, shallow, and naive. With such a foundation, forgiveness takes on rich significance and power.

In the Sermon on the Mount, Jesus said, "You have heard that it was said, 'You shall love your neighbor and hate your enemy.' But I say to you, love your enemies, bless those who curse you, do good to those who hate you, and pray for those who spitefully use you and persecute you" (Matthew 5:43, 44). The popular "hate your enemy" idea was actually a biased interpretation of divine counsel, such as that concerning the Ammonites and Moabites: "Because they did not meet you with bread and water on the road when you came out of Egypt, and because they hired against you Balaam . . . to curse you. . . . You shall not seek their peace nor their prosperity all your days forever" (Deuteronomy 23:4, 6). Of course, resentful hearts twisted this counsel into something more vicious than God intended. But He did say, in effect, "Don't ever help them! Remember what they did to you!" God is no milquetoast.

> *To work through the forgiveness process, see the "Forgiveness" worksheet in the toolbox.*

But while justice is a partial expression of God's character, forgiveness is a more complete expression. Justice is the foundation of God's throne (see Psalm 97:2); mercy builds on that foundation, and forgiveness results. The cross of Jesus is described as the place where "justice and mercy were reconciled."[4] At the Cross these traits achieve a perfect balance. Jesus as our Representative absorbed our punishment and as our Savior extended forgiveness. Justice demanded satisfaction; mercy longed to save. Forfeited justice would have sabotaged God's throne and with it the stability of the universe. But mere justice apart from mercy would have done the same thing, for His authority rests on His character of love. So it devolved upon our Creator to find a way to punish sin while still forgiving sinners. That way was for God to bear His own death penalty.

The good-natured, human kind of forgiveness can be a win-win situation: I overlook your sins; you keep liking me; we nosh a little, schmooze a little, and go home happy. But God's forgiveness is a win-lose situation: we win; He loses. It sharply contrasts with mere human forgiveness in that it mandated death. In order to forgive, God had to take the consequences of sin in to and on to Himself. This means that God extends forgiveness, not as a pal with no capacity for hard feelings, but as a holy Hero whose offense at sin is superseded only by His love for sinners.

Define it

Both the Old and New Testaments contain multiple words translated as "forgiveness," but one, *calach,* refers only to divine forgiveness. In other words, one human can never *calach* another. This in itself conveys a message. The only One with the ultimate right to exact and, therefore, avert justice, is God. The rest of us can only wish on our enemies what we ourselves deserve. Only God stands innocent of any sin and therefore free to execute punishment. Humans can punish sin only as He defers to them this authority, as in church discipline or state jurisprudence.

Therefore our forgiveness of one another finds its source in the Divine. When we forgive, we accept that Jesus bore the punishment of that person's sin, and we choose to align ourselves with Him in spirit and will. We can't bear people's sin, but we can forgive the people, which means that we do everything in our power to see that their sins are removed through the grace of Jesus.

Let's take a simplified look at the original languages[5] behind our word *forgiveness.* The Hebrew *kaphar* means "to cover." *Nasa* means "to bear, to take away." *Calach,* referred to above, means "to pardon" as in a legal debt. The Greek word *apoluein* means "to release." The word *charizomai* changes the noun *charis,* or grace, into a verb, as in "to grace" with undeserved favor. *Aphesis,* from the Greek word *aphesis,* means "to send away." Boiling that down, we see that forgiveness is

1. to cover;
2. to send away;
3. and to grace.

For a pen-picture of this, recall the woman taken in adultery (John 8). Jesus shrouds her naked shoulders with His own robe, sends away her would-be executioners, and graces her with a second chance, saying, "Go and sin no more" (verse 8). What a fitting and precise picture of forgiveness! Covered, sent away, graced. That she was, and so are we.

In His Magna Carta on forgiveness in Matthew 18, Jesus used a parable involving debt and debt cancellation. This conveys the idea that sin demands a payment, or a "wage," as stated in Romans 6:23, "the wages of sin is death." Sin puts us in debt to God, a debt that can be satisfied only by our death. Jesus as the Representative of humanity died our death—"One died for all, then all died" (2 Corinthians 5:14)—and so paid our debt, making it possible for God to cancel the debt to us.

One of my precious loved ones owes me five thousand dollars, incurred as the result of a drunk driving charge, a night spent in jail, and the many associated costs. I may forgive that debt eventually (don't tell her). If and when I do, I will have effectively paid five thousand dollars. As all parents know, the money must come from somewhere! (Our credit-crazed society risks forgetting this.) Knowing we could never pay and live, God the Father absorbed the debt of our sin into Himself in the form of the crushing loss of His own Son.

To flesh out our definition of forgiveness based on this debt idea: God covers our sin, absorbing the debt into Himself, sends away the punishment for it, and graces us with a second chance. Behind the touching picture of Jesus forgiving the woman taken in adultery towers a Cross. He could forgive her because of it.

Receive it

To receive this forgiveness seems natural, simple, and obvious. God requires only that we confess our sins and believe in Him. Simple, right? Right. But very unnatural. Recall the post-Fall carnal impulse to self-justify. As gushing water drowns bugs in the gutter, so God's forgiveness destroys pride. Notice Jesus' parable in Matthew 18. The real-estate entrepreneur, symbolizing God's forgiveness of all sin, forgave the property manager ten million dollars of debt. Rather than melting in gratitude, the manager said, "Give me some time! I'll pay you everything." In these few words he echoed the essence of the post-Fall human condition. The entrepreneur freely poured out his forgiveness, but the flow was blocked by the manager's desire to fix himself, to pay his own debt. Ultimately, the entrepreneur withdrew the offer of forgiveness.

How precisely like God's dealings with humanity! Freely He forgives in sending Jesus "when we were enemies" (Romans 5:10). Poured-out forgiveness soaks into receptive, repentant hearts, but it rolls off the proud like beads of water off oily skin. Days turn into years as the Holy Spirit, in motherly fashion, pleads, warns, coaxes, and cries. Finally, probation and opportunity end. Forgiveness is withdrawn. And for what cause? Self-righteousness, denial, and unbelief. In the end, the unpardonable sin is the unconfessed sin, be it as common as a cherished resentment or a habit of off-color joking.

You don't have to persuade God to forgive you; like the entrepreneur, He forgives even while we remain self-righteous, impenitent, unconverted, ungrateful, and oblivious

To identify your own self-righteousness, see the "What Are Your Favorite Fig Leaves?" worksheet in the toolbox.

to His sacrifice. Even those of us who walk with Jesus harbor unconscious sin, so it is only "through the Lord's mercies we are not consumed" (Lamentations 3:22). We all on some level cry, "I'll pay you all!" revealing obliviousness to the real cost of sin. As the human race collectively cried, "I'll pay you all!" Jesus canceled our debt, hanging all alone on a cross. Jesus brought to the human race "divine forgiveness of all sin."[6] In this sense, God forgives us all, penitent or not.

But for His forgiveness to work a transformation in our personal lives, to truly heal us from sin's devastation, we must be individually, personally forgiven. "If we confess our sins, He is faithful and just to forgive us our sins and to cleanse us from all unrighteousness" (1 John 1:9). Repentance and confession format our minds in preparation to download grace. They plow up the packed mud of our hearts to prepare for the heavenly seed. Facing our sins as they march forth from our own mouths like so many death-row inmates solemnifies our souls in preparation to hear the divine sentence. And the sentence is "Forgiven," praise His name! As grace pours down like warm sunshine, Jesus covers our cowering shoulders with His own pure white robe. And the guilt that clings to us like a second skin He miraculously detaches and sends away. Praise *El Nahsah,* "the God who forgives!" "There is therefore now no condemnation to those who are in Christ Jesus, who do not walk according to the flesh, but according to the Spirit" (Romans 8:1).

> I will greatly rejoice in the Lord;
> My soul shall be joyful in my God;
> For He has clothed me with the garments of salvation;
> He has covered me with the robe of righteousness (Isaiah 61:10).

"As far as the east is from the west, so far has He removed our transgressions from us" (Psalm 103:12).

Do you want transformation? Confess your sin. Renounce your self-righteousness. Admit your ingratitude. Denounce your denial. Be intentional, specific, and honest. Let your mouth speak the truth before God, and let the tears flow. Then read out loud the promises and rejoice that you stand before God justified—just as if you'd never sinned.

Your automatic thoughts and feelings may tell you you're guilty, but this is where faith comes in. So many of us suffer from chronic guilt feelings; we assume that these feelings reflect God's opinion of us. We find ourselves in a feedback loop in which we project our guilty feelings onto God and assume He condemns us, which leads us to cut ourselves off from Him, which just leaves us prey to temptation and sin, which feeds our guilt all over again.

God's requirements for forgiveness are simple, just, and reasonable. Once you've complied with them, you're free to believe, talk, and behave like a forgiven person.

Part of this new experience entails forgiving other people. It's your chance to road test your own forgiveness.

> *For a more complete discussion of overcoming guilt and shame, read week 9, "The Care and Feeding of the Conscience."*

Give it

When I was about twelve years old, a girl I'll call Wanda bullied me without mercy. One incident involved Wanda and a group of girls she'd whipped into a frenzy, who dragged me out to the baseball field during recess, and through physical and sexual abuse, robbed me of every shred of dignity. I still remember the blue-and-green striped sweater dress I wore, smudged with dirt, grass caked in my tangled hair, and I remember crying until my eyes nearly swelled shut.

About a year ago Wanda contacted me because a mutual friend had died. Her note chatted on as if to an old buddy: "I have two teen boys . . . the marriage to their dad didn't work out . . . I run a bed and breakfast here in Statesville . . ." My heart grew cold in my chest. All I knew about accountability and boundaries, all the "you hurt me once, shame on you; you hurt me twice, shame on me" expressions, seemed like a perfect fit. *I want nothing to do with her,* I thought.

But then Jesus' teachings flooded my mind: He said, "Forgive us our debts, as we forgive our debtors. . . . If you forgive men their trespasses, your heavenly Father will also forgive you. But if you do not forgive men their trespasses, neither will your Father forgive your trespasses," and "whenever you stand praying, if you have anything against anyone, forgive" (Matthew 6:12, 14, 15; Mark 11:25).

The still, small Voice urged me to forgive Wanda. For a moment in time, two systems of logic collided in my mind. Forgiveness seemed irrational, silly even. But then the light dawned. I thought of the forgiveness of Jesus toward me, and I forgave.

Mary Magdalene wrestled with seven demons. The sketchy facts suggest to me that Mary, having been seduced by a high-profile Pharisee, she fled her childhood home in the Jerusalem suburb of Bethany to a faraway city called Magdala. There she became a successful prostitute. Perhaps, she first saw Jesus at the Sermon on the Mount; we don't know. Perhaps, she heard, "Blessed are the poor in spirit, for theirs is the kingdom of heaven," and fell in love with Him on the spot (Matthew 5:3). Try as she might, though, she couldn't stay "clean." She'd been seduced by a clergyman, Simon the Pharisee.[7] As the perpetrator went on to bask in the sunshine of human approbation, she struggled with the hideous consequences of the abuse. I believe this inequity gave birth to a root of bitterness.

Some believe her deliverance was instant and complete; I know better. More likely, she relapsed many times on the road to recovery, and the demons came out one by one. It seems the demon bitterness left last. The devil's only remaining toehold in her life was a disposition to coddle an old wound, holding in her heart a certain delicious resentment. From what I know of human nature, the disdain of the disciples for prostitutes probably produced cold attitudes and comments, which acted like triggers for her reactive cycle. Down, down, down she'd descend into old patterns; until one day she realized that she was becoming more and more like her abuser—a sexual predator. Finally, she knew her foundational demon to be unforgiveness. One last encounter with the Deliverer left her a forgiven and forgiving follower.

At Simon's party she stood under a shower of ridicule from the misled disciples. Simon himself despised her as she poured the precious spikenard ointment on her Messiah. But it was as if Jesus had filled her field of vision. She poured out her gratitude to God in spite of the reproach of man. She'd been healed of bitterness. In the innermost sanctum of her soul, grace received spilled out in grace bestowed. She forgave her offender.

As can we.

DISCUSSION QUESTIONS

1. How did you feel when you read the opening stories of the Amish, Debbie Morris, and the Scottish prisoners?

2. Do you know by experience what the Bible means by a "root of bitterness"?

3. Is there a person, or persons, you're tempted to be bitter against?

4. Do you tend to think that bitterness will protect you against being hurt again?

5. When you went through the "Forgiveness" worksheet, which things commonly mistaken for forgiveness—trust, excusing, approval, forgetting, and feeling—applied to you? Give an example.

6. Why do you think we must receive forgiveness in order to bestow forgiveness?

7. Why do you think we must bestow forgiveness in order to receive it?

8. Why do we need faith in order to give and receive forgiveness?

9. Can you think of a time when you were torn between an attitude of justice and one of forgiveness? How did you resolve it?

10. What about Mary Magdalene's story ministers to you most?

---

1. Wikipedia contributors, "Amish School Shooting," Wikipedia, accessed February 24, 2011, http://en.wikipedia.org/w/index.php?title=Amish_school_shooting&oldid=415575895.

2. This story is the subject of the book and movie *Dead Man Walking*.

3. "Debbie Morris Interview," *Frontline*, accessed Sept. 12, 2010, http://www.pbs.org/wgbh/pages/frontline/angel/interviews/dmorris1.html.

4. Ellen G. White, "The Unsearchable Riches of Christ," *Signs of the Times*, May 14, 1902.

5. The English etymology goes like this: forgiveness morphed from Greek to the Latin *perdonare*, in which *per* means "for" and *donare* means "give" (or "donate"), to the Saxon *forgivan* and then finally to our English *forgive*. *Pardon* and *forgive* are essentially the same word.

6. Ellen G. White, *Christ's Object Lessons* (Washington, D.C.: Review and Herald® Publishing Association, 1941), 244.

7. In Luke 7, Mary anoints Jesus at Simon's party, and Simon thinks evil. Jesus tells a parable in which one person is ten times more indebted. Both were forgiven. It's my belief that Jesus in this parable tried to show Simon that he, Simon, was ten times guiltier than Mary. This seems to allude to him as perpetrator upon her. They must have been related, or she wouldn't have been allowed at his party. I take these evidences to mean that Mary suffered childhood sexual abuse at the hands of a male relative.

Will Power

I have a long personal history of having a bad temper. No, I don't have violent, mouth-foaming temper tantrums or even frequent outbursts. Rather my temper has manifested as occasional frustration-born verbal volleys (yelling), mostly directed at my husband. It's a sad fact that we often behave the worst with "safe" relationships, the ones least likely to reject us for bad behavior. Oh, that we'd do what James Taylor advocated and "Shower the people you love with love." But that's a subject for another time.

One such temper outburst occurred in front of our young children. It was over the television. I wanted it out of the house, but my husband clung to it for football purposes. I walked into the den one day to find my cherubs ogling some nightmare-inducing sci-fi movie preview (OK, I was overprotective). I called Michael in to witness the atrocity and exploded about the TV, forgetting that watching their parents argue is much worse for kids than watching scary television ads. Little eyes turned from the sci-fi movie to the sci-fi mother ranting and waving her arms like a short-circuiting robot.

Stung in my conscience afterward, I sought out my children to apologize. Strangely, my youngest said, "Daddy had a short temper."

Why is she mentioning Mike's short temper when I was doing most of the yelling? I wondered.

But then she continued, "And you had a long temper."

I'm happy to say that time has subdued my "long" temper. Mike rarely hears those shrill, lacing words these days. As a couple, we've learned what marriage expert John Gottman says is even better than not arguing; we've learned how to exit an argument before it escalates.[1] The general mellowing effect of age has helped with this, as has the maturing of our marriage; but the little marvel the Bible calls "self-control" has helped the most. I've been to Jesus' anger management school and learned my lesson—pretty much.

> *For more comprehensive help in managing anger, see "Mind Your Anger" in the toolbox.*

Definition

Depending upon the translation, the word *self-control,* or *temperance,* comes from the Greek word *egkrateia.* Notice the *krat* in the center of the word. *Kratov* in Greek means "strength," and *egkrateia* means "with strength." In other words, self-control is power—personal, individual power and self-determination, or simply willpower.

"The fruit of the Spirit is love, joy, peace, longsuffering, kindness, goodness, faithfulness, gentleness, *self-control.* Against such there is no law. And those who are Christ's have crucified the flesh with its passions and desires" (Galatians 5:22–24; emphasis added).

"But also for this very reason, giving all diligence, add to your faith virtue, to virtue knowledge, to knowledge *self-control,* to self-control perseverance, to perseverance godliness, to godliness brotherly kindness, and to brotherly kindness love" (2 Peter 1:5–7; emphasis added).

Think of it analogously: *akrates* can mean "incontinent." We've all been there! As babies, before the brain had time to forge that essential connection to the organs, we had no continence, or "contain-ence." "Like a city whose walls are broken down is a man who lacks self-control" (Proverbs 25:28, NIV).

Self-control can involve positive actions in addition to restraint. It includes refraining from the bad *and* doing the good; passing up the ice cream *and* choosing the walk around the block; holding the sharp tongue *and* saying, "I love you." Whether restraint or action, it requires an energy to which many of us are strangers.

Whose power is willpower?

A million-dollar question presents itself: Where does the power for these things come from? From our own will, or from God? The answer is yes and yes. It's a mysterious, gorgeous, synergistic, intertwining of both human and divine. Philippians 2:12, 13 lays out this partnership beautifully: "Work out your own salvation with fear and trembling; for it is God who works in you both to will and to do for His good pleasure."

A direct translation of the first half of this would read something like, "Perform for yourself salvation." Now that sounds heretical, doesn't it? Especially in the face of what I've been sharing about the ineffectiveness of humanity's natural fig-leaf drive to fix ourselves! But apparently God calculated the risk. He would never say anything that could be mistaken for self-salvation if we didn't need to hear it. Apparently, dwelling solely on God's part in the plan of salvation fails to paint a comprehensive picture.

I once visited a friend's Bible study. The subject matter was the spiritual fruit of self-control. "We can't claim to have self-control," the leader said. "God does it all. All we can do is come to Him, and He takes over. After that point, it's all Him and none of us."

"But that would make us into robots!" I protested, pulling out various texts to defend my position. It was to no avail. The sentiment of the group was toward a God-takes-over model of divine empowerment.

The event prompted me to think more rigorously about the whole concept of self-control. First of all, it's called *self*-control, so it must involve *self*. Second, one of the distinguishing marks, if not *the* distinguishing mark, of God's governance is freedom. Put in relational terms, when we submit to Satan, he takes away our free will; when we submit to God, He returns our free will. Yes, God "takes over," but only with our ongoing permission. God is the Supreme Gentleman.

Of sin, Paul said (I think sarcastically), "Do you not know that to whom you present yourselves slaves to obey, you are that one's slaves whom you obey, whether of sin leading to death, or of obedience leading to righteousness?" (Romans 6:16). Simplified and colloquialized, that might read, "Duh! Don't you know that when you make yourself a slave of sin, you become a *slave*?" In other words, sin leads to the loss of freedom. Think of the top ten addictions: alcohol, tobacco, drugs, gambling, food, video games, the Internet, sex, shopping, and work. Some of these are innately sinful, some only sinful if used excessively. But all, when put before our relationship with God, become idols to which we become captives. We lose our freedom; our wills are held in iron bondage.

Just last night I spoke to a slave named Todd. Todd's mother and grandmother had spoiled him, and at the age of twenty-five he still lived at home for free. His work income expendable, he spent it on multiple addictions. But the consequences turned the pleasures bitter. He finally lost the respect of his family when he left his aging aunt at the bus stop for several hours in the cold. "I was at a party. . . . I totally forgot about my aunt," he mourned, concluding, "this addiction has control of me!" Because parental discipline founds self-discipline, permissive parenting typically turns out adult children with poor self-control. Todd was a classic case of poor parenting compounded by personal mistakes.

Fortunately, Todd's conscience felt appropriate pangs of guilt. He begged me, "What do I need?" I said, "You need to understand the true force of the will." And then I paraphrased the following quotation from *Steps to Christ:*

> This is the governing power in the nature of man, the power of decision, or of choice. Everything depends on the right action of the will. The power of choice God has given to men; it is theirs to exercise. You cannot change your heart, you cannot of yourself give to God its affections; but you can choose to serve Him. You can give Him your will; He will then work in you to will and to do according to His good pleasure. Thus your whole nature will be brought under the control of the Spirit of Christ; your affections will be centered upon Him, your thoughts will be in harmony with Him.[2]

Notice that in the midst of the list of things we can't do, we find something we can do. We can give God our will. After that point, our "whole nature" experiences a transformation at God's hands. Giving God our will, then, is the critical point in this process. But how do we give God our will? Not much is said about it here, perhaps, because it's really that simple.

Spiritual intimacy with God

Some things we learn by doing. Aristotle said, "For the things we have to learn before we can do them, we learn by doing them." John Dewey, considered the father of experiential education, said, "Give the pupils something to do, not something to learn; and the doing is of such a nature as to demand thinking . . . learning naturally results."[3] Long before Aristotle or Dewey, Jesus urged experiential knowledge: "This is eternal life, that they may know You, the only true God, and Jesus Christ whom You have sent" (John 17:3). The word for *know,* the Greek *gnosis,* is a Jewish idiom for sexual intercourse.

Certainly sexual intercourse isn't a head-knowledge event! We don't spend hours in class in preparation, then keep the manual by our side as a reference to follow step by step. "Wait a minute, honey, I have to look something up!" *Hmm . . . I'm not sure what happens next! Oh! Here it is—page 126.*

No! We learn by doing.

Knowing God—blending our wills with God's will in spiritual intimacy—we also learn by doing. I often find myself urging people to simply experiment with giving

For help with having a devotional life, find "Devotions Made Simple" in the toolbox.

themselves to God. "Oh, taste and see that the Lord is good" (Psalm 34:8), I quote to them. "What do you have to lose? You can always go back to your own miserable way of doing things." I hope that once they get the feel, the kinesthetic sense, of serving God, they'll actually like it!

Will plus grace equals change

Most of us mouth the words *we have free will* quite easily. But in the next breath, we'll say things like, "I can't resist this brownie à la mode," "I couldn't help yelling back," or "I'm just not motivated to exercise." This doublespeak reveals that we understand free will *technically* but not *experientially*. We mentally assent to it without walking in it. Yet free will lies at the very core of our being.

As much as we're helpless to save ourselves, as much as without God we can do nothing, apparently the reverse is true. Without us, He can do nothing in terms of changing our characters! The great controversy between good and evil revolves around free will. God will do anything for us *except* choose for us. But He will give us power to choose. He will infuse our weakness with His infinite power if we simply cooperate. And so, we see this mysterious formula, welling up from the depths of God's heart: Will plus grace equals change.

Leave the human will to fend for itself, and it remains either flaccid or perverted. The desires of the flesh and the whims of the feelings dominate our spiritual lives and control our behaviors. But align the will with grace, and it sets the entire person back in order, with the governing powers ruling the flesh.

This power-of-the-will phenomenon unlocks the mystery of motivation. The cry of "I'm not motivated" is never actually true. As behavioral psychologists say, "All behavior is operative," meaning human beings are constantly in the process of trying either to

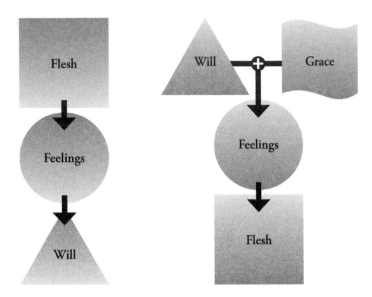

obtain or avoid something. Even the limp-willed are motivated—motivated to *avoid* the discomfort and risk involved in making an effort. When we say, "I'm just not motivated" what we really mean is, "I just don't *feel* like it!" And the more we live by what we feel like doing, the less we feel like doing the right thing.

Abraham Maslow theorized that the human-need hierarchy determined behavior, such that when foundational needs were met, the person would naturally progress to higher motivations. In other words, once a person had food and safety, he or she would naturally pursue social connections and self-esteem, ultimately reaching potential through self-actualization. This sometimes happens, but how many people stall out at the food and safety point, full-fledged couch potatoes lacking social lives or personal fulfillment? How many Americans eat themselves to death rather than build a well-rounded life? Or use alcohol, sex, or mass media to soothe away deeper longings?

Learned helplessness

Of course, some circumstances demand compassion. In the case of severe childhood trauma, a condition called *learned helplessness* can keep a person locked in self-defeat, seemingly bereft of self-control. In one experiment, "a group of subjects was exposed to a loud abrasive noise that they were unable to shut off. . . . Later, they were placed in a situation where they could shut off the noise by moving a handle."[4] Many, however, never lifted a finger. Repeated past failures and trauma led to despondency.

Learned helplessness appears frequently in a condition called *borderline personality disorder* (BPD). BPD features extreme relational and emotional instability and often impulsive, self-destructive behavior. Therapists often use something called *dialectical behavioral therapy,* a complex system of exercises based on Buddhist and humanistic principles, as treatment. One of the exercises is called opposite action. When a person feels impelled to engage in impulsive, self-destructive behaviors, he or she does the opposite. Instead of cutting himself or herself, he or she makes a healthy salad. Instead of bingeing, he or she takes a shower.

I believe that the most therapeutic element of this exercise is that it helps individuals rediscover their free will. They find they can actually make self-determining choices! Amazing. I often give clients exercises such as making their beds faithfully or cleaning one small part of the house. They often like the resulting sense of self-control. Even those from chaotic or abusive childhoods can unlearn their learned helplessness and discover the willpower that God has blessed them with.

For help in learning how to exercise your will, see "Exercise Program for the Will" in the toolbox.

For help in thought control, see "F.A.R. Thought Control" in the toolbox.

Not all people subjected to childhood trauma become helpless. Clinicians have identified one of the characteristics of those who rise above difficulty as an *optimistic explanatory style,* meaning that they explain events in a positive manner. People with *pessimistic explanatory style*—who see negative events as permanent ("it will never change"), personal ("it's my fault"), or pervasive ("I can't do anything correctly")—are most likely to suffer from learned helplessness. Fortunately, our explanatory style can change.

Will weakeners

Like all cognitive functions, the will works within the context of a biological system—specifically the executive system of the cerebral cortex. Anything that compromises that system, weakens the will and makes self-control more difficult. The enemy of mental health knows how to erode our cognitive fine-tuning through "socially acceptable" practices. Here are a few big culprits.

Alcohol. Even a sip or two of alcohol assaults the frontal lobes, weakening judgment and deteriorating self-control. People lose inhibition with blood alcohol levels as low as .01 percent (the legal driving limit in the United States is .08 percent). Losing inhibition is good, right? Not when you're trying to drive. But "drink responsibly" is an oxymoron. Alcohol destroys the ability to make responsible decisions. So change that slogan to "Drink not."

Nicotine. A central nervous system stimulant, nicotine changes metabolic activity in areas of the brain that manage impulse control—particularly in women! In fact, women who smoke can become more aggressive and rash. True, nicotine, like caffeine, can at first increase alertness. But unnatural highs always end in unnatural lows—and addictions. Don't fool yourself; nicotine is not your friend.

Caffeine. Caffeine binds to adenosine receptors to prevent fatigue from setting in, causing the body to activate the fight-or-flight system. Alertness increases, but not necessarily intellectual acuity. It also spikes dopamine levels, eventually causing a letdown effect. Even if you sleep, caffeine can prevent deep sleep, creating a kind of chronic fatigue. And the list of caffeine's woes goes on. Start weaning yourself!

Media. In less than one minute of television viewing, our brain waves switch from beta waves—brain waves associated with active, logical thought—to primarily Alpha waves. Alpha waves are the brain waves present in hypnosis and some kinds of meditation. This explains why people look like zombies when they watch TV. User discretion advised.

Electronic games. Preliminary research suggests that video, online, and other electronic games tend to stir up the fight-or-flight response while compromising frontal lobe activity. With gaming options multiplying by the day, observers are noting "video game brain," in which key parts of the frontal region of players' brains become chronically underused. This condition can alter mood, behavior, and ultimately, character. Electronic game addiction is fast being recognized by mental health providers—in fact, treatment programs are multiplying as fast as video games themselves.

Poor diet. The brain runs on glucose. The best diet to keep a steady, even level of glucose is a diet consisting of fruits, nuts, grains, and vegetables in as simple and natural a state as possible. The refined, sugar- and fat-rich Western diet causes rapid fluctuations in blood sugar levels, which, in turn, affect cognition and willpower. Animal fats cause

For a list of brain-building foods, see the "Happy Brain Food" document in the toolbox.

vascular changes that affect oxygen and glucose supply. Refined, animal-product based diets cause degenerative diseases, which then affect the brain. In more ways than can be listed here, diet affects the brain and spirituality!

Today, harden not your heart

So many of us have failed to fully appreciate the treasure of free will. Like sleepy, fat dogs, we live by impulse, feeling, and momentary comfort. But while we sleep, the consequences multiply like fleas, and we pay a dear price in lost opportunities and wasted talents. I often ask people, "How is this working for you?" The answer almost never varies from "Terrible." What we sow, we reap. As I see it, we pay sooner or later for our choices; we might as well pay up front by putting up with a little self-denial. "Today, if you hear His voice, do not harden your hearts" (Hebrews 3:15). This could be translated as, "Don't make your wills stubborn." You've heard His voice. Don't harden your heart; don't make your will stubborn. Come to know Him. Give Him your will. Learn by doing. Enjoy the better life God has for you.

Listen to a woman named Edith Eva Eger talk about the power of choice. Edith had every reason to give up: she survived Auschwitz; she watched her mother die; a German guard broke her back; she endured a death march to Austria and, finally wasting away to forty pounds, was thrown on a heap of bodies, taken for dead. An American soldier saw her hand move and summoned help, so that she lives today to tell her story.

Edith remembers that some in the camps resorted to cannibalism to fend off the starving. "I chose to eat grass," she says. "And I sat on the ground, selecting one blade over the other, telling myself that even under those conditions I still had a choice—which blade of grass I would eat."[5]

Edith says, "The biggest concentration camp is in your own mind."[6]

I say we end the war and walk out.

DISCUSSION QUESTIONS

1. What has been your greatest need in the area of self-control?

2. How do you think self-control connects to spiritual growth? Can a person with no self-control be a healthy Christian?

3. Have you ever "presented" yourself as a slave to something, then been dismayed that you were stuck? Give an example.

4. Why do addictions often lead to extremely selfish behavior?

5. What do you think is the meaning of the statement, "Everything depends upon the right action of the will"?

6. Can you think of an experience in which you came to know God experientially? Share that experience.

7. Can you think of a time when God helped you use self-control and reason to govern over your fleshly or emotional desires? Share that experience.

8. Do you think you're someone who suffers from learned helplessness or from a feeling that you can't change anything, no matter how hard you try? Explain.

9. What will weakeners—alcohol, nicotine, caffeine, media, electronic games, and poor diet—would you like to give up, if any?

10. As you contemplate God's gift of free will, what do you feel? Gratitude? Fear? Awe? Confusion? Explain.

---

1. See, for instance, "Gottman's Marriage Tips 101," *Gottman Relationship Institute,* accessed February 25, 2011, http://www.gottman.com/dept.aspx?d_id=49804.

2. Ellen G. White, *Steps to Christ* (Washington, D.C.: Review and Herald®, 1956), 47.

3. John Dewey, *Democracy and Education* (Stilwell, Kans.: Digireads.com, 2005), 92.

4. "Learned Helplessness," WikiEd, accessed February 25, 2011, http://wik.ed.uiuc.edu/index.php/Learned_Helplessness.

5. Gerald Corey and Marianne Schneider Corey, *I Never Knew I Had a Choice,* 9th ed. (Belmont, Calif.: Brooks-Cole, 2010), 377.

6. "Survivor of Holocaust Shares Story," *Reflector Online,* accessed October 24, 2010, http://www.reflector-online.com/2.13177/survivor-of-holocaust-shares-story-1.1781796.

Let Us Reason Together

I'll admit that I'm probably one of the more than twenty million adult Americans who has wrestled with a mood disorder.[1] Dad was transferred when I was ten, and the move to a new, more urban school district brought bullying, rejection, and loneliness. Just as I recovered socially, a teenage romance and breakup re-devastated me. These events probably laid the foundation for a long-lasting battle with depression. Science confirms that the earlier the onset of depression, the more chronic it is likely to become.

I couldn't even label the wound in my brain, much less heal it. It felt as if a thunderhead of sadness loomed over me. I had no idea when it would break or what would happen when it did; I just lived in constant fear of disaster, developing unconscious strategies to deflect the pain. Those defenses led me into a very risky, experimental lifestyle throughout my teens.

At nineteen, I encountered Jesus on my personal Damascus road. I was broken. Conversion left behind pieces of my former self, as if my personality had been disassembled like a toy. People who met me as a new Christian thought I was a quiet person, but really I was a fairly extroverted person in a lingering state of shock. I had encountered a blinding light in Jesus, and I was stunned and speechless. It took a few years to rebuild my personality as a Christian.

Some years later, I confronted my old demons. I believe this was God's doing. He filters our trials and coddles the weak (see 1 Corinthians 10:13; 12:22, 23). This means that life's hard blows are God's backhanded compliments that we can take them. But I surely didn't feel complimented when I confronted the depression demon as a more mature Christian. Certain life crises prompted discouragement. Suicidal thoughts popped into my mind involuntarily, like mushrooms in a damp summer lawn. I never considered acting on them, but I wanted to.

Suicidal thoughts are not something a Christian wants to own. Even now it's hard to admit. The worst part was that I was a Seventh-day Adventist who observed a lifestyle proven to help me live "six years longer." I didn't even drink soda or eat hot dogs. And I was thinking, *I want to die? How un-Adventist is that?*

We clinicians call this type of thing *secondary disturbance.* People become disturbed, then they become disturbed about the disturbance: "I'm not supposed to be sad (anxious, angry, you fill in the blank)! I'm a Christian!" But as I said above, God was allowing me to face my past demons, which were jangling my old synaptic pathways.

It took some time and effort, but I'm happy to tell you that I've been depression free for many years. One of the reasons is that I learned how to use reason.

A history of cognitive behavioral therapy

The field of psychology has always been concerned with the mind. After all, *psyche* means "the immaterial part of man." Blood vessels, bones, glands, lungs, stomachs, livers, and uteruses can be measured, weighed, and quantified. This is more difficult with thoughts, feelings, desires, beliefs, and motives. One can't open a bag and say, "Here, take my motives," put desires in a petri dish to culture them into beliefs, or shake thoughts and feelings together in a test tube to see if they explode. These things lie beyond the pale of a science lab with its scales and test tubes. For a period of time, the field of psychology rejected introspection and attempted to focus entirely on measureable behaviors. But in the late 1900s, behaviorism gave way to the cognitive revolution, and the inner life of human beings once again became the focus of counseling. The psyche, the immaterial, difficult-to-pin-down part of us, is here to stay. To ignore it is to circumscribe and belittle human beings, the fearfully and wonderfully made images of God.

The most influential figure of the cognitive revolution was the brilliant, fiercely logical, atheistic, and, at times, profane, Albert Ellis. He was able to help human beings learn to use one of their most important God-given faculties, that of reason. He introduced a therapy called *rational emotive behavioral therapy* (REBT). Above all, REBT stressed control of the thought life, routing out irrational thinking. This conquest of irrational thoughts passed through the hands of other experts such as Aaron and Judith Beck, and morphed into today's cognitive behavioral therapy (CBT).

Ellis designed exercises to destroy irrational fear. One exercise for shy people involved dragging a banana on a leash through a shopping mall. He called it "shame-busting." He had overcome his own shyness by forcing himself to go to the Bronx Botanical Garden every day for a month and talk to women he found sitting alone on park benches. At the end of the month, only thirty had walked away; one hundred stayed to chat. Most essentially, Albert Ellis was fear free because he'd defeated his own irrational thoughts about women.

Rational, balanced, truthful thinking stabilizes us. The cognitive theorists didn't originate this principle. Long before they lived, Jesus said, "You shall know the truth, and the truth shall make you free" (John 8:32). Before the Incarnate Christ spoke, His prophet Jeremiah said, "Behold, I will bring . . . health and healing; I will heal them and reveal to them the abundance of peace and truth" (Jeremiah 33:6). Notice the link between truth and healing. And Isaiah said, "Let us reason together" (Isaiah 1:18).

King Nebuchadnezzar presents an interesting case study of this principle. If he lived today, he'd probably receive the diagnosis of *narcissistic personality disorder,* which is essentially pathological pride, vanity, and grandiosity. Listen to his pompous words: "Is not this great Babylon, that I have built for a royal dwelling by my mighty power and for the honor of my majesty?" (Daniel 4:30). As the story goes, severe mental illness befell him the moment he spoke these words; we might say a personality disorder led to a psychotic episode. We next see him unkempt, on all fours, eating grass, homeless, and nonverbal. Whether labeled as *dissociative fugue, delusional disorder,* or *boanthropy,*[2] he had clearly lost his mind. But notice the connection between his acknowledgment of the truth about God and the restoration of his sanity: "But at the end of that period, I, Nebuchadnezzar, raised my eyes toward heaven and my *reason returned* to me, and I blessed the Most High and praised and honored Him who lives forever" (Daniel 4:34, NASB; emphasis added).

Defining reason

Let's probe the meaning of the word *reason*. One dictionary defines it as "the power of comprehending, inferring, or thinking especially in orderly rational ways."[3] As early as the thirteenth century, it meant the "intellectual faculty that adopts actions to ends."[4] So our current use of the word *reason* has to do with cause-effect process.

The Bible also identifies reason as a cause-effect phenomenon. Interestingly, its primary Hebrew word, *yakach,* can also mean "judge," "reprove," or even "rebuke." The current cultural climate in the West has made *judge* a dreaded word, a pejorative term, but Old Testament times conveyed a more positive connotation. Read passages such as Leviticus 19:17, "You shall not hate your brother in your heart. You shall surely rebuke your neighbor, and not bear sin because of him." Did you get that? Don't hate him, rebuke him! Hate *contrasts* with rebuke! Or we might recast the concept as a positive and say that we show our love to a brother by judging or rebuking his actions. It sounds pretty counterintuitive, but read on.

For instance, when, as a mother, have I lovingly rebuked my children? When they engaged in self-destructive or self-defeating behaviors. "No, no! Alison! You can't play in the middle of the highway!" "Kimmy, the dog food is for the doggy, not for you!" I told my children what would hurt them until they knew it for themselves. Likewise, when a friend, client, or loved one, blinded by prejudice, ignorance, or passion, engages in self-harm, I rebuke them out of love. I look at their lives and *reason* from cause to effect, then warn them, "Overwork will kill your spirituality," "Flirting with a married man will hurt your soul and your reputation," or "Alcohol could be contributing to your depression." To remain silent in such situations isn't as "nice" as it seems. We seem so stuck these days on being nonjudgmental that we sometimes leave people to further harm themselves through their own bad choices.

Romans 12:1 says that presenting our bodies a living sacrifice to God is our "*reasonable* service" (emphasis added). In 1 Peter 3:15, Paul admonishes us to "sanctify the Lord God in your hearts, and always be ready to give a defense to everyone who asks you a *reason* for the hope that is in you, with meekness and fear" (emphasis added). The word *reason* in this verse is translated from the Greek *logos,* the same *logos* we find in psycho*logy,* neuro*logy,* or physio*logy. Logos* can mean "word," "speak," or, as Trench's *Synonyms of the New Testament* expands, "to speak by linking and knitting together in connected discourse of the inward thoughts and feelings of the mind." Notice the "linking and knitting together" involved in reasoning. In other words, psycho-*logy* is the linking or knitting together of facts about the human psyche.

It's all about knitting. We're seeing a pattern here. Reason, by all accounts, is the ability to connect, to knit together, cause and effect.

Much of counseling involves reasoning with people, helping them think connectedly. Some people's random speech patterns can resemble an attic full of curious but unrelated things. Such individuals seem to be constantly hurrying to bring down another strange, new item, which has no significance to the last object: "Here's my graduation gown! Oh, look at my family Bible! Do you think we should throw away these encyclopedias?" Listening to disconnected speech can exhaust the listener, so often people with tangential speech find themselves rather isolated and lonely. Sadly, their disconnected thoughts lead

For some guidance in choosing a good counselor, see "Finding a Good Counselor" in the toolbox.

to disconnected relationships. Often for such people learning to think connectedly, in a reasoning manner, begins a more positive chapter of their lives. And fortunately, the brain is flexible, or as neuroscientists say, "plastic," even into old age. Old dogs *can* learn new tricks!

Love that frontal lobe!

Although not a discrete organ, reason has a neurological basis. The frontal lobe of the cerebral cortex rests above your eyebrows and behind your forehead, or frontal bone. The cranial bones are the hardest in human anatomy, clearly to protect the "image of God" capacity we possess. In fact, the body protects the brain at all costs. For instance, the weight and protein content of the brain remain relatively stable during long-term starvation. The body breaks down organs and tissues before it sacrifices the brain. God designed human anatomy to preserve the "house" of the character.

As I've point out before, the very essence of who we are, the soul, the character, resides in a physical organ. To sabotage the body, particularly the physical organ of the frontal lobe, is to harm the character. Abundant research reveals that frontal lobe injuries

For a more detailed explanation of practices that compromise brain function, see the previous week.

lead to immoral and even aggressive behaviors. Most of us will never suffer a traumatic brain injury. But sadly, many of us cause slow frontal lobe injuries on ourselves with substances and practices that compromise brain function.

This brings us back to the beginning—correct, rational thinking. Cognitive behavioral therapy has received strong empirical support.[5] This simply means that it helps people function better. Now, as a counselor, I must balance functionality with thoroughness. I don't want to prematurely sew up a wound with a cancer still deep in the tissues, so to speak. Not every psychological problem can be treated quickly. But even when dealing with deep wounds, I must also help a person feel better during the healing process. They must make it through the day without a meltdown. And for this, CBT is one of my best tools.

The thought-feeling connection

The connection between reason, thoughts, and feelings can be illustrated by a boy walking a dog. Ideally, the dog heels, and the boy decides where to walk. The dog is precious, fun, exciting, and valuable, but is not capable of making decisions. But too often the dog walks the boy, and both end up in the swamp. Many of us who fail to place reason before emotion end up in the same murky water.

Emotions can produce thoughts. A horror film, for example, can lead to an obsession with zombies. Hormonal activity causes people to think they're in love. Political propagandists use emotion-stirring music to indoctrinate. Emotional arousal gives birth to thoughts that match the emotion. But much of emotional conditioning, especially through the media, bypasses reason.

Some worship styles strive to produce intense emotions, often to the exclusion of disciplined teaching of truth. If believers realized that this causes people to place emotion before reason, they might change their approach. Think about it: If my emotional high tells me that God is with me, what does an emotional *low* tell me? That He has left me! This is how emotion-based religion can lead to serious spiritual and mental health problems.

In psychology, we call this *emotional reasoning*. Emotional reasoning says, "I feel sad, so something horrible must be happening," or "I'm anxious. This must be a dangerous place." Emotional reasoning looks to feelings as a source of conclusive evidence. While we should respect our emotions, we should pass them through the filter of reason and evidence. Another analogy I use likens emotions to a two-year-old. "Do you know a two-year-old?" I'll ask.

"Yes, my niece, Bethany," someone will respond.

"She's cute, isn't she?" I ask.

"Really cute," he says.

"Adorable."

"Yes!"

"You listen to her, right?"

"Oh, yeah."

"You care about her, right?"

"Yeah."

"Do you let her drive the car?"

"No!"

"Why not?"

"We'd all die!" he says, now understanding my point that while emotions are precious, to be listened to, and not to be ignored, they mustn't be allowed to drive.

Another extreme in the thought-feeling continuum is failing to experience our emotions at all. Some people so fear their emotions that they repress them, locking them in the basement, so to speak. Clinical and anecdotal experience tells me that women are more inclined to follow emotions and men are more inclined to repress them. Women tend to wallow; men tend to stuff. Learning how to use the gift of reason can actually free "stuffers" (men or women) to experience emotions because reason provides structure without which emotions become too threatening and all-consuming. Likewise, our worship of God, if grounded in truth, actually frees us emotionally. "God is Spirit, and those who worship Him must worship in spirit and truth" (John 4:24).

Thoughts and feelings apart from the discipline of reason can resemble young siblings without parental supervision—things go bad quickly.

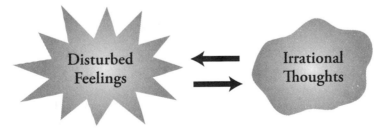

With reason out of the picture, feelings and irrational thoughts form a self-defeating feedback loop.

Reason brings the thoughts back into harmony with truth, and the feelings mold to rational thoughts. In this more structured environment, feelings actually strengthen, deepen, and expand.

It's very difficult to directly change emotions. My mother used to say, "Be cheerful!" I hated it. It actually triggered the opposite emotions of frustration and irritation. I have a family picture in which I am smiling a very unconvincing clenched-jaw smile. I think Mom had just said, "Be cheerful!" If she had said, "We're going for ice cream after the shoot!" I would have smiled sincerely because I would have had a *reason* to smile. You can't turn your emotions off and on like a light switch. But if you change your thoughts, your emotions tend to follow. Granted, they follow slowly—like two-year-olds wandering behind their mothers, dawdling to look at bugs and flowers—but they follow!

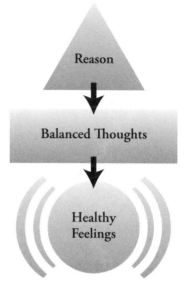

Often depressed or anxious people harbor extremely negative thought patterns, such as "No one loves me," "I'm ugly, fat, and stupid," or "Nothing I try ever works." Tragically, these thoughts tend to set up a feedback loop in which their worst fears become reality. A little examination reveals how this self-fulfilling prophecy syndrome works. A friend named Joe repeated a near mantra: "I'm lonely and will never be loved." Because of this belief, he behaved in a loveless manner, and people validated his belief by withdrawing from him. He believed they rejected him, but in reality they rejected his attitude and behaviors. When he finally started thinking differently, he acted differently, and ultimately felt different. Finally, Joe started building relationships, one positive interchange at a time.

Negatively biased, distorted thoughts are called *misbeliefs*. These misbeliefs act like hard, impenetrable ground; the seeds of truth don't penetrate it. If we hold misbeliefs, we may be able to recite facts in a cold, sterile way, but we don't really *believe* them. Our hearts remain unchanged. So many Christians can recite Bible verses by the score without feeling anything! This is because deeply held misbeliefs exist below the surface. Until we can unearth them from the depths of our psyches, and plow them into fallow ground, nothing really changes. In other words, we must examine our own core beliefs.

Find, argue, and replace

In a clinical setting, I use a three-part process to help clients learn thought and emotional regulation. I use the acronym FAR, for find, argue, and replace. There are many ways to approach the process of replacing irrational thoughts with reason, but this one works well for me and for most of my clients.

Find. The first step of the process is to find misbeliefs. As I pointed out a minute ago, these misbeliefs tend to lurk in the unconscious and, like wild animals, evade detection. It can help to take the finding process in three steps: First, find the event; second, find the feeling; and third, find the thought. Finding the *event* means identifying the problematic circumstance or happening. (Use the "Event-Emotion-Thought Record" worksheet in the toolbox). Finding the *feeling* involves identifying the feeling that comes as a result of the event. (Use the "Feeling Words" document in the toolbox). Finding the *thought* entails identifying the distorted thinking that couples with the disturbed feelings.

For instance, Joe can readily identify the loss of his job as a cause for depression. But he lost his job over a year ago and could have recovered by now. The reason his depression continues is that he harbors certain misbeliefs that have paralyzed him and make finding a new job difficult. Joe identifies his feelings as bewilderment, despair, and devaluation. Now Joe begins the process of identifying the thoughts that underpin the feelings. Typically, these distorted thoughts involve ourselves, other people, the future, and God. Here are Joe's thoughts: *I'm a loser; other people don't see me as valuable; I'll never find a stable job; and God doesn't care about me.*

Argue. Now Joe is ready to argue with his thoughts. I use a list of "Distorted Thoughts" (found in the toolbox). The list enumerates and defines such thought patterns as *catastrophizing, overgeneralizing,* and *mind reading.* I help people like Joe identify their thought patterns and learn to hold themselves accountable for them. "Learn to argue with your irrational self!" I say. This process resembles what 1 Corinthians 10:5 describes as, "casting down arguments and every high thing that exalts itself against the knowledge of God, bringing every thought into captivity to the obedience of Christ." "Casting down" is from the Greek *kathaireo,* and can mean "demolish." It's a forceful process, this learning to dismantle our misbeliefs. I liken it to hoeing the hard, crusty ground. We must be prepared to sweat.

One technique I use to facilitate this involves changing context. I might say to Joe,

"You're telling yourself that because you lost a job, you're a loser. If I lost my job, would you call me a loser?"

Joe would say, "No, that would be unfair and cruel."

Then I'd say, "So you're being cruel and unfair to yourself. Tell yourself to stop that!"

Replace. Often the process of identifying core beliefs provides great relief. It resembles putting toxic waste in containers, taping them shut, and labeling them. Once contained, the individual can start to replace the distorted thoughts with truth. Truth is typically more nuanced and detailed than a misbelief. *I'm a loser!* is replaced with *I have failed and will fail, but I have also succeeded and will succeed. I'm not perfect, but I do make a contribution.* Once the thoughts are brought under the control of reason, the emotions conform to the truthful, balanced thoughts and likewise become more balanced. We call this process *emotional regulation.*

Psalm 139:23, 24 says,

> For a synopsis of the "F.A.R. Thought Control" exercise, look in the toolbox.

Search me, O God, and know my heart;
Try me, and know my anxieties;
And see if there is any wicked way in me,
And lead me in the way everlasting.

"Wicked way" is translated from the Hebrew *otseb derek,* and can mean "habit of pain, toil, and idolatry." Through the guidance of God's Spirit, we can find within ourselves the habits of pain and toil that cut us off from God and contribute to our suffering and the suffering of others.

For many years of my life, irrational, distorted, unbalanced thinking caused me pain and toil. Because I lived in connection with others, my pain hurt them too. Part of self-control and good stewardship entailed managing my thought life. When I finally learned to tell myself the truth, my depression lifted like fog in sunshine. I believe every one of us can benefit from using this God-given power of reason.

DISCUSSION QUESTIONS

1. Do you recognize in yourself a tendency toward irrational or distorted thinking?

2. Do you think Nebuchadnezzar's pride contributed to his mental breakdown? If so, how?

3. The concept of reason involves tracing from a cause to an effect. What cause-effect process has affected you recently? Explain.

4. Why do you think the current moral climate in our world has caused us to become "allergic" to warning people or even reproving them?

5. Can you think of a time when either you reproved someone or they reproved you to good effect? Share the experience.

6. Do you tend to have disconnected thought and speech patterns? How has this affected your relationships?

7. What traumatic experiences in your life may have initially caused you to develop negative thought patterns? Give details.

8. Have you allowed emotion to "drive the car"? Explain and give examples.

9. From the "Distorted Thoughts" document, which thought pattern(s) are you the most likely to fall into? Give an example.

10. What "ways of pain" has the Lord revealed to you—ways in which you make your own mood and situation worse? Give examples.

---

1. R. C. Kessler et al., "*DSM-IV* Disorders in the National Comorbidity Survey Replication," 617–627.

2. In R. K. Harrison's *Introduction to the Old Testament* (Grand Rapids, Mich.: Eerdmans, 1969), he speaks of a 1946 mental institution featuring an otherwise normal patient with "pronounced anti-social tendencies. . . . His daily routine consisted of wandering around the magnificent lawns . . . and it was his custom to pluck up and eat handfuls of the grass as he went along" (1116).

3. Merriam-Webster's Online Dictionary, s.v. "reason," accessed October 26, 2010, http://www.merriam-webster.com/dictionary/reason.

4. Online Etymology Dictionary, s.v. "reason," accessed October 26, 2010, http://www.etymonline.com/index.php?term=reason.

5. The health care trend of evidence-based treatment, where specific treatments for symptom-based diagnoses are recommended, has favored CBT. Wikipedia's page on cognitive behavioral therapy has a good bibliography of references for further study. See http://en.wikipedia.org/wiki/Cognitive_behavioral_therapy.

Faith It Till You Make It

A friend once told me she rejected the Bible. "All that stuff about Creation, the Flood, the Red Sea—it's so outrageous." Ironically, a few minutes later, she began to read me a very sentimental newspaper clipping about Santa Claus and how precious little children so innocently believe in him. As she read, she began to cry, moved by the faith of the little ones. I stifled a laugh. She admired faith in Santa and ridiculed faith in the Bible! What a contradiction.

I didn't take it personally; I know we humans need to believe in something. If not God and His Word, it can be any number of things from Santa Claus to Bigfoot to our variable annuities.

Defining faith

Faith is difficult to define. The lexical definition is as flat as root beer without bubbles: "persuasion, i.e. credence; moral conviction . . . assurance, belief, believe, faith, fidelity." Metaphors of faith vary widely, comparing it to a fight, a race, eating, drinking, a door, a shield, a seed, a hand, and a ship.[1] Notice that some of these metaphors indicate receiving (eating, drinking, opening) and some acting (fighting, racing, grasping, shielding). Faith apparently morphs into whatever mode the situation demands. It can receive, it can give, it can rest, and it can take action. It's bigger and more basic than its manifestations.

So apparently faith is more about what it *does* than what it *is*.

God showed us faith for an entire Testament before He labeled it. The Hebrew word for faith, *aman,* appears only twice in noun form (in the Old Testament).[2] In contrast, the Greek noun *pistis* appears 244 times in the New Testament. In other words, Abel, Enoch,

Noah, Abraham, Sarah, Isaac, Jacob, Joseph, Moses, and Rahab *show* us faith[3]; Matthew, Mark, Luke, John, Jesus, and Paul *name* it.

I studied dance in college.[4] A famous New York City dance troop performer named Beverly Schmidt Blossom came to our school to perform. I saw her sitting and eating an orange before the performance. She looked unimpressive—even homely. Then, under the spotlight, she blossomed into a work of art. Beauty exuded from every twirl and bend, sculpted by what seemed like a million muscles flexed throughout her body. Beverly looked fantastic when she moved. So does faith. It's small and unimpressive, like a mustard seed, until it's put into action, at which point it shimmers with powerful, mountain-moving beauty.

It's my hope that this chapter will help you to learn how to put the seed of faith, buried in your heart, in motion. Once you do, mountains of entrenched, troublesome hang-ups, headaches, habits, and even character flaws will move out of your way.

Faith becomes saving faith

God bestows each human being with the ability to believe. We exercise this ability through the access of our free will. What a risk God took! The very power the Creator bestows can be turned against Him, exercised toward damning delusions and godless fallacies. For example, the Muslim extremists responsible for the September 11 attacks acted in the name of Allah; they were possessed with the expectation of an instant virgin-filled paradise. The medieval Inquisition stretched over several centuries, killing and torturing in the name of God. The Aztecs brought human sacrifice into their golden age, killing twenty thousand people a year to appease their gods. The list of religious atrocities throughout human history reads like a sci-fi war epic. Alongside these wicked deceptions, the tamer lies multiply like flu viruses. In a twisted, sad way, our very ability to believe lies proves the existence of faith. But like all God-given faculties, there's a healthy, proper use of faith. This proper use demands a connection with God. Through the empowerment of the Holy Spirit and the guidance of God's Word, faith becomes *saving* faith. Otherwise, in a state of disconnect, it's damning faith as we believe nonsense.

Saving faith can be conceptualized in an acronym (I know acronyms are cheesy, but this one really works!):

Facts
Assent
Internalize
Trust
Heart

Facts. Faith demands an object; saving faith's object is the truth of Scripture. "So then faith comes by hearing, and hearing by the Word of God" (Romans 10:17). "These [stories of miracles] are written that you may believe that Jesus is the Christ, the Son of God, and that believing you may have life in His name" (John 20:31).

Many forms of spirituality champion faith, yet they don't clearly identify faith in what. The agnostic rock star Sting sings a hit song, "If I Ever Lose My Faith in You." What does he believe in? He's not even sure. People are told to believe in a higher Power. That power can be anything: a doorknob, a toad, or a muffin. But is a muffin really a higher Power? No. Such faith has no true object; faith without an object is a groundless mind game. It's faith in faith itself, which is a kind of spiritual cannibalism in which one eats one's own hand rather than the apple it plucks from the tree.

Assent. In the next step of believing, we assent to, or agree with, the facts. We consciously, intentionally, unreservedly, acknowledge their truth. Regardless of the weight of evidence, this is still a choice. Like soldiers sleeping through enemy stealth incursions, human beings have a profound capacity for denial. Facts may be blaringly obvious; but to fully benefit from them, we must say Yes to them.

The evidence for God is strong but not overwhelming. There is room for doubt. But thank God because no room for doubt means no room for faith either. If God removed all doubt, cultivation of faith would become impossible.

Don't wait for irrefutable evidence. Philippians 2:10 tells us that "at the name of Jesus EVERY KNEE WILL BOW" (NASB). Every knee! When the weight of evidence is overpowering, when God Himself appears before people, projecting on heaven's IMAX movie screen the panoramic view of their lives, including every dirty little secret, they will crumble to their knees and acknowledge He is Lord. But, by then, it will be too late to exercise faith.

Internalize. "Even the demons believe—and tremble" (James 2:19). The devils know and assent to the facts, yet their "faith" has no saving value; unholy fear still jangles in their diabolical nerves. For them, truth isn't personal. Notice that the letter *I* rests in the middle of the word *faith*. *I* internalize faith, assimilating the spiritual nutrients of the gospel until they become part of me. The righteousness of Jesus coheres with my very essence.

Even my dog believes what she can't see. Every time I put on my walking shoes, she "by faith" begins to frolic around in preparation for her favorite activity—going for a walk. But I could preach twenty sermons to her and she'd just cock her cute little head, never grasping by faith the saving grace of Jesus Christ. I'm not saying she won't be in heaven; I'm simply saying she won't get there by internalizing the truth the same way I do. As a human that's my unique ability.

Here's an interesting verse about faith: "Now faith is the substance of things hoped for, the evidence of things not seen" (Hebrews 11:1). Distill this statement down to nouns and verbs, and it reads, Faith is substance; faith is evidence. Notice that faith *itself* is evidence. Evidence of what? Evidence that the object of faith exists. Here's what the verse seems to be saying: the fact that humans *believe* proves that a suitable object of faith exists. The faith proves the object.

My grandmother used to spend Sundays on our porch, reading the Bible out loud all day long. Her Christian Scientist beliefs prevented her from getting glasses, so she sat stooped over the words, peering through a magnifying glass, practically sweating a drop with each word. I couldn't help but wonder what would possess a person to spend the day reading the Bible. As extreme as some of her beliefs may have been, she had tremendous faith; her faith gave me evidence of a living Savior.

I've bought used cars that were missing the radios. The holes in the dashboards prove that there were radios somewhere out there. My point is that the capacity proves the existence of its object. Our capacity for faith proves the existence of the object of faith— Jesus. We have this unique spiritual capacity; Jesus fits it perfectly.

Paul prayed that Christ would dwell in our hearts through faith. When he said "dwell," he used the Greek word *katoekito*, which means to "dwell permanently." Essentially, this means "to internalize." I remember that when we moved several years ago, I put my piano in storage until we found a house in which to dwell permanently. Not until that point did we lug in the (very heavy) piano. Did you know that Jesus wants to move into your heart and life *with His luggage*? He wants to dwell permanently in your heart. As a result, you will be "strengthened with might through His Spirit in the inner man . . . rooted and grounded in love . . . able to comprehend with all the saints what is the width and length and depth and height—to know the love of Christ which passes knowledge; that you may be filled with all the fullness of God" (Ephesians 3:16–19). Look at those verbs: *strengthened, rooted, grounded,* and *filled.* It sounds like mental health to me.

Trust. Things are getting warmer now. Not only do I accept and receive Jesus, but I bond with Him and trust Him. I learn to cast my burdens upon Him, to leave my life in His hands. In order to step into the Red Sea, the Israelites had to leave their lives in the hands of God. They had to trust Him with their stuff as they took on His stuff.

Most of us have trust issues. I think of Matt. In all my years on this earth, I've never heard a story like his. The first time I met him he had a look of complete distrust in his eyes—as if opening the door made me a dangerous person. Bit by tiny bit over a period of months, his story of horrible childhood abuse tumbled out. With each new disclosure he became terrified that I would reject him, asking, "Are you going to hate me? Are you going to leave me?" At first, I reassured him because he had no history with me. Now that he can draw from previous experience, I've asked him to lean on that evidence rather than look for constant verbal assurance. In doing this, he'll have to exercise trust. It's intelligent trust, it's informed and careful, but it still requires risk.

So with our natural distrust of God. He gives just enough evidence to awaken trust without giving so much evidence that it becomes unnecessary. Just as no room for doubt means no room for faith, no room for risk means no room for trust.

Heart. Faith warms up even more when we see that it includes heartfelt love. According to Galatians 5:6, faith works by love (*pistis di agapēs energoumenē*). This could be stated, "Faith's engine is *agape* love." What is this *agape* love that keeps faith in motion? God's love differs from human love, not just in type and characteristics but in position. God's love lies at the foundation of all relationships. It acts like the soil in which all loves grow. This means that when our feelings dry up, become strained, or even disgusted, the river of *agape* can continue to flow into that relationship. *Agape* "never fails" (1 Corinthians 13:8).

Agape works by choice rather than by feeling, impulse, or natural affection. God loves

Laodicea even though He feels like vomiting (Revelation 3:16). But it's not as if God is holding His nose, gritting His teeth, and "loving" us in spite of constant disgust. Just as our deepest ties feature complex feelings that can include simultaneously deep passion, anger, tenderness, and repulsion, God can hold mixed emotions toward us.

What keeps God's love-engine going? My engineer brother recently explained his hybrid car to me: "It gets its power partly from gas and partly from electricity, but it also captures the kinetic energy from the wheels as the car coasts down a hill, storing it in the battery. When this energy-capture process becomes more efficient, we'll have self-powered cars."

God's self-powered "engine" has already achieved this design. He loves us out of sheer downward-motioned commitment, and capturing the energy of that choice *feels* more deep than a mother, father, friend, and lover combined and multiplied a trillion times. And this love can only deepen throughout the ages as God continues to actively love us. His choice increases His desire to choose; God's ongoing investment in us fuels His love, making it much more than a cold, righteous dedication. He likes us! We tickle His heart with affection! He "will rejoice over [us] with singing" (Zephaniah 3:17). My husband never sings in public, but he has a rich baritone voice, with which he occasionally breaks into love songs. No one hears but me, his beloved. God has a love song for each one of us, and He breaks into it from time to time. Listen and be blessed.

Faith in motion

By love, love awakens. Feast your heart on the love of Jesus, and you'll find the strength to make a lasting commitment. Once you consecrate yourself, continue to live by faith in Him, even when the feelings wane. The energy of your dedication will fuel again the feelings of love, adoration, and affection for God. This is how faith works by love. His sacrifice for you will awaken in you a desire to surrender all to Him.

While salvation is by faith and not by works, works can encourage faith. Putting that same thought into psychology parlance, behavior has a reflective effect on belief. One somewhat hilarious manifestation of this phenomenon emerged when certain Botox clients experienced a mood lift—not just because they looked better, but because *they couldn't frown*! When they smiled more, they felt happier. Our inner life flows out in actions, but our actions also flow inward and influence our inner life. When we experience ourselves acting on our convictions, we reinforce those convictions. Our choices to act on beliefs ratify those beliefs in the council of our own hearts. Consider Romans 10:6, 8–10: "The righteousness of faith speaks in this way. . . . 'The word is near you, in your mouth and in your heart' (that is, the word of faith which we preach): that if you confess with your mouth the Lord Jesus and believe in your heart that God has raised Him from the dead, you will be saved. For with the heart one believes unto righteousness, and with the mouth confession is made unto salvation."

The mouth is an organ of action. This passage says that when the mouth acts on what the heart believes, salvation occurs. It's not that the action merits salvation; it's that the action builds faith, which provides an avenue for Christ's saving grace to be poured into our lives.

For a worksheet to help you with this, see "Overcome Fear Through Faith" in the toolbox.

We have enough information now. We have sufficient reason to believe. But remember, faith moves. Faith *works*. It's not just a fact registered in our brains. We must act on faith to fully understand it. So let's act. Let's take that first step, whether it is talking to a neighbor, eating more raw food, or apologizing to an offended brother. As we move, our faith will grow. Believers look so beautiful when they dance.

DISCUSSION QUESTIONS:

1. Can you remember an experience in which you put faith into motion? Share it.

2. When people misuse the faculty of faith, they become vulnerable to lies. What lies have you believed in the past? How did you finally "see"?

3. Which of the five steps of faith—faith, assent, internalize, trust, and heart—have you achieved, and which are you still working on?

4. Why do you think so many of us have difficulty internalizing faith?

5. Have you asked Jesus to dwell permanently in your heart by faith? If so, what changes came about in your life as a result of that decision?

6. Do you have trust issues? Who or what do you have trouble trusting? How has distrust worked for you, meaning has it helped you or backfired? Explain.

7. In what areas of your life have you walked by feeling instead of faith? Explain.

8. Do you believe that God actually likes you? How does that thought affect your state of mind?

9. In what areas can you "act faith" rather than waiting for your feelings to change? Give specific details.

10. How has faith "worked by love" in your life? In other words, how do faith and love connect in your experience? Give details.

---

1. Faith is like a fight (1 Timothy 6:12; 2 Timothy 4:7); a race (Hebrews 12:1, 2); eating (John 6:44–58); drinking (John 7:37); an open door (Acts 14:27); a shield (Ephesians 6:16); a hand (Hebrews 4:14); and a ship (1 Timothy 1:19).

2. Deuteronomy 32:20 and Habakkuk 2:4 in the King James Version.

3. See Hebrews 11.

4. Grand Valley State College in Allendale, Michigan.

The Care and Feeding of the Conscience

I recall that the Holy Spirit had convicted me deeply to come clean with a certain woman. I resisted. This woman had often judged me harshly, and I knew that admitting any sin or weakness would lay me open to more censure. My tiny sin, in comparison to her pharisaical judging, seemed unworthy of mention. But my conscience wouldn't leave me alone. Finally, through a series of events, I ended up singing a duet for church with that very woman. Ironically, the song focused on the need to respond to God's call or be ultimately lost. Suddenly, I imagined myself on the wrong side of heaven, being left out because I suppressed the work of the Spirit in my heart.

That evening I sheepishly made my way to her and confessed my secret. The secret involved other people. I said little about them, but she pieced the story together. She felt betrayed and cried bitter tears. A series of events followed in which many buried sins came to light; the Spirit of God moved through the community. I wish I could say peace followed, but things actually became worse before they became better. Yet, in spite of interpersonal chaos, my inner world was calm. I had the peace of a clear conscience.

Years before, King David harbored dirty little secrets of adultery and murder until the prophet Nathan rebuked him. Repentant, David said, "When I kept silent, my bones grew old through my groaning all the day long" (Psalm 32:3). Scientists might say that David's guilt led to bone marrow suppression, which led to a deficiency of infection-fighting white blood cells, as his "bones grew old." Since then, medical science has firmly established a link between guilt and immune-system depression. For instance, one study showed self-blamers to have elevated tendencies to produce inflammation; another study showed immunoglobulin A, needed for strong immunity, plummeted with increased guilt.[1] No wonder David felt such relief when forgiven. According to him, his suppressed bones rejoiced (Psalm 51:8).

If guilt has this much power, ought we not to respect it? That little phenomenon called the conscience makes us capable of integrity and faithfulness. It steers our lives toward moral excellence and high spiritual attainment. But ignored, disrespected, or misinformed, it can wreak havoc, leading to full-blown psychiatric disorders, fanaticism, and even terrorism. We would do well to care for the conscience. Delicate as a baby, it's as powerful as a king.

After sin, God mourned, "Behold, the man has become like one of Us, to know good and evil" (Genesis 3:22). Like any conscientious parent, our heavenly Father would have spared us exposure to the dark side of life. He would have preferred us to remain in childlike, innocent obedience. He didn't want our minds to be sullied with sin.

I empathize. I sheltered my kids to such an extent that my daughter, upon seeing a Salvation Army Santa Claus, cried, "Mommy! It's Samuel!" (that is, the prophet Samuel from the Bible). In spite of my efforts, the knowledge of the world eventually seeped into their little minds. However, the juxtaposition of it against their innocence made for some great humor, such as when, after hearing a workman use some bad language, one child tried to copy him by calling the other a "stupid shift!" Thankful for the mispronunciation, I couldn't help but mourn the jading of my children.

As my daughters grew, I changed my approach. I began to value a moderate (and inevitable) exposure to evil, so long as I could identify it as such. I told them we could watch certain movies together, as long as whenever an inappropriate word was used, I could bleep it out. They absolutely hated it, but a deal was a deal. I even showed them *Schindler's List* (fast-forwarding through the sex scenes) so that we could discuss the reality of evil, the Holocaust, and racism. In my way, I was training their consciences through gradual exposure to evil, preparing them to manage the full onslaught of choices they would face as adults.

Definition

"Conscience is an aptitude, faculty, intuition, or judgment of the intellect that distinguishes right from wrong."[2] The word never appears in the Old Testament, but it pops up thirty times in the King James Version of the New Testament, always in the form of the Greek word *suneidesis*. Interestingly, the first lexical definition of *suneidesis* reads like this, "the consciousness of anything."[3] Really? *Conscience* and *consciousness* are almost synonymous?

Think about it. To be conscious of something means to know the truth. Truth offends the guilty—only a clear conscience can bear it. The only way for us to know the truth, therefore, is to have a clear conscience before God. To bear a guilty conscience is to compromise our faculty of perception so that we can't possibly be conscious of reality. This is all the more reason to keep a clear conscience; our very grasp of reality, our sanity, hangs on it.

The sin-sanity connection

Notice the pattern: evil and unrepentant, Pharaoh irrationally believed that he could fight a God who had caused the ten plagues. King Saul sold out to Satan, ultimately falling prey to the witch of Endor's delusion. Nebuchadnezzar rebuffed the Spirit and ended up in long-term psychosis. Crazed with jealousy, Herod tried to kill the immortal God by slaughtering the innocents of Bethlehem. The Jewish leaders, in spite of overwhelming evidence, lied about Jesus' resurrection. The antichrist believes he can usurp God's throne. Truly, a defiled conscience blunts one's perceptions.

In each of these cases, evil bore fruit in complete delusion. These wicked men created super-sized lies to rationalize away their super-sized guilt. In contrast, Jesus bore the sins of the world but couldn't accommodate it through lies, for He was the Truth. The Truth had no capacity for denial. He faced our sin head-on, and it crushed His soul.

We all partake in one foundational lie—that of self-righteousness. On a fundamental level, we all believe that we can manage without God. Only God can reveal to us the flimsiness of our fig leaves—not a pleasant revelation. We tend to regard these ego-destroying experiences with horror. In reality, seeing our own nothingness before God becomes the cornerstone of true spiritual growth.

As much as healthy spiritual experience involves some appropriate guilt, the conscience is delicate and subject to disorders. Let's get an overview from Scripture of the various conditions of the conscience:

- The New Testament writers often speak of a "good conscience" (Acts 23:1; 1 Timothy 1:5, 19; Hebrews 13:18; 1 Peter 3:16, 21).
- Paul spoke of a "conscience without offense" (Acts 24:16).

- A "weak" conscience refers to a conscience inclined toward fanatical or false guilt (1 Corinthians 8:7, 10, 12).
- Paul also spoke of a "pure conscience" (1 Timothy 3:9; 2 Timothy 1:3).
- An "evil conscience" refers to a conscience defiled by sin (Hebrews 10:22).
- A "seared" conscience refers to a conscience so long abused that it becomes insensate, effectively dead (1 Timothy 4:2).
- A "perfect" conscience refers to a conscience that has reached full maturity (Hebrews 9:9).

True guilt and false guilt

From this list we can see that the conscience can be "good" (*agathos*), "pure" (*katharos*), "void of offense," and even "perfect." A good conscience comes as a result of turning away from sin, receiving forgiveness from God, and living in obedience to Him. It functions in conjunction with reason and faith, is informed by the Word of God, and is empowered by His Spirit. When a person in this condition feels the pangs of guilt, we call it conviction. That conviction leads him or her to repentance and to appropriate confessions of sin and making right the wrong. A healthy believer resolves guilt in a timely fashion and lives, for the most part, in joyful, guilt-free communion with God.

At the other end of the spectrum we find an "evil" and even a "seared" conscience. A hot iron cauterizes flesh, forms a hard scar, and robs it of sensation. The hot iron of sin can damage spiritual nerves. What else explains the amoral condition of sociopaths? The infamous Khmer Rouge tyrant Pol Pot, his death toll up to three million, nearly a quarter of Cambodia's population, said, "My conscience is clear." But, in reality, his conscience was *dead*—insensible and unable to feel. It had been seared with a hot iron.

What is a "weak" conscience? From the Greek *asthenes,* which can mean "sick," a weak conscience is a conscience riddled with false guilt. It seems some of the believers in Corinth couldn't bear to watch their brethren eat meat sacrificed to idols. Their weak conscience became defiled; and they guiltily began to eat the same meat, putting themselves in a state of self-condemnation. Paul saw this as a damaging experience and urged believers not to lay a stumbling block before the feet of the weaker brothers. At the same time, he himself could conscientiously eat such meat, and he educated believers toward the same liberty (see 1 Corinthians 8:7–9).

Paul didn't accommodate the weak consciences of his brothers so they could remain weak. He hoped to preserve his relationship with them, so that he could ultimately educate and help them. Through this accommodation, their consciences could mature into good consciences. Likewise, those of us who harbor false guilt can grow less fragile and more resilient as we come to know God and His Word while interacting with other believers.

One of the key features of false guilt is emotional reasoning, which thinks like this: if I feel guilty, I must *be* guilty. This approach can prove to be disastrous. I've worked with countless sufferers of false guilt, but one sticks in my memory. His name was Moish. A vagabond who visited a city ministry where I worked, Moish had a sweet, charitable spirit and lovable personality. He also had a guilt complex about eating. He probably weighed all of 120 pounds, but he never ceased to obsess about his supposedly sinful gluttony. Anorexia in males is rare and the spiritualized form of it is even rarer; but he had both. Like so many, Moish felt a chronic sense of unworthiness that seemed to intensify with each calorie consumed. Any time he read or heard about Judas, he identified completely with him; yet he was, in character and spirit, the antithesis of Judas.

Have you ever known someone, or *been* someone, with a guilt complex? Let me share a few unhealthy patterns that tend to produce false guilt:

Emotionalism. A religious or life experience that constantly pursues an emotional high and that tends to overinterpret those emotional states as being right with God, free, or filled with the Spirit. This sets a person up for basing conviction of guilt on their feelings as well.

Impressions. People who overrely on impressions to guide them through life can be taken over by the impressions. Impressions must be compared with the Scriptures and should be subjected to peer review within the faith community as well. One man was impressed to quit his job and subject his family to a life of poverty, reducing their already squalid existence to near starvation. In the end, he lost family, friends, reputation, and almost life itself. Living by unquestioned impressions is a wide-open invitation to fanaticism.

God's voice. Similar to living by impressions, some people seem to say, "The Lord told me" quite often. We all have moments when the Holy Spirit reveals something to us. These are thrilling moments. But, in my mind, such language should be used cautiously. It puts a person in an unchallengeable position; if you question that person, you seem to be defying God. It's wonderful when God speaks to us personally, but these days He most often uses the Written Word.

Mind control. Cults, gangs, and, unfortunately, some families are controlled by a dominant personality or personalities who effectively manipulate the consciences of all around them. When subjected to this control for a long period, people literally lose the ability to reason and judge for themselves. Parents do well to begin teaching their children to choose for themselves at a very early age.

For a document with information about training a child's will, see "Teaching Children to Choose" in the toolbox.

If you suffer from false guilt, hear this message, loud and clear: God would like to free you from false guilt just as much as He'd like to reach your conscience with true conviction. Let me say it in another way: for your spiritual and mental health's sake, learn to deflect false guilt just as readily as you accept responsibility for actual sin. The end-time crisis, recorded vividly in the books of Daniel and Revelation, reveals a state of affairs where the beast power will manipulate and control the masses, telling God's people that *they* are responsible for the plagues—which are actually falling because of the beast! (See Revelation 13:11–18.) Part of our preparation for the crisis ahead of us is learning to distinguish conviction from its counterfeit.

Like any other human capacity, overuse can lead to breakdown. If our consciences fire away day and night, they become exhausted. Guilt requires a large amount of nervous energy from us. Ideally, occasional guilt is quickly resolved. Chronic, nagging guilt—true or false—can wear out the machinery. This is why the conscience must team up with reason and faith to retain its balance.

For help with overcoming chronic guilt, see "A Good Conscience" in the toolbox.

As a new Christian, trying to do the right thing, guilt hung over me like a foreboding, dark cloud. The very legalistic ministry where I worked fed my hyperconscientiousness. Lack of a broad knowledge of the Bible led me to focus on certain parts to the exclusion of other balancing parts. I read about Jesus' forty-day fast in the wilderness and became convinced that God required me to fast forty days. Of course, at 110 pounds this may have killed me, but my impression overwhelmed the voice of reason. Although I never successfully completed the fast, eating became more and more guilt driven, until I weighed only ninety-five pounds. Many tried to reason with me—parents, doctors, church members, friends—but I felt that to yield to them would be to disobey God.

Finally, I caught a horrible case of the flu and was unable to eat. My weight plummeted to eighty-five pounds. Then I realized my life was on the line. Fortunately, God had sent a young man into my life who'd been down a similar road. He knew how to help me. Actually, he married me first (we're still married!); then he took me to Montana, where we planted tree seedlings in the mountains. With the fresh air, the natural surroundings, and his steady, kind support, I finally saw my fanaticism. I began to realize that God's requirements were reasonable, sensible, and merciful.

A friend of mine makes guitars. He plays them too—masterfully! Similarly, God creates and then makes music with our souls. God has crafted within us an instrument capable of playing in tune with His Spirit. Even more, He will train and strengthen us to make holy music as our consciences come into harmony with His mind. His Spirit is striving with us at this moment, leading us to deeper and deeper repentance and greater and greater surrender.

A clear conscience allows us to engage in the difficult work of self-realization. Deep in the layers of our unconscious minds, we hold secrets unknown even to ourselves. Corrupt motives, deeply engrained selfishness, and hidden sins lurk in the dark corners of our psyches. One sin at a time, God brings these things to our awareness, all for the purpose of bringing us to the point of saying, "I'd rather have Jesus than *that*." Only the knowledge of His full acceptance and love, the knowledge that His righteousness covers our sins, can provide the security and support needed to face our personal darkness. This is why we must keep Jesus at the center of our field of vision. If we do so, soon and very soon, we will see Him face-to-face.

DISCUSSION QUESTIONS

1. Share an experience in which the Holy Spirit convicted you of a wrong and gave you no peace until you made something right with another person.

2. Have you ever kept back from confessing an obvious sin to God, even though you knew very well that you couldn't hide from Him? How did the situation resolve? Share that experience.

3. *Conscience* and *consciousness* have similar meanings. Having a guilty conscience makes it hard to be fully conscious of the truth. When has your guilt kept you from facing reality?

4. Of all the kinds of consciences listed (good, without offense, weak, pure, evil, seared, and perfect), which best describes the condition of your conscience?

5. Do you struggle with false guilt? If so, what things do you wrongly feel guilty for?

6. Do any of the patterns that tend to produce false guilt—emotionalism, impressions, God's voice, or mind control—apply to you? Explain.

7. Were you raised in such a way that you were trained to choose for yourself? Explain.

8. Were you raised in a shame-based, guilt-ridden environment? If so, how is that affecting you now?

9. We all harbor deep in our unconscious minds hidden sins, selfish motives, and other things that would shock us. What is your willingness level to face those things?

10. How does the message of Jesus' forgiveness, righteousness, love, and grace encourage you to face the truth about yourself?

---

1. Christel Nani, "Link Established Between Guilt and Illness: Research, Case Studies, Expert Tips," Expressions of Soul .com, accessed February 28, 2011, http://expressionsofsoul.com/article-C.Nani-GuiltAndIllness.htm.

2. Wikipedia contributors, "Conscience," Wikipedia, accessed February 28, 2011, http://en.wikipedia.org/wiki/Conscience.

3. New Testament Greek Lexicon, s.v. "Suneidesis," accessed February 28, 2011, http://www.searchgodsword.org/lex/grk/ view.cgi?number=4893.

Recovering Self-Respect

My friends and I anticipated the Bayside Middle School ski trip with a kind of devious excitement, simply because we planned to engage in many illegal and forbidden activities. A complete sellout to peer pressure, I jumped on board and, for the first time in my life, became falling-down drunk. The wild night passed by in a blur, only to find regret waiting at sunrise as my schoolmates told me of things I'd supposedly done. I doubted the truth of some of them, but the holes in my memory kept me from any bold denials. I knew one thing—that whether my follies were big or small, I'd made a total fool of myself.

Heartbroken and humiliated, I spent hours alone, skiing down cold white slopes or trying to warm away the sadness with cups of overpriced hot chocolate bought in the chalet. Nothing seemed to dent my dark mood until the Muzak system chimed in with the Crosby, Stills, and Nash hit "Carry On."

"Carry on! Love is coming! Love is coming to us all."

In the absence of any real knowledge of the Bible or spiritual things, these words came to me as God's message. They took the edge off the feelings of self-loathing and social insecurity that had been triggered by the unforgiving ridicule of my peers. Someone—God—was telling me I should keep going and that something better lay ahead. That something was love. In my shattered state, being loved was enough. I didn't have to be perfect, good, or cool. If someone loved me, I could carry on.

At the foundation of true self-respect lies this principle: we can value ourselves because One greater than ourselves valued us first. Created for worship, we thrive in the light of God's smile. Attempts to generate our own sense of worth fail; ultimately, they become self-worship. But to be loved—*that* creates an unshakable sense of significance.

The evil twins of shame and pride

Before we can truly recover self-respect, we have to eliminate our self-sabotaging behavior and thinking. Often what we do to fix our wounded self-image actually makes it worse. As was mentioned earlier, our human parents "knew that they were naked," and "sewed fig leaves together and made themselves coverings" (Genesis 3:7). Represented in these two events we see the strange mix of shame and pride that characterizes human nature. While the fallen pair felt the disgrace of their sin, they simultaneously sought to lift themselves from the dust of it, to elevate themselves by their own power. There in the Garden, the first insecurity and pride complex was born.

As human history marches on, we see more and more extreme forms of this condition. Narcissistic personality disorder (NPD), sometimes called *malignant self-love,* features "an inflated sense of self-importance and an extreme preoccupation" with one's self.[1] But strangely, NPD is thought to stem from feeling an extreme fear of rejection and from a fragile self-esteem; under the egomaniac cowers a self-loathing bundle of insecurities. Very few of us would qualify for a diagnosis of NPD, but all of us have at least a mild case. I think of my high-school class valedictorian who received his first C in college and proceeded to jump out of a tall building to his death. His perfectionism couldn't tolerate the slightest failure. Pride made him as brittle as thin ice.

Pride will ultimately destroy any true self-worth because it puts the focus on you rather than on God's love for you. Insidiously, this form of self-valuing tends to thrive on competition—on comparing ourselves with others. Through pride we effectively take our value out of God's hands and put it in the hands of faulty human beings. A bad idea—a very bad idea.

Our worth never changes in God's eyes, but, in the human realm, it fluctuates like the stock market, creating instability. A pretty girl ages, a rich man loses his wealth, and an athlete passes out of his prime. We "compare ourselves with those who commend themselves," and this comparison of ourselves with other human beings is "not wise" (2 Corinthians 10:12). Someone better always seems to come along. All these things make our sense of worth very fragile. So the question is, How can we develop a solid, stable sense of self-worth?

Defining self-respect

Self-esteem, self-worth, self-image, self-regard, self-concept, self-awareness, self-respect, self-acceptance, self-confidence, self-this, and self-that. Frankly, the terms make me dizzy with all of their definitions and connotations. Of course, we must use words, so I have my favorites. I prefer the terms *self-respect* and *self-worth* to indicate the sense of value one obtains when he or she believes God's love. Self-esteem's current use can mean something as innocent as believing in one's basic rights; it can also mean pure, narcissistic pride. Because it's a mix of good and bad, I don't want to either belittle it or advocate it. So I don't generally use the term *self-esteem.*

Mental health advocates often regard self-esteem as a psychological panacea. But the scientific literature doesn't really support this belief; the data is confusingly mixed. Teens with high self-esteem, for instance, don't necessarily get better grades or refrain from high-risk behaviors. While high self-esteem does correlate with extroversion and the ability to make friends, people with high self-esteem are more likely to end friendships when conflict enters the picture, which can be a bad trait. Shockingly, perpetrators of domestic violence tend to have high self-esteem.[2] Basically, self-esteem doesn't deliver on the promise of fixing what's wrong with us.

Regardless of what we call it, a healthy, godly, positive self-worth comes from God—not from ourselves. *That* is the issue. No insightful person would deny the reality of self-awareness or say that positive self-regard is categorically evil. We all have a self-image, and that self-image must be at least passably positive for us to avoid extreme feelings of discouragement. But because we are sinful, corrupt, infirm, defiled, sick, broken, and fallen, the source of our self-image must originate in something outside of ourselves. Our positive self-regard must at least initially reflect the positive regard of another toward us.

We can see throughout Scripture God's positive regard for us. It's as if He's saying, "You're much more valuable than you think!" Read aloud the following statements of how God values you:

- "I will make a mortal more rare than fine gold, a man more than the golden wedge of Ophir" (Isaiah 13:12).
- "Are not two sparrows sold for a copper coin? And not one of them falls to the ground apart from your Father's will. But the very hairs of your head are all

numbered. Do not fear therefore; you are of more value than many sparrows" (Matthew 10:29–31).

- "You also, as living stones, are being built up a spiritual house, a holy priesthood, to offer up spiritual sacrifices acceptable to God through Jesus Christ" (1 Peter 2:5).
- "You are a chosen generation, a royal priesthood, a holy nation, His own special people, that you may proclaim the praises of Him who called you out of darkness into His marvelous light" (1 Peter 2:9).

God enjoins an affirmative response to the value He places on us. He calls us, even commands us, to respect and care for ourselves. While pride and selfishness are unholy, self-respect and self-care are acts of worship, as much our responsibility as paying tithe or attending church. When we care for ourselves, we exercise God-given stewardship over His creation. We thus love and honor Him, who loves and honors us, creating an ever-deepening cycle of value from heaven to earth and back again. This self-care includes care for all the aspects of our being: our marvelously designed bodies, our intricate souls, and our image-of-God spirits:

- "I will praise You, for I am fearfully and wonderfully made; marvelous are Your works, and that my soul knows very well" (Psalm 139:14).
- "Present your bodies a living sacrifice, holy, acceptable to God, which is your reasonable service" (Romans 12:1).
- "Do you not know that your body is the temple of the Holy Spirit who is in you, whom you have from God, and you are not your own?" (1 Corinthians 6:19).
- "Beloved, I pray that you may prosper in all things and be in health, just as your soul prospers" (3 John 2).

Vertical and horizontal self-respect

Clearly, God values us and desires that we value ourselves accordingly! I like to use the cross to illustrate how this works. First, the cross has a vertical beam: this can symbolize God's valuing of us by giving us His only Son. Though we face the world alone with no human support or regard, though we're fired from our jobs, divorced, hated, rejected, or imprisoned, we still have the assurance that God gave His most prized possession to

save us, thus proving that no sacrifice was too great if He might
have our fellowship for eternity. The message of the Cross
irrefutably conveys my value in God's eyes.

But—and I say this delicately—this isn't enough. Yes,
God values us, but He also created us to be social creatures
that need to make a difference in the human realm.
Symbolically, the Cross also has a horizontal beam. This beam can
symbolize the authentication of our value in the human realm.
Because Heaven affirms my value, I'll make a difference for good in
this world. Because God said I have a purpose and a future, I'll go
about to establish that. I can make a difference! The difference may
not garner human applause, but it will be felt in the human realm.

SERVICE

WORSHIP

Low self-esteem

Some of us struggle mightily with low self-esteem. Speaking for myself, it's been an
off-and-on companion throughout my life. However, for the most part, it has stayed away
in recent years. I don't miss it. I was one of those people who generated a constant stream
of self-deprecation. Someone would say, "You look nice," and I'd respond, "Get your eyes
checked."

I finally realized that low self-esteem wasn't as virtuous as I'd thought, nor was it
true humility. In fact, many of my self-denigrating comments were calculated to extract
compliments from people: "I'm ugly." "No! You're beautiful." Sometimes I was trying to
defend against criticism; if I insulted myself, it protected me from other peoples' insults—
or even their constructive advice, which also wounded my overly sensitive ego. At any
rate, as opposed to conveying humility, the self-denigration conveyed wounded pride,
which, for all its "woundedness," was still pride.

Low self-esteem is actually inverted pride. People with low self-esteem genuinely
feel bad about themselves, but they hope that if they just try hard enough, they'll prove
their worth. Often they hope that if they can just be pretty, smart, talented, fashionable,
athletic, competitive, powerful, or rich enough, they will indeed achieve a sense of
worthiness. In other words, low self-esteem and pride rest on the same foundation of self-
value for self's sake.

Scientific research has correlated low self-esteem with bad behavior such as aggression.[3] I can understand this. I thought my low self-esteem made me a "safer" person, but it created in me such a self-worth vacuum that, like a starving man stealing bread from other starving people, I compensated in hurtful ways. I took into my own hands—and out of God's hands—the task of declaring my worth. Did you know that God rebukes our low self-esteem in His Word? He says,

"I have also called you by your name;
I have given you a title of honor
Though you have not known Me. . . .

"Woe to the one who quarrels with his Maker—
An earthenware vessel among the vessels of earth!
Will the clay say to the potter, 'What are you doing?'
Or the thing you are making say, 'He has no hands'?" (Isaiah 45:4, 9, NASB).

Allow me to paraphrase: "I've declared you of value! I've given you honor and a purpose! How dare you argue with Me. You're a created being, and you're insulting Me, your Creator. Now stop it!"

Jesus' parable of the talents (Matthew 25:14–30) speaks to people with low self-esteem. A man gave one servant five talents, another two, and another one. The servant with five talents invested and doubled his talents. The servant with two also doubled his investment. The servant with one "hid his lord's money" (verse 18). The man called his servants to account for their investments, commending the wise investors but condemning the one who failed to use his talent. Now, notice this: the man says, "You wicked and lazy servant. . . . So you ought to have deposited my money with the bankers, and at my coming I would have received back my own with interest" (verses 26, 27). He didn't rebuke the servant for having little, but for doing nothing with the little he had. I believe Jesus here speaks to low self-esteem sufferers, saying that our comparative poverty of gifts doesn't excuse us from service. We needn't worry if our gift is small or large. We must simply concern ourselves with how we use what we have.

God gave me a talent for songwriting, particularly writing lyrics. I believe He called me to music ministry, but the path has been fraught with conflict. I've spent much of my musical career fighting insecurities about my performance ability. I've been harder on myself than God is (and most people)! At the same time, I've based too much of my worth on how well I could perform. Finally, I've wasted boatloads of energy on comparing myself to other performers who could sing or play better than I. I've done everything I'm trying to teach you not to do! And all the time I tried to find my own self-esteem, I missed out on simply accepting God's assessment of the situation, which was, "I gave you a gift, now use it with an eye single to My glory."

To help you find your gifts, see "God's Plan Life Purpose" in the toolbox.

I've finally arrived at the place where I accept my limitations as a musician while still appreciating and respecting my gift. Average ability cultivated and used with humility can carry the gospel much more effectively than great ability alone. Ultimately, the love that infuses our gift makes it effective.

For some suggestions in getting started in serving others, see "Using Your (Average) Talents."

Spiritual pride

The most insidious pride of all is spiritual pride—a sense of standing before God in our own righteousness. Unfortunately, on a baseline level, we all cherish this pride to some degree and in some form. Fortunately, God has a remedy for it. It's called the law. As we compare ourselves to the perfection of God's law, we realize how short we fall. Listen to Paul as he does this: "I was alive once without the law, but when the commandment came, sin revived and I died" (Romans 7:9). We use the phrase *I died!* to indicate extreme shame or embarrassment, as in "I said his name wrong again and *I died* of embarrassment!" I believe Paul meant "I died" in the same way. In the words of Ellen White, "His self-esteem was gone."[4] The contrast between God's holiness and his own sinfulness provoked a state of extreme humiliation or low self-esteem.

Fortunately, God doesn't leave us in this state of groveling. The God of second, third, fourth, fifth, sixth, and seventy-times-seven chances follows the demolition of our pride with the restructuring of our souls in Christ. God works on the principle of something better. He takes away pride only to replace it with a new born-again identity. Paul adamantly refuses to blame the law for his "I died" experience. He says, "Is the law sin?

Certainly not! On the contrary, I would not have known sin except through the law. . . . For sin, taking occasion by the commandment, deceived me, and by it killed me" (verses 7, 11). Simplified, this passage would read, "Sin killed me through the law."

These are mysterious words but are worth probing. Paul's sin killed him by causing him to be "deceived." How was he deceived? Apparently, sin led Paul to overidentify with his sin and think that the destruction of his spiritual pride meant the end of him as a person. He thought, as we all do at times, *What will be left of me without my pride?* Notice in verses 20 and 25, he triumphantly says, "It is no longer I who do it, but sin that dwells in me. . . . I thank God—through Jesus Christ our Lord! So then, with the mind I myself serve the law of God, but with the flesh the law of sin." Once Jesus enters the picture, Paul's shame turns to gratitude. Through the gospel, he may cease to identify with his sin. The love of God frees him to form a new identity in Christ. In other words, when he looks to himself for self-worth, he ultimately crashes and burns. When he looks to God, he finds a stable, sound sense of self, based on God's value of him.

An interesting study revealed two reactions to wrongdoing: a shame-based reaction and a guilt-based reaction. The researchers pointed out that shame-prone people tend to globalize wrongdoing by saying, "I'm worthless" and "You're worthless." In contrast, the guilt-prone person can feel remorse for a wrong done without lapsing into self-loathing.[5] They can differentiate between self and behavior: "What I did was wrong, but that doesn't make me worthless," "She did something bad, but she's still God's child." The shame-prone have more defenses and insecurity in relationships, but the guilt-prone tend to have secure, trusting relationships. Here's a quotation from the study: "Guilt-proneness involves a working model of self that is humble about personal limitations; shame-proneness involves a more narcissistic working model of self."[6]

In other words, pride underpins a shame-based existence. God has something much better for us than this rickety, rotting foundation for our value. He has a new identity in Christ for us, a sense of self derived from God's pronouncement from the cross that we have infinite value in His eyes. Shame on the devil for his cheap substitutes! God would give us a self-respect that doesn't waver when we perform poorly and that can recover from even moral lapses and spiritual failures; a self-respect that gets up after falling and continues on because it's not about us, it's about God and His infinite, passionate, unfailing love for us.

DISCUSSION QUESTIONS

1. Have you ever felt so bad about yourself you wished you could die? Share the experience.

2. How are shame and pride connected in the human heart?

3. Some people tend toward pride, entitlement, and overconfidence; others tend toward low self-worth, shame, and self-consciousness. Which tendency do you possess?

4. Read out loud the promises on pages 100 and 101 that reveal how God values us. How do the promises make you feel?

5. How have you successfully cared for yourself physically, emotionally, socially, and spiritually? In which areas do you need to do better?

6. Jesus paid an infinite price for you, declaring you of value. Service to other people authenticates that. Have you ever felt that sense of significance that comes when serving others? Share the experience.

7. Do you consider yourself someone who suffers from low self-esteem? Do you engage in any poor ways of coping with the low self-esteem, such as self-deprecation, bragging, or withdrawal? Explain.

8. Does it help you to know that in Isaiah 45:4, 9, God rebukes those who devalue themselves and question His purpose in their lives?

9. Why do you think it's harder to use small talents than big ones?

10. When you do wrong, do you have a guilt-based reaction (accepting responsibility for the wrong and making it right) or a shame-based reaction (personalizing the wrong and overidentifying with it)? Explain. How does Romans 7:20, 25 say you can move toward a healthier response to guilt?

1. MedlinePlus Medical Encyclopedia, s.v. "Narcissistic Personality Disorder," accessed February 28, 2011, http://www.nlm.nih.gov/medlineplus/ency/article/000934.htm.

2. Roy F. Baumeister et al., "Exploding the Self-Esteem Myth," *Scientific American,* January 2005, 84–91.

3. M. Brent Donnellan et al., "Low Self-Esteem Is Related to Aggression, Antisocial Behavior, and Delinquency," *Psychological Science* 16, no. 4 (April 2005): 328–335, accessed December 19, 2010, http://persweb.wabash.edu/facstaff/hortonr/articles%20for%20class/donnellan%20low%20se%20and%20aggression.pdf.

4. Ellen G. White, " 'Go and Tell Him His Fault Between Thee and Him Alone,' " *Advent Review and Sabbath Herald,* July 22, 1890, 2.

5. Steven J. Sandage and Everett L. Worthington, "Comparison of Two Group Interventions to Promote Forgiveness: Empathy as a Mediator of Change," *Journal of Mental Health Counseling* 32, no. 1 (January 2010): 35–57.

6. Ibid., 35.

Healing Past Hurts

I remember Nancy Knuckles as a frazzled single mom, preparing lunch for a gaggle of antsy children at a spiritual retreat we both attended. In a funny, neurotic way, she seemed to have a handle on things. It came as a shock years later to learn that those antsy kids had grown up into young adults who murdered their mother. Clifford Linedecker's *Killer Kids*[1] reports Nancy as a religious fanatic who punished with beatings and psychological torture, even stuffing her children into laundry bags and leaving them for hours in a closet. According to sources, the twists and turns of family pathology resulted in daughter Pamela's decision to strangle her mother with the help of a boyfriend. Son Bart then wrapped her head in a plastic bag, after which the kids and their friends stuffed her already stiffening body into a steamer trunk and threw her into Salt Creek in Elmhurst, Illinois.

There must be a better way of dealing with childhood abuse!

Parenting places upon human beings a solemn responsibility to build the characters of their children after the likeness of God. Parents, psychologically speaking, stand as God to their children. This dynamic, attested to by the story of Nancy Knuckles, can go horribly wrong. Like a baton in a ruthless relay, parents often pass to their children curses instead of blessings. Approximately one-third of children from abusive homes go on to abuse. In Nancy's case, the abuse turned back on her.

But, wait. In our awareness of these things, we must take care not to allow sad stories to fill our field of vision. We must be solution focused. The fact is that one-third of abused children do not abuse; they do not pass the behavior on to the next generation.[2] Why do some people replicate the past and others do not? Even more broadly, how do we deal with—and heal from—past hurts? How do we root out from our souls the dysfunctional patterns that impel us to pass the baton on to the next generation? All of us inherit a package of individual traits from our genetics and environment. Just as one child lives in the sunshine of parental love and another gasps under the hail of abuse, those packages differ. Some have it harder than others. But all have past wounds from which we need to heal. How can we make sure our disadvantages don't become disasters? In this chapter, I'll try to give a biblical, balanced, helpful answer to this question.

Nature, nurture, and beyond

Science identifies biological factors (*nature*) and environmental factors (*nurture*) as the two contributors to our individual trait package. What makes us who we are? Is it nature? Is it nurture? A little of both? Or something additional? Actually, the scientific model falls short of the complexity of the truth. Both biology and environment play roles; but so does choice. The nature-nurture debaters never seem to mention this. Thank God, we have the option of self-determination. We possess a mysterious, wonderful free will that mingles with nature and nurture, producing the complex reality of our present selves. We'll explore nature, nurture, and choice one by one.

Nature

Every living organism begins with a substance called deoxyribonucleic acid (DNA); it's an acid that carries genetic information in cells. You've seen the double helix figure that looks like a twisted ladder—that's DNA. Select a short segment of that ladder and you have a gene. Your mother and father each gave you twenty-three chromosomes, which were "cut and pasted" into the new "file" of forty-six chromosomes that is *you*.[3]

Genetic traits can be either dominant or recessive. I come from a (dominant trait) brown-eyed family, but my brown-eyed sister's second son has these "I'm drowning!" (recessive trait) blue eyes. My own second child has the same eyes—slanted upward slightly, as if an afterthought of God. My sister and I not only roll our tongues but spontaneously, unaided by fingers, mold them into a tricornered hat shape. Genetics also accounts for the three "bumpless" vertebrae in my back and my shorter leg. I recall watching a doctor examine my first child, then six years old. He found the same missing vertebrae bumps, then lined up her legs to show me that one was shorter. A chip off the old block.

My gene pool forked into my two daughters, one receiving the music gene and one the writer's gene. Almost before she could walk, Alison sang incessantly. It was a little weird to hear a two-year-old singing her own made-up arias in the bathtub, but she hit all the high notes uncannily on pitch. Today, she's a classically trained, full-time traveling singer-songwriter. Kimmy didn't seem as driven to make music, but she filled up journal after journal from the time she had a private thought. Of the two, she's far more verbal; a conversation with Alison usually lasts a few minutes, whereas with Kimmy it can go on for an hour, with her doing most of the talking.

To establish genetic causality for mental disorders requires an exacting, expensive process. At this point the National Institutes of Mental Health (NIMH) have established the heritability of several disorders: schizophrenia, attention deficit hyperactivity disorder, bipolar disorder, early onset depression, autism, anorexia nervosa, and panic disorder.[4] No doubt others will be added to the category in the future. But make note: scientists emphasize that people inherit a *disposition* toward these diseases rather than the disease itself. We'll return to that issue.

The biological factors in mental health reach far beyond genetics. For instance, premenstrual syndrome (PMS) can be a factor in a host of disorders, such as depression and addictions. I know a woman with premenstrual dysphoric disorder, an extreme form of PMS. She's one of the sanest people I know, except for "that time of the month," when she simply comes unglued. Another woman had panic attacks about putting her baby in the microwave—until she was treated for her low thyroid level, and the panic attacks stopped. My point is simple: biology, or "nature," factors heavily into mental health.

> *To assess your biological, psychological, social, and spiritual causes for mental health problems, see "Mental Health Checklist" in the toolbox.*

Nurture

Nature begins with prenatal influence. Our earliest home environment happens to be that warm, dark place we call the womb. At no developmental stage are we more susceptible to our surroundings than this one. Certain disorders, such as fetal alcohol syndrome, develop prenatally. Beyond these extremes, a host of traits are communicated through the umbilical cord; after all, mother and unborn child share a bloodstream. Ellen

White said of the mother, "If before the birth of her child she is self-indulgent, if she is selfish, impatient, and exacting, these traits will be reflected in the disposition of the child."[5]

The birth process itself matters. Birth is a demanding, often traumatic event requiring physical and emotional support for mother and child. If the mother has few financial and social resources, if the birth is a difficult one, or if the child wasn't planned, a normally stressful event becomes overwhelming. Both mother and child can develop psychological complications from inadequate care in childbirth.

Humans need adequate touch stimulation, especially in infancy. One of many causes of a condition called *failure to thrive* (FTT) is inadequate touch and face-to-face contact with the primary caregiver. The infant will "give up" on life, lose interest in eating, and eventually die. Surprising as it might seem, cuddling and talking baby talk to an infant does much to foster brain development and bonding ability. God designed breast-feeding to facilitate this bonding. Of course, He made babies cute, soft, and squeezable; can you imagine cuddling a baby-sized version of your old crusty self?

The home environment weighs heavily in the development of the child's character. Relationships within the home literally teach the child, by example and experience, how to bond. When parents fail to attach to their infant, the child can pay the price in a condition called *reactive attachment disorder* (RAD). A child with RAD either withdraws totally or bonds indiscriminately; in either case, the child's trust-building machinery misfires.

Children learn by imitation. For instance, when they observe their parents working through conflict, accepting one another, forgiving one another, and just generally enjoying a healthy bond, they learn to do the same. I remember a certain childhood drama that replayed itself often. My mom and dad's conversation would heat up, drawing from me a response of, "Mom and Dad, stop arguing!"

"We're not arguing; we're just *discussing*!" Dad would say, lips curled and eyes glaring.

The fact that my parents knew how to argue without becoming overly hostile (sorry, Dad, but you *were* arguing) actually helped me in my marriage. Mom and Dad didn't get along perfectly—but they did stay together. I can't think of a better gift to give our children. Mike and I occasionally argue (see the "Will Power" week), but we work things out. My children, in turn, work through conflicts with their friends. The trait of working through conflict has been passed through the generations.

This principle works negatively too. I know a father and husband who emotionally divorced his wife (he was too "Christian" to legally divorce her) and turned his two sons against their father so completely that when he'd speak, they'd pretend they hadn't heard him. The home, designed by God to be heaven's prep school, became hell's boot camp as the sons learned the poisoned thinking and behavior of their father.

Any life trauma or major stressor, particularly in childhood, is part of the nurture package. Abuse, relational trauma, rejection, bullying, academic pressure, poverty, divorce, natural disasters, personal misfortune: any or all of these things can affect the nurture portion of an individual's development. People exposed to these problems can develop *post-traumatic stress disorder* (PTSD) or the less-severe *acute stress reaction*. For instance, the bullying I suffered as a fifth-grader has given me a tendency to be extremely fearful of powerful, aggressive personalities.

To summarize, prenatal factors; congenital factors; early, mid, and late childhood home influences; primary caregiver relationships; and life experiences, all wadded together, constitute the nurture section of the nature-nurture complex. Fortunately for those of us with childhoods that make Bart Simpson's seem wholesome, neither nature nor nurture have the final say in who we become.

Choice

Enter the beautiful, blessed reality of human free will. Choice has, within limits, the final say in who we become. Our choices essentially direct the choir of our inherited tendencies. A choir director can't turn sopranos into basses, but he can awaken and cultivate the natural voice. Likewise, our choices can't change our inheritance, but they can direct it.

Recently, scientists have begun to understand something called *gene expression.* Epigenetics—as the science of gene expression is called—essentially says that we can activate or de-activate our genes. Here's a brief explanation: Every cell in your body contains a nucleus with your DNA—your entire genetic code. This DNA expresses itself differently in various parts of the body. In your eye cells, the eye-color part of your DNA expresses itself; but it's switched off in your liver cells, because your liver doesn't need to know your eye color. Because of this switching off, only 10 to 20 percent of genes are active in any given cell. This prevents genes of one cell type from being expressed in another cell type. Otherwise, our livers might be baby blue.

Similar to a global positioning system (GPS) losing function when you drive through a tunnel, certain biological processes can "turn off" genes. For instance, adults often lose the ability to digest milk because certain aspects of aging turned off their production of lactase. These "off switches" can be brought into our cells through our food, environment, or bodily processes.

Most important, our *choices* affect gene expression. Specifically, we can activate certain diseases, including mental disorders (such as addiction), by choosing to engage in those behaviors. While we may have the gene for alcoholism, it is the choice to drink, and thus exposure to alcohol, that brings about changes that snowball into addiction. I know a man who so fears his tendency toward alcoholism that he even abstains from cough syrup.

It's not our fault; it *is* our responsibility

Let's bring all these factors into to the arena of inner healing. As we learned in earlier chapters, we have been created with the purpose of reflecting the character of God. Our failure to do this is called sin. Secular psychology ignores this concept for the most part, but the Bible teaches that true healing includes moral regeneration. In other words, we can't fully heal without dealing with our sin problem. Our typical human response to genetically and environmentally inherited wounds is to worsen them by *sinning* in response to *sin*. *Sinners* do that very well. In 1966, Marine Corps sharpshooter and University of Texas student Charles Whitman, after killing his mother and his wife, climbed the university tower and shot forty-six innocent passersby. An autopsy revealed a glioblastoma in his brain. Psychological assessments revealed that Whitman had a perfectionistic, abusive father. In addition to the tumor, he probably inherited the father's hostile temperament both genetically and environmentally. Then he raged in response to rage. He sinned in response to sin.

How can we break the momentum of this reactive cycle? How can we rise above inherited tendencies to evil? How can we heal from the internal damage of sin? I would suggest three steps: (1) gain insight, (2) receive comfort, and (3) take responsibility.

1. Gain insight. As a first step, we must connect the dots between our past hurts and present patterns. Ellen White said, "God would have His servants become acquainted with the moral machinery of their own hearts."[6] David prayed, "Examine me, O Lord, and prove me; try my mind and my heart" (Psalm 26:2). Because "thoughts and feelings combined make up the moral character,"[7] acquaintance with our "moral machinery" requires that we have emotional and cognitive self-awareness.

But notice that we acquire this self-awareness in partnership with God. "You examine me, God," David prayed. We need both God's laser of truth and His balm of love in our process of self-discovery. This process can be catalyzed by fasting, prayer, counseling, and Bible study, but God's timing also plays a part. He knows when to confront us with the past and arranges circumstances for this purpose. A friend visited her childhood home in Germany, and when she began speaking German with her relatives, forgotten scenes of childhood sexual abuse flooded her memory. She believed that God had prepared her emotionally and spiritually for that revelation.

Psychodynamic therapy, or insight-oriented therapy, stresses the need for self-understanding and exploration of the past, particularly childhood. It has empirical support[8] but, like all therapies, can be taken too far. One friend became clinically depressed when she "dug around too much." I know of multiple situations in which counseling led clients to cut off contact with their parents or divorce their spouses. While at times a cutoff may be necessary, we must remember that the object of revisiting the past is to become *better* rather than *bitter*. We need to *walk through* the past without *wallowing in* it. As much as we need insight into how others' actions toward us have affected us, we need even sharper insight into how our own reactions have compounded the damage. Being sinned against hurts us, no question. Especially severe childhood abuse and neglect take a heavy toll on future health. But our destructive responses to sin sustain the worst damage. In the end, "the heaviest burden that we bear is the burden of sin."[9]

As a counselor, I witness the impact of past trauma daily. Often as people pour out their stories, they feel a sweet release. The tissue box gets frequent use in my office—sometimes even by me! I know as I listen that the empathy I feel and show is the most therapeutic element of the counseling process. Depending on the depth of the wound, I might allow the "ventilation" to go on for weeks or even months. But, eventually, the time comes when I encourage the client to identify his or her own destructive reactions. This is almost always difficult. We generally dislike taking responsibility and prefer to blame others. At the same time, taking responsibility helps us gain back the power lost through being wounded by other people. Dwelling upon what I can change breeds hope and courage; dwelling upon what I can't change breeds despair, fear, and frustration. I can't change the past. I can't ultimately change other people. But I can, by the grace of God, change myself by making better choices.

2. Receive comfort. This process is a finely tuned dance. I try to be careful not to rush wounded people toward taking responsibility. Victims of abuse especially tend to overblame themselves. They've often been trained by their abusers to whitewash the abusers' sins and blame themselves for the abuse. Such individuals need to see the matter clearly before accepting their own responsibility. Often their lives are a tangle of others' sins and their own flawed ways of coping. Untangling can feel like combing a head of matted hair—painful and slow. I don't rip through the hair. One abuse victim I know developed a sexual addiction. The abuse clearly led to the addiction. Once he gained this insight, the pressure of guilt lifted enough for him to start the process of recovery.

Jesus knows our needs. To our weakness, He's no stranger. The Scriptures teach that God's Son, the "brightness of His glory and the express image of His person" (Hebrew 1:3), "shared in the same" "flesh and blood," was "made like His brethren," and "suffered, being tempted," so that He could "aid those who are tempted" (Hebrews 2:14, 17, 18). This means something very simple and very encouraging; when we go to Jesus with our tempted souls, He resonates. He empathizes. Somehow He retains His spotless purity, yet knows the struggles of sinful human beings.

Most of us try to purge ourselves of sin before coming to Jesus. This is like being so ashamed of my crooked teeth that I try to straighten them in order to impress the orthodontist. Pertaining to our sin-inflicted wounds, the crooked must approach the Straightener in our crooked state or be doomed to everlasting crookedness!

3. Take responsibility. Our sinful tendencies give our carnal natures a specific shape, as unique as a fingerprint. One man's great sin is alcohol; a woman caves in to gossip; a youth, to lust. Sin can take innocuous forms (eating too many sweets) or heinous forms (pedophilia). One man I know developed a foot fetish—a sexual fascination with feet—which he battled constantly. Sin can morph into as many forms as there are individuals in the world.

We can't change the shape of our carnal nature, but we can choose whether or not to feed it. Feed it, and it grows. Starve it, and it weakens. It's not our fault that we receive genetic and developmental disadvantages. It's not our fault when we suffer abuse that sets us up for addictions, emotional scars, and relational problems. The wounds of the past *are not our fault.* But what we do with them is our responsibility. We can let our lower nature react, feeding the beast within, obtaining momentary gratification, but ultimately sacrificing everything dear to us. Or we can starve the beast and feed the spirit.

The Gospel of Matthew depicts a wonderful metaphor of human choice. Pilate stood Jesus next to Barabbas. What a strange juxtaposition—the innocent, holy God-man and the dark, vicious thief. Pilate then said, "Which one do you want me to release to you?"

"Barabbas!" the people shouted.

"What should I do with Jesus called Christ?" Pilate pleaded.

"Crucify Him!" they screamed.

"Why? What evil has He done?"

"Crucify Him!" (see Matthew 27:15–23).

We know that Pilate released Barabbas and crucified Jesus. Our destiny hangs today on the same choice. We can't change the shape of our inner Barabbas, but we can choose whether or not to free him. We can crucify Jesus out of our hearts and free Barabbas to actuate our worst tendencies. Or we can crucify Barabbas, the carnal nature with all its hate, lust, envy, and pride, and free Jesus to live within us. Crucify Jesus, free Barabbas. Crucify Barabbas, free Jesus. We must ultimately choose one or the other.

You know which choice I recommend. If you crucify Barabbas and free Jesus, you'll allow into those dark crevasses of your soul the healing presence of Love. He can heal those hurts too deep to speak out loud and feed those hungers that are never satisfied. He can even break generational strongholds to create a new legacy for your children. The promise is, "If they confess their iniquity and the iniquity of their fathers . . . if their uncircumcised hearts are humbled, and they accept their guilt—then I will remember My covenant with Jacob, and My covenant with Isaac and My covenant with Abraham I will remember; I will remember the land" (Leviticus 26:40–42). Through the gospel, the baton passing of sin to sin from one generation to the next can stop with you.

DISCUSSION QUESTIONS

1. People don't always respond negatively to childhood abuse and trauma. What do you think makes the difference between a constructive and a destructive response?

2. When you completed the "Mental Health Checklist," what present, changeable contributors did you identify?

3. Do you know any prenatal, birth, or childhood traumas that may contribute to some of your present struggles? If so, what are they?

4. Did you come from a hug-filled, affectionate home or a more reserved home? Was love expressed verbally? How do these things impact you now?

5. Were there any parental or other behaviors you learned to imitate in positive ways? Have you carried on the legacy of any negative behaviors, such as criticism, anger, withdrawal, and so on?

6. Have you experienced, through the power of choice and God's grace, overcoming any negative behaviors? Explain.

7. Can people experience emotional healing apart from moral and spiritual healing? Share your thoughts on that.

8. So far in this book, have you gained insights about your "moral machinery"? Share your experience.

9. Have you ever gotten stuck wallowing in past hurts? Explain.

10. Does knowing the love of Jesus make you more inclined to take responsibility for your choices? Explain.

---

1. Clifford Linedecker, *Killer Kids: Shocking True Stories of Children Who Murdered Their Parents* (New York: St. Martin's Press, 2005).

2. The remaining one-third are vulnerable to repeating the pattern of abuse but do not continue the abuse. J. E. Oliver, "Intergenerational Transmission of Child Abuse: Rates, Research, and Clinical Implications," *American Journal of Psychiatry* 150, no. 9 (September 1993): 1315–1324.

3. Speaking of cut and paste, this is a kindergarten explanation.

4. See, for instance, U.S. Department of Health and Human Services, "The Fundamentals of Mental Health and Mental Illness," in *Mental Health: A Report of the Surgeon General—Executive Summary* (Rockville, Md.: U.S. Department of Health and Human Services, Substance Abuse and Mental Health Services Administration, Center for Mental Health Services, National Institutes of Health, National Institute of Mental Health, 1999), accessed March 1, 2011, http://www.surgeongeneral.gov/library/mentalhealth/chapter2/sec3.html#bio_influences.

5. Ellen G. White, *Temperance* (Mountain View, Calif.: Pacific Press®, 1949), 171, 172.

6. Ellen G. White, *Testimonies for the Church* (Mountain View, Calif.: Pacific Press®, 1948), 4:85.

7. White, *Mind, Character, and Personality,* 2:593.

8. Jonathan Shedler, "Getting to Know Me: What's Behind Psychoanalysis," *Scientific American Mind,* November 2010, 53. This article reports on a study that compiled the results of twenty-three randomized trials, involving 1,431 patients who suffer from depression, anxiety, stress-related physical ailments, and other psychological problems. The study showed a greater effect size for psychodynamic therapy than either CBT or antidepressants.

9. White, *The Desire of Ages,* 328.

Identity Shift

Who are you? Without rattling off generic data like your name, address, marital status, and vocation, describe your essence in a few sentences. What are your core identifying characteristics? What makes you an individual? What distinguishes you from the masses of humanity?

It's not easy, is it?

The topic of identity formation, particularly in adolescence, provides much vigorous debate for social scientists. One simple, well-understood psychological phenomenon fuels the dialogue—we human beings become who we think we are. We fulfill our own self-prophecies. We mold to our own self-concepts.[1]

When self defines self

The psychologists of ancient Babylon understood this. When the seventeen-year-old Daniel and his three buddies found themselves deported from Judah to serve in Nebuchadnezzar's court, the idol worshipers determined to brainwash the teens. In order to persuade the captives to identify with the pagan gods and forget their own Yahweh, their names were changed.

- *Daniel,* "judged by God," became *Belteshazzar,* "Bel's prince."
- *Hananiah,* "Yahweh who is gracious," became *Shadrach,* "command of the moon god."
- *Mishael,* "Who is like Yahweh?" became *Meshach,* "who is what Aku is."
- *Azariah,* "Yahweh has helped," became *Abed-Nego,* "servant of Nego."

Can't you almost hear the PhDs plotting? "Give them new names, get them to see themselves as Baal worshipers. Once we have their identities, we have their souls!" Modern-day priests of Baal have captured most of God's children by persuading them to identify with the habits of earthly gods. Like the deities of Babylon, our pantheon of celebrities live lives of excess, selfishness, licentiousness, and pride. They love, then hate, one another. They marry, have affairs, and divorce. Like the heathen gods, the gods of this age are projections of our own human weakness. To worship them is to worship various aspects of self. To identify with them is to identify with self and to create an endless growth-preventing cycle of self mirroring self.

This world urges us to find our identity in some aspect of our personhood, whether our race, gender, sexual orientation, religion, family line, or nationality. In contrast, Jesus calls us to something much higher and better. He calls us to find our identity in Him. This in-Christ concept has the ability to revolutionize our lives. Finally, the futility of self defining self can be shattered, and our hearts freed from Babylonian captivity.

"In Christ"

The phrase *in Christ* appears eighty-five times in the New King James version of the New Testament, building upon the Old Testament concept of corporate oneness. Let me explain. In the Eastern mind, individuals shared an identity with their leader. For instance, when judgment came upon the Philistine king Abimelech, he said, "Lord, will You slay a righteous *nation* also?" (Genesis 20:4; emphasis added). To kill the king was to kill the nation. To be *in* someone was to share his fate.

Building on this foundation, Paul explained in 1 Corinthians 15:22 that "as in Adam all die, even so in Christ all shall be made alive." Adam, the first head of humanity, fell into sin. We share his fate, which is death. We also share his nature, which is fallen. Fortunately, Jesus became the second Head of humanity, the Second Adam. And by faith we share His fate, which is life, and His nature, which is divine. We pass from death to life the moment we believe, when we are "born of the Spirit" and become "partakers of the divine nature" (John 3:6; 2 Peter 1:3, 4).

One psychologist describes conversion as "a change in which the self becomes identified with the sacred."[2] While conversion has many aspects, I'm focusing on what happens to us in terms of identity. It is my belief that through conversion, we have the privilege of identifying ourselves as new creatures in Christ. At the same time, we have a realizing sense of the decadence of our humanity. Through the work of the Spirit, we see the moral decay of our flesh and our ugliness without God. At the same time, we see ourselves purified, covered, transformed, and holy in Christ.

Mephibosheth: A case study

An interesting case study in 2 Samuel illustrates this identity shift. David's best friend, Jonathan, had a little five-year-old named Mephibosheth. Remember that Jonathan's father, King Saul, had fallen into rebellion against God and had lost his calling to David, God's anointed king. During that time, David and Jonathan became best friends, even though Jonathan knew that David would take the throne instead of himself. They cut a covenant, meaning they literally cut their arms and sprinkled in crushed rock so that a scar would result.

When Saul and Jonathan died in battle and David claimed the throne, Saul's family fled the palace in a kind of mass hysteria. In the rush, Mephibosheth's nanny fell, crushing the child's feet. Lack of medical care resulted in his feet being deformed. Humanly speaking, this doomed Mephibosheth to a life of social ostracism as associates interpreted his physical infirmity as a judgment from God. He settled in Lo Debar, a slum a few days' travel north of Jerusalem, to live out his days in obscurity. *Lo Debar* means "no pasture," a place of desolation; and *Mephibosheth* means "shame." This was not a pretty life.

One day King David caught sight of the covenant scar on his arm and remembered his promise to care for Jonathan's family. He sent for Mephibosheth via a royal chariot. Mephibosheth had no idea of David's intentions and assumed the worst. Arriving at the palace, he flung himself at David's feet, willing to become his slave. "Don't be afraid!" David assured him. "Because of a promise I made to Jonathan, I'm going to return everything you lost because of Saul's rebellion. You're also going to eat at the royal table every day."

Mephibosheth rubbed his eyes and tried to grasp David's words. This meant that his fate under Saul, his "head," would be reversed. It also meant that his shameful wounds, ironically acquired as a result of fleeing from his condemned state under Saul, would be covered by the pure, white tablecloth of the king. No one would see his feet. Mephibosheth would look just like royalty. In fact, because of the love of the king, he *was* royalty.

Upon hearing these words, the broken man again flung himself to the ground, crying out, "Who am I that you should care for a dead dog like me?" Keenly aware of his unworthiness, Mephibosheth referenced his flesh—condemned, ugly, diseased, and broken. Day by day, though, as servants of the king ushered him to the royal table, the truth sunk in: his identity stretched beyond his fallen state. Because of the love of the king, he was a son of royalty. This ultimately changed him from an enemy of the king to one of his most loyal friends (see 2 Samuel 19:24–30).

Likewise, we flee from the palace of God because of our condemned state under Adam. That very fear of condemnation, our internal shame, drives us to sin, causing weaknesses, addictions, and infirmities. We sequester ourselves away to a spiritual Lo Debar, a place of desolation, to live out our futile existence separated from God. But one day He calls us. In fear, we beg for our lives. "Fear not," He says, and tenderly informs us that He's made a covenant with Jesus; all we lost in Adam will be restored. More than this, Jesus' white robe covers our deformities, and we feast at His table as sons and daughters of God. Grace restores. Mercy redeems. Love heals.

Because of God's blood covenant with Jesus, because of His eternal scars, we can have eternal healing. Because of our status in Christ, we have the joy of seeing ourselves as new creatures. In 2 Corinthians 5:17, Paul said, "Therefore, if anyone is in Christ, he is a new creation; old things have passed away; behold, all things have become new." Once a new creature in Christ, we become so many things that even Houdini couldn't say them in one breath! We're justified, dead to sin, alive to God, free from condemnation, free from sin and death, joined to God, one body, approved by God, sanctified, wise, established, triumphant, enlightened, reconciled, free, blessed, chosen, sitting in heavenly places, filled with good works, and even perfect! And the list continues.

> *Check it out in the toolbox: "All the Things We Are in Christ."*

God's promise of change

Is God creating some kind of heavenly spin zone, spewing out fictitious, high-gloss versions of our shabby little selves? Is He merely Photoshoping away our spiritual pimples? No! How could the Truth lie? Rather, God sees what we will become and counts it as done. He says, "What we will be has not yet appeared; but we know that when he appears we shall be like him, because we shall see him as he is. And everyone who thus hopes in him purifies himself as he is pure" (1 John 3:2, 3, ESV). The Spirit of the Lord transforms us "from glory to glory" (2 Corinthians 3:18). God sees the final product of that transformation and applies it retroactively to us now. Just the act of believing this, of hoping in Him, catalyzes that transformation, purifying us "as he is pure."

As I think about these things, I feel like jumping up and down for joy.

God doesn't see us as failures. He knows we'll have final triumph in Him. Notice what He says about Abraham, recorded in Romans 4:20, "He did not waver in unbelief" (NASB). It almost makes one ask, "Are we talking about the same Abraham?" Abraham's unbelief in producing Ishmael through Hagar is one of the most oft-referenced acts of unbelief in the Bible! And God says Abraham didn't waver? Does God have amnesia? No, but He does have omniscience. He takes in the big picture. He isn't looking at Abraham's Hagar lapse when He makes His final assessment of the man. Why? Because Abraham did learn his faith lesson. He, like God Himself, showed his willingness to give his son. He finally graduated to father-of-the-faithful status, and God applied that final attainment retroactively to his entire life.

God "calls those things which do not exist as though they did" (verse 17). God knows the final state of sanctification you will reach in Him. He applies this to your life record now and proclaims you perfectly faithful and victorious in Christ. The Great I AM doesn't work within the confines of human time and so isn't perturbed by your temporary failure. He sees you as you are in Christ—the final, finished, glorious product of the heavenly Sculptor's masterful hand.

Think about it. What hope would there be for any of us without this? If we had to base our identity on our current performances, all we could do to change that identity would be to perform better. But fixing our eyes on our own behavior is, in itself, self-centered. Self-centeredness is sinful. So we wind up trying to overcome sinful self by focusing on sinful self. This is about as futile as trying to make pimples disappear by staring at them. Self-centeredness can be very miserable.

Honest self-assessment can be a good thing. But we must also fasten our hope to God's promise of change. In Him, we are "complete in Christ" (Colossians 1:28, NASB).

• "Being confident of this very thing, that He who has begun a good work in you will complete it until the day of Christ Jesus" (Philippians 1:6).

- "His divine power has granted to us everything pertaining to life and godliness, through the true knowledge of Him who called us by His own glory and excellence" (2 Peter 1:3, NASB).
- "I will give you a new heart and put a new spirit within you. . . . I will . . . cause you to walk in My statutes" (Ezekiel 36:26, 27, NASB).
- "I will put the fear of Me in their hearts so that they will not turn away from Me" (Jeremiah 32:40, NASB).

It is your privilege as a believer in Jesus to regard every departure from Christlike behavior as a temporary lapse into your old life rather than a self-defining act. In other words, every time you sin, you revert back to the person you no longer are in Christ. So, why go back to your old ways? The sooner you leave them behind, the better.

My daughter's story illustrates this well, and she's given me permission to include a condensed version of it. It's hard to be so open, by the way, but I find that I help more people when I'm willing to share personal experiences.

Kimmy's story

Kimmy's childhood resembled the *Little House on the Prairie* TV series. Loving parents, a country home, shelter from the world, Bible stories, prayer—everything moved her toward a life of faith. But her world shattered into a million pieces when we relocated. At the age of thirteen, she entered a new school, a new neighborhood, and a new world. Her typical resilience drained away through the hole in her young faith, a hole that widened until it swallowed her. My straight-A, bright light of a child began to settle into the role of bad girl. She had been my little "marsupial," so closely connected to me with bonds of love. Now she hated me.

One misbehavior after another put her at odds with teachers and youth leaders. People have asked, "Did she fall in with the wrong crowd?" "No," I respond, "she *was* the wrong crowd." My parenting pride was humbled to dust as she became a kind of pariah in our Christian community. Finally, the boarding school expelled her for smoking pot in her room.

As tough as Kimmy appeared to be, expulsion from the Christian boarding school still stung her confused little heart. She medicated her sorrow with street drugs, sliding into full-blown cocaine addiction and polydrug use. I began to feverishly search for an appropriate therapeutic boarding school or residential treatment. This search was overdue. She was now eighteen years old, and the options had thinned out. Looking back, I realize I should have acted sooner.

One night she disappeared through the window, not returning till the next day after a church member's son found her, frightened and strung out, at a rave party. Fear had broken her defiance. She'd seen things she still wishes she could forget. The drugs coursing through her veins had robbed her of the ability to grasp reality, and she wondered if her reason would ever return. She was basically scared speechless. I said, "Kimmy, you'll die if you don't change, and I don't think you'll change until you accept Jesus." Weary from five straight years of repelling Him, she said, "OK, I'm ready. You're right. Nothing else has worked." We prayed together.

Kimmy had a long battle ahead of her. I wish I could say she snapped out of her party lifestyle, but she relapsed several times. For one thing, she was a drug addict, and there were physiological hurdles to jump. Second, her entire social network had been formed during her party life, so social dynamics dragged her down. Finally, her most ferocious opponents became her own thought patterns of unbelief, long held and deeply entrenched.

My husband and I could see all of this. We kept repeating Paul's words to her, "If anyone is in Christ, he is a new creation; old things passed away; behold, all things have become new" (2 Corinthians 5:17). Over and over, through valley and height, failure and recovery, we repeated these words. Several times Kimmy claimed, "I'm not really a Christian because I can't do it. It's too hard!" But we would counter with, "God has claims on you. He knows what you will be, and He sees you now as a new creature."

Today, Kimmy says, "Getting addicted to drugs makes you feel like your brain is toast, your future is ruined, and life as you know it is forever stained with the aftermath of sin. When my parents told me I was a new creature, it put a brilliant twist on an otherwise hopeless tale. It helped me see that I could have a fresh new start, as a gift from God, and that I was going to be re-built. My future suddenly turned from bleak to bright, and instead of wishing to die, I couldn't wait to see what He had in store for me as a new creature."

Imagine if that first night I had said, "God forgives the past, but you better prove yourself now!" And then imagine if after her first relapse, her dad piped in with, "I guess you never really changed at all, did you?" Those words would have dealt a deathblow to the basis of Kimmy's faith by denying God's promise of regeneration and putting the focus on her performance.

Today, Kimmy lives for Jesus. She's been drug free for a year and is mastering her tendencies toward depression. Each day she discovers a new talent or interest. She loves to share her testimony one-on-one and sometimes before large crowds. Best of all, our family relationships are healed, and the love is again flowing. We talk regularly and pray together. In short, she's becoming in present reality what we told her she was in Christ.

I realize this idea could morph into presumption. We could settle into our sins, and just claim to have some kind of mystical "new creature" floating around in the heavens. We could believe spiritual fiction, severing our supposed changed status from our unregenerate experience. But we mustn't allow fear of presumption to keep us from the joys of true faith. The truth is that God's Spirit provides a pipeline from heaven to earth, such that God's picture of who we will be becomes tangible, observable fact day by day. God's mystery unfolds day by day in the lives of believers. It is "Christ in you, the hope of glory" (Colossians 1:27). Mephibosheth, Abraham, and Kimmy all affirm its power.

DISCUSSION QUESTIONS

1. Describe your identity in three or four sentences.

2. Why do you think the leaders of Babylon changed the names of the Hebrew youth?

3. Do you believe you're unconverted, in the process of conversion, or converted? Explain.

4. Why do you think we withdraw from God when we feel guilty and ashamed, as opposed to going to Him who can take away all of our sin?

5. Which entries did you mark on the "All the Things We Are in Christ" worksheet? How does it feel to know that God will make you new?

6. What's wrong with trying to get better by focusing on our performance?

7. How does it feel to know that "He who has begun a good work in you will complete it" (Philippians 1:6)?

8. What are the risks involved in telling ourselves and other people we're new creatures in Christ?

9. Have you had certain people in your life who believed in you even when you lost faith in yourself? Share your experience. How did this affect you?

10. How do we get from struggling and failing to victory in Christ? Give some examples of past victories.

---

1. For instance, according to A. Pierro, L. Mannetti, and S. Livi, "Self-Identity and the Theory of Planned Behavior in the Prediction of Health Behavior and Leisure Activity," *Self and Self-Identity* 2, no. 1 (January-March 2003): 47.

2. Kenneth Pargament, *The Psychology of Religion and Coping: Theory, Research, Practice* (New York: Guildford Press, 1997), 248.

Made for Love

The subject of biblical psychology overwhelms me. I find the vastness of it intimidating. In writing this book, I struggled to decide which subjects to include. A comprehensive book would be thick enough to knock down a small building, so I decided to break the subject into at least two books—this one on individual psychology, and the second, on relationships. But as a foretaste of the next book and a fitting finish to this one, this chapter contains a glimpse into relationship psychology. After all, the highest expression of mental health is to love and be loved.

I must tell you that the distinction between individual and relationship psychology is essentially artificial. God designed each of us with powerful social drives, such that relationship and individuality mingle together like toast and butter. One of the great theorists, Alfred Adler, realized this. After helping Sigmund Freud found the psychoanalytic movement, he began to advocate new ideas, one of which was "social interest"—referring to humans' interest in relationships. Freud tended to see people as stand-alone units; Adler saw them in the context of their social network. Freud so resented Alder's departures that he issued an ultimatum to all members of the Vienna Psychoanalytic Society: "A vote to drop Adler from the society or you yourself will be expelled!" It seems that Freud himself needed a little relationship counseling.

God made us to be like Him in character. His character is love. According to 1 John 4:16, "God is love." Love so accurately summarizes and encapsulates God's character that this verse *equates* them, as in God = love.

But love doesn't exist within God to be admired as an isolated trait; it spills out of Him in the milieu of relationships. The crown jewels of England on display in the

Tower of London didn't convey the glory of England as effectively as did Princess Diana's mingling with AIDS orphans in Zambia. I suppose God could have left love on display in heaven in a locked case, but He sent it to earth to mingle with the terminally ill.

To fulfill our purpose—to be like Jesus, to reflect God's character—demands that we enter the wild world of human relationships. But fear not. In this chapter you'll see how God endlessly and ingeniously crafted human beings for successful bonding. I'm going to divide the chapter into the three phases of human love: family, friendship, and romantic. The Greek language uses different words for these: *storge, phileo,* and *eros.*

Storge: The family bond

Just as the Father, Son, and Holy Spirit blend Their perfect individualities to form a unit, the human family blends separate beings into one. The nuclear family functions more effectively than any other social unit in human history. The natural affection between family members serves as a primer for bonding with future friends and lovers. Sadly, ungodly forces within society increasingly assault the family unit. Biblical descriptions of the degraded state of humanity in the last days include *astorgos,* or "without natural affection" (see Romans 1:31 and 2 Timothy 3:3). As the family structure crumbles, people forget how to love.

A study of family bonding reveals that nature pushes us powerfully toward intimacy. Take, for instance, a mother and father bearing their first child. At her child's birth, a mother feels a rush of endorphins, oxytocin, and endogenous opiates in her brain, which give her a certain "high" and pushes her toward nurturing behaviors. I remember that wave of emotion I felt for my newborn. All she could do was eat, cry, and defecate—and all I wanted to do was love on her. Now I know it was hormones; nature literally drugs women to drive them to bond with their infants.

Amazingly, God has built into babies a preference for female facial features and the female voice, impelling the child toward the milk truck, so to speak. The baby instinctively searches for the nipple, which slides into the tiny palate perfectly. Doses of oxytocin rush into the baby's throat, along with all the other goodies in mother's milk. Oxytocin is called "the cuddle hormone" because it gives us that warm, fuzzy, bonding feeling. As the baby nurses, his or her eyes and the mother's eyes lock in a fond gaze. Opioids, or pleasure hormones, flood the infant's brain, forming a positive association with feeding, which motivates further breast feeding. The mother's prolactin, secreted during nursing, relaxes the mother so that she's inclined to linger with her baby rather than get up and go. You can just feel the love, can't you?

Amazingly, the father also experiences endocrine and neurological changes that press him into intimacy with his family. His vasopressin levels increase when living with the pregnant mother. Vasopressin has earned the reputation as a monogamy hormone because it tempers the effect of testosterone, the prowling hormone. Opioids are released in the father during bonding behaviors (such as cuddling, hugging, and rocking), thus encouraging those behaviors. God induces a kind of family "high" to get them into bonding mode!

Once opioid bonding has occurred, separation becomes stressful for the infant. Babies cry, not because something's wrong, but because something's right. Even this separation stress has a function—it impels us toward bonding. Without that bonding, stress hormones such as cortisol can inhibit healthy brain and social development.

Throughout childhood, cortisol moves the child back to the mother for regular doses of affection. I recall one particular day I was sitting at my desk when my four-year-old wandered into my office. Soon she was knocking up against my knees as I worked. She wasn't crying, fussing, or doing much of anything but hovering near me. I put down my papers, picked up my child, kissed her head, squeezed her tight, gave her a razz on the neck, and put her down. As if recharged, she ran off to play.

A psychologist named John Bowlby pioneered the attachment theory of child development. Essentially, this theory taught that an interruption in the bond between the child and mother or mother figure—especially between birth and three years of age—caused compromises in brain development and the future mental health of the child, particularly in the area of social skills. Bowlby was right. Humans need nurture throughout childhood, especially the first three years.

As the child learns language, verbal communication becomes central to home life. Good communication furnishes the building material for more mature relationships. Blessed is the home where family members actually talk! These families have become rare, largely due to the overuse of mass media. The problems that come with the way people use mass media abound—violence and immorality in the programming, health problems due to lack of exercise for those using media, Internet pornography, sexting—I could write reams about how all these things eat away at the heart of society. But my concern for now is what media *displaces*. Parents in "wired" homes spend on average four minutes a day of uninterrupted time with their kids. Recently, kids' electronic media use has jumped to more than fifty-three hours a week.[1] Do the math: that means kids are spending almost eight hours a day in giving their attention to media, *more than one hundred times the amount of time spent communicating with their parents*! Glowing screens displace face-to-face, verbal communication with family members. Parents would do well to clear their houses of televisions and limit computer time.

I don't want to brag about my family. Just like all families, we have skeletons in our closets—skeletons with warts, no less. But my daughters' friends marvel at the closeness between my daughters and me. One day I realized that we talk on a deep, meaningful level at least an hour a week. I wondered how many of my counseling clients would need my services if they had such bonds with their mothers. I'd go out of business! The way these close communicative bonds formed was by talking. From the time they could lisp, I engaged my girls in conversations of all sorts. They asked me about everything, from "Mommy, how did you meet Daddy?" to "Mommy, what's a harlot?" (I read the Bible to my kids.) As they've matured, the conversation has continued; today, they stun me with their insights. The skills of communication, intimacy, and relationship building develop just like the skills of speaking Japanese or playing the ukulele—with practice.

Phileo: The friendship bond

God is the Author of friendship. After all, Jesus had friends. In the home of siblings Mary, Martha, and Lazarus (see John 11:1, 2), He found a place to relax. He formed close, horizontal bonds with His disciples. Even Abraham was called a "friend of God" (James 2:23). If the Monarch of the universe could be a Friend to humankind, how much more can we befriend one another by following His pattern? "Be kindly affectionate to one another," we're told (Romans 12:10). That word is *philostorgos,* a combination of *phileo* and *storge.* As I pointed out above, the family serves as a training school for relationship building throughout life. Drawing from the love we learned in our families, we *philostorgos* one another as brothers, sisters, and friends.

As we grow into late childhood and adolescence, we develop intense interest in peers—potential comrades of similar station in life. Because these peers come from outside our family system, we must gather information about them—thus the near obsession of kids with their social network. The peer orientation of the teen years means that the young person is preparing to dive into an endless pool of strangers and forge their own relationships. Don't worry, parents; God planned this!

I remember the shift well. I enjoyed high status with my children until they were about ten years old, when I gradually became less interesting. It was as if their biological clocks had said, "Get ready to leave your parents! Prepare to live without them! Find other people!" As much as it hurt, I reminded myself that their friendships served as a practice run for the daunting task of finding, and bonding with, a life partner. I hasten to add that friendships remain important throughout life. Sociological research confirms over and over that social connectedness correlates with happiness.[2]

Now, I know someone will read all of this with a broken heart. Loneliness affects up to 20 percent of Americans.[3] I'm concerned about this, but I am more concerned about the fact that in the last twenty years, the rate has tripled![4] As methods of communication multiply, actual communication dwindles. Candidly, this fact led me into the counseling field. I knew I had a gift for face-to-face communication and that the demand for it was increasing.

Beyond the need for intimate one-on-one friendships, humans have an innate hunger for community. Every social forum—bars, social clubs, cliques, gangs, to name a few—testify to this need and our ingenious methods of satisfying it. According to sociological research, church life best meets this need. The Greek word *koinonia,* often translated "fellowship," ironically means "communication." This *koinonia* sums up our need to belong to, and communicate with, a unit greater than ourselves. We have an innate drive to live in *koinonia* with a larger body. We crave belonging.

I realize that malfunctioning, pathological churches exist, but overall, a church is a safer place than the world. This song title sums it up: "It Stinks in the Ark (But It Sure Beats the Ocean)." Reams of research validate the multifaceted benefits of church attendance and involvement.

One study out of Detroit studied seven hundred women and found that regular church attendance significantly correlated with less depression and better global health.[5]

A study on 445 youths in Baltimore showed that if their *mothers* attend church, the youth tended to be more functional and healthy.[6] A study of Latinos correlated church attendance with better health and dietary practice.[7] A study on senior citizens showed that the support received in church reduced the impact of financial strain. This study went so far as to research the effect of support from secular networks. The effect wasn't as strong! Apparently, the quality of support in church sets it apart from bars and Rotary Clubs.[8] Finally, we must remember that it is more blessed to give than to receive. The findings of another study on seniors indicated that *their service to others,* facilitated by church involvement, reduced stress.[9]

On the last point, quantities of research also validate the therapeutic benefit of service to others. I'll let a favorite author sum it up: "Doing good is a work that benefits both giver and receiver. If you forget self in your interest for others, you gain a victory over your infirmities. . . . The pleasure of doing good animates the mind and vibrates through the whole body."[10]

I can remember a discouraged time when I wanted to stay home from church. Sabbath morning arrived, and my bathrobe called out to me. Self-pity seemed like a needed refuge. The problem was that I was preaching that day. I went out of duty. I didn't regret that decision. As I worshiped God, communicated with fellow believers, and ministered to other people, I forgot my problems and felt great. Sure, the problems returned, but at least I got a little break from them.

Here's an interesting fact: recent discoveries show that most people have the capacity for only about 150 friends.[11] I've found that the greatest individual benefit comes from churches with a congregation size of between 50 and 150 members. As churches increase in size, members tend to feel insignificant and invisible, with fewer demands placed upon them; and therefore they have less incentive to give of themselves. If you can attend a smaller church, do it.

For some help in building social and relationship skills, see "Social Skills 101" and "Relationship Skills 101" in the toolbox.

Eros: The romantic bond

The most delicate yet torrid of human loves is sexual, or romantic, love. The Greek word *eros* never appears in Scripture, but anyone who has gasped through the book Song of Solomon knows the idea is there. God made sex and rejoices in its beauty. He says, "Husbands, love your wives, just as Christ also loved the church and gave Himself for her" (Ephesians 5:25). God uses the act of marriage, the man giving himself to the wife, as a metaphor of Christ's holy love for His own bride. Marriage and sex in marriage are holy in God's eyes.

Marriage is the stepping-stone from family of origin to family of choice. Just after God put the finishing touches on Eve and brought her to Adam, He said, "Therefore a man shall leave his father and mother and be joined to his wife, and they shall become one flesh" (Genesis 2:24). He predicted well. During the subsequent six millennia, man after man left his parents, cleaved to a wife, brought forth children who grew, left, and cleaved. Today, that leaving and cleaving has filled the earth with people.

But most of the leavers and cleavers have failed to follow God's design. Human passion has raged like a grass fire, consuming everything in its path. Apart from divine guidance and power, human relationships either end or continue in a perverted pathological form. The well-known 50 percent divorce statistic gives a partial picture of the mortality rate of romantic relationships. Add to that the nonmarriage romances that fail, and the marriages that remain legally intact but psychologically shattered; I would dare say that most romantic, sexual relationships in this world fail.

"The love of Christ controls us" (2 Corinthians 5:14, NASB) means that Jesus' love holds us together. Just as a loving God directs the trillions of flying particles of the material universe, He directs the moral and spiritual course of His children. Only the Designer can help us live according to His design. Only He can hold our souls and our relationships together.

Sexual love keeps us alive. Not individually, of course—no one ever died without sex (although many thought they would), but as a race. Collectively, we depend upon *eros* to perpetuate our existence. The problem is that the very thing that gives life when it stays within boundaries, brings death when it breaks them. Every form of immoral erotic love, as alluring as they may be, bears the hideous fruit of physical illness, psychopathology, social disorder, and ultimately spiritual death. Sexuality within heterosexual monogamous marriage alone bears the fruit of health and prosperity.

The benefits abound; married people live longer—an average of seven years for a man and four years for a woman. Amazingly, married people have more money. Married people tend to be safer from crime and violence; this is due, it is thought, to having someone to watch out for the other. Marriage tends to stabilize people socially and emotionally and engender better self-care; for instance, single men drink twice as much as married men. Finally, married people have better sex lives! Feeling secure in a committed relationship has a way of releasing our inner wild child.[12]

At this moment in time, many of earth's young people feel the first surges of hormones that will soon transform them into fully reproductive beings. They will find partners with whom their passions will burn. A sharp spike in the neurotransmitter dopamine will attend one of the greatest pleasures known—orgasm. No other animal in creation knows that rich, crazy, deeply satisfying sensation. The bonding hormone oxytocin will pour forth in rich supply during sex, a gift from God to forge and support the emotional connection. Harnessed by the love of Christ, sexual urges will lead to sexual encounters within the sacred confines of marriage. God's holy purpose for human sexuality will be fulfilled. But in most cases, that won't be so. These young people will reap the consequences of living outside of God's design.

Agape: The ultimate bond

Relationships often disappoint. Many of us face a dull, gray loneliness every day of our lives. Broken bonds litter the past and prophesy of doom for the future. In such times we must remember that while God created us for human relationships, He put in place a contingency plan for times when those relationships fail. That plan is a personal connection with Jesus. He says, "Yes, I have loved you with an everlasting love; therefore with lovingkindness I have drawn you" (Jeremiah 31:3).

Fortunately, there is a fourth kind of love: *agape.* It towers over human loves like a mountain over foothills. Human loves are morally neutral, but *agape* carries within its heart the law of God. While family, friendships, and romantic love can be perverted by selfishness, by definition *agape* sacrifices itself for the good of others. Because of our sinful state, human loves must be fed by the streams of *agape,* be directed by its principles, or be doomed to fail.

For a worksheet on how agape works in relationships, see "Qualities of Agape" in the toolbox.

At such times as our human relationships do fail, we have a soft place to fall. Jesus says, "I will never leave you nor forsake you" (Hebrews 13:5). Do those words sound sweet to your embattled ears?

Ending at the beginning

This book began with the truth that we have been made in God's image and are called to be molded into His likeness by His Spirit dwelling within. How fitting that we should end with a revelation that His character is love—pure, unfailing, self-giving love. This means that as we come to reflect the character, or the inner life, of God, we will begin to love the way God loves.

The first step toward that purpose is a step we will take every day for the rest of our lives. That step is a step toward Jesus, the Fountain of living water, the endless Source spring of all that is good.

> *For a tutorial on prayer, see "Prayer Basics" in the toolbox.*

DISCUSSION QUESTIONS

1. How has it affected you personally to know that Jesus left heaven and came to earth to die so that He could show you *agape* love?

2. Do you feel your family of origin bonded well? Rate on a scale of one to ten, ten being the best, how well you bonded as a family.

3. How have the relationships in your family of origin affected the way you relate to people today?

4. What practices compromised (for example, drug and alcohol use, mass media overuse, etc.) the bonding in your family of origin, if any? What practices do you currently engage in that may be compromising you socially and relationally?

5. Do you feel you have at least three close bonds? If not, what things can you do to increase your intimacy skill set?

6. Do you feel you have a community? If so, what is it? Do you feel you belong? Explain.

7. Do you have a means of serving others? If so, what is it? How do you feel when you engage in it?

8. Have you been married or otherwise coupled? Have you successfully bonded with another romantically? If not, are you looking for that component in your life?

9. On the whole, has sexuality been a blessing or a curse to you? If a curse, can you move toward a more biblical, pure sexuality?

10. We're made in God's image, created to reflect His character. That character is *agape* love. Express your commitment to fulfilling this purpose in your life.

---

1. Greg Toppo, "Kid's Electronic Media Use Jumps to 53 Hours a Week," *USA Today,* accessed January 26, 2011, http://www.usatoday.com/tech/news/2010-01-20-1Avideokids20_ST_N.htm.

2. See, for instance, "Connection & Happiness," *This Emotional Life,* accessed March 3, 2011, http://www.pbs.org/thisemotionallife/topic/connecting/connection-happiness.

3. John Cacioppo and William Patrick, *Loneliness: Human Nature and the Need for Social Connection* (New York: W. W. Norton & Co., 2008), 5.

4. J. Olds and R. S. Schwartz, *The Lonely American: Drifting Apart in the Twenty-first Century* (Boston: Beacon Press, 2009).

5. Juliana van Olphen et al., "Religious Involvement, Social Support, and Health Among African-American Women on the East Side of Detroit," *Journal of General Internal Medicine* 18, no. 7 (July 2003): 549–557.

6. Stuart R. Varon and Anne W. Riley, "Relationship Between Maternal Church Attendance and Adolescent Mental Health and Social Functioning," *Psychiatric Services* 50 (June 1999): 799–805.

7. E. M. Arrendono et al., "Is Church Attendance Associated With Latinas' Health Practices and Self-Reported Health?" *American Journal of Health Behavior* 29, no. 6 (2005): 502–508.

8. N. Krause, "Exploring the Stress-Buffering Effects of Church-Based and Secular Social Support on Self-Rated Health in Late Life," *Journals of Gerontology: Series B, Psychological Sciences and Social Sciences* 61, no. 1 (January 2006): S35–S44.

9. Neal Krause, "Church-Based Social Support and Mortality," *Journals of Gerontology: Series B, Psychological Sciences and Social Sciences* 61, no. 3 (May 2006): S140–S146.

10. Ellen G. White, *Messages to Young People* (Nashville, Tenn.: Southern Publishing Association, 1930), 209.

11. See, for instance, Stan Schroeder's article "Your Brain Can't Handle Your Facebook Friends," accessed March 3, 2011, http://mashable.com/2010/01/25/brain-facebook-friends/.

12. Richard Niolon, review of *Why Married People Are Happier, Healthier, and Better Off Financially,* by Linda J. Waite and Maggie Gallagher, *PsychPage* (blog) October 23, 2010, http://www.psychpage.com/family/library/brwaitgalligher.html.

ALL THE THINGS WE ARE IN CHRIST

Use a highlighter or underline to mark the rows that apply to you. Then look up the promises on the right and claim your new creature status in Christ, believing that "He who has begun a good work in you will complete it until the day of Christ Jesus" (Philippians 1:6).

Do you feel . . .	In Christ, you are . . .
Dead?	Living—Acts 17:28
Unjustified?	Justified—Romans 3:24
Alive to sin and dead to God?	Dead to sin and alive to God—Romans 6:11
Condemned?	Freed from condemnation—Romans 8:1
Trapped by sin and death?	Free from the law of sin and death—Romans 8:2
Separated from God?	Joined to the love of God—Romans 8:39
Separated from believers?	One body—Romans 12:5
Disapproved of by God?	Approved of by God—Romans 16:10
Unsanctified?	Sanctified—1 Corinthians 1:2
Stupid?	Wise—1 Corinthians 4:10
Betrayed and let down?	Recipients of promises—2 Corinthians 1:20
Unstable?	Established—2 Corinthians 1:21
Defeated?	Triumphant—2 Corinthians 2:14
Ignorant?	Enlightened— 2 Corinthians 3:14
Alienated from God?	Reconciled to God—2 Corinthians 5:19
Used by Satan?	The righteousness of God—2 Corinthians 5:21
Corrupt?	Uncorrupt—2 Corinthians 11:3
Enslaved?	Free—Galatians 2:4
Cursed?	Blessed—Galatians 3:14
Orphaned?	Sons of God—Galatians 3:26

ALL THE THINGS WE ARE IN CHRIST (cont.)

Unfaithful?	Faithful—Ephesians 1:1
Alone on earth?	Blessed in heavenly places—Ephesians 1:3
Insignificant?	Chosen—Ephesians 1:4
Forgotten or resented?	Redeemed, forgiven, graced—Ephesians 1:7
Earthbound?	Sitting in heavenly places—Ephesians 2:6
Untalented or unresourceful?	Created for good works—Ephesians 2:10
Far from God?	Near to God—Ephesians 2:13
Written out of God's will?	Heirs of God—Ephesians 3:6
Unforgiven?	Forgiven—Ephesians 4:32
Unholy?	Saints—Philippians 1:1
Sad, depressed, or discouraged?	Rejoicing—Philippians 3:3
Flawed?	Perfect—Colossians 1:28
Unimportant?	Called according to God's purpose—2 Timothy 1:9
Empty?	Filled with good things—Philemon 6
Badly behaved?	Having good conduct—1 Peter 3:16

BIBLICAL MODEL OF HUMAN NATURE

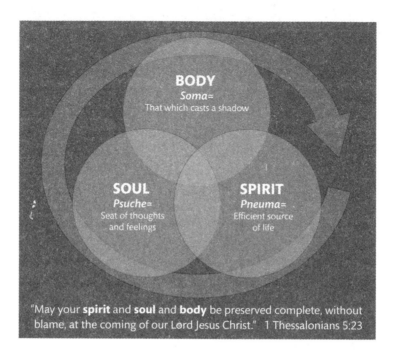

BODY
Soma=
That which casts a shadow

SOUL
Psuche=
Seat of thoughts
and feelings

SPIRIT
Pneuma=
Efficient source
of life

"May your **spirit** and **soul** and **body** be preserved complete, without blame, at the coming of our Lord Jesus Christ." 1 Thessalonians 5:23

According to the above passage, human nature is tripartite, including body, soul, and spirit. The body can be thought of as the "house we live in." The soul is the inner life, including feelings, affections, appetites, drives, desires, passions, attitudes, temperament, and disposition. The spirit is the aspect of human nature that connects with the divine mind and includes the will, reason, faith, and conscience.

Notice that these three dimensions overlap. The Bible teaches a wholistic view of human nature—that the parts exist in conjunction with one another. For instance, the soul exists in the context of the body, and both depend upon God for life. What impacts one dimension, impacts the other dimensions.

Contrary to popular teaching, the soul doesn't retain consciousness outside the body. The notion of the soul flying off to heaven at death originated with Greek philosophy. This belief results in the attitude that it does not matter how we treat our bodies. However, the Bible is clear that immortality is a gift from God (1 Timothy 6:16).

For further study on human nature, read the following biblical passages:

- Genesis 2:7
- Job 14:10–14
- Job 27:3
- Job 33:4
- Job 34:14, 15
- Ecclesiastes 12:7
- Isaiah 42:5
- John 1:4
- John 11:11–24
- Romans 12:1, 2
- 3 John 2

Choose your study style, depending upon your temperament and interests.

The artist

You're an artist if you're creative, unconventional, and expressive. Try prayer walking for ten minutes, then putting scripture to music, reading a passage and journaling on it, or even creating some kind of drawing or sculpture depicting what you read. Make sure to have some plan of which passages to address, such as those found in "the marathoner" or a list of poetic passages, such as those found in the 199 Favorite Bible Verses series. (For a few dollars you can buy a book of 199 Favorite Bible Verses for women, men, teens, mothers, grads and leaders. See www .christianbook.com.)

The scholar

You're a scholar if you love to acquire expert knowledge on a specific topic. Choose a book of the Bible that holds special interest for you. Day by day develop a comprehensive knowledge of the book. Do online research to understand the history of the book, the author of the book, and the literary style of the book. Journal your findings or write them in a research paper format to share with others. You might even volunteer to teach a special class at your local church or library. Pray for opportunities to share what you learn.

The pilgrim

You're a pilgrim if you're devotional and worshipful by nature. Journals are an excellent tool for you. Keep a prayer journal in which you write specific prayer requests, also making note of when they're answered. Keep a list of Bible promises to claim in behalf of your prayer requests. There are good lists online at http://www.scripturepromises.com and http://www .encouragingbiblequotes.com. Put your hands on these promises and read them out loud during your prayer time.

The marathoner

You're a marathoner if you like to set goals and complete a task. You're an ideal candidate for reading the Bible through in one year. Simply set aside up to an hour a day in which to pray and read a section of the Bible. There are many Web sites that assist with this, such as http://www .ewordtoday.com/year/ and http://christiananswers.net. Do a Google search for "read the Bible in one year." BibleGateway has a plan that will actually send an e-mail reminder: http://www .biblegateway.com/resources/readingplans/.

DEVOTIONS MADE SIMPLE (cont.)

The linguist

You're a linguist if you like to deeply probe a spiritual issue or mystery. Use http://www
.topverses.com to find "top verses overall." This is a list of hundreds of the best-loved Bible verses.
Using the Web site http://bible.worthwhile.com begin to write down each verse in the original
language, keeping a journal of your findings. You might then put them in your own words, thus
making your own translation.

The journalist

You're a journalist if you want to get the whole story with all the details. Purchase a set of The
Conflict of the Ages series by Ellen G. White. This series begins in Eden and comments on each
era of Bible history. Each chapter has a list of the Bible passages on which it's based. Read those
Bible passages along with the commentary, chapter by chapter, until the series is finished.

Here are some other great Web sites to check out:
http://www.biblegateway.com
http://www.searchgodsword.org
http://www.studylight.org
http://www.biblestudytools.com

A Study of Mental Illness Versus Demonic Activity

Some say the Bible doesn't support the idea of mental illness and that all erratic behavior results from demonic activity. Some take the opposite stance, believing that what Jesus called demon possession was really not yet understood pathology at work. Could this be one of those issues in which the answer isn't "either-or" but "both"? Is it possible that denying one or the other oversimplifies a complex, multidimensional problem? Could it be that we can be crazy or demon plagued—or sometimes simultaneously a little of both?

Some believe that acknowledging mental illness absolves people of responsibility for their behavior. "We're not sick," they object, "we're sinners!" Yet God speaks of our sin problem in pathological terms:

The whole head is sick,
And the whole heart faints.
From the sole of the foot even to the head,
There is no soundness in it,
But wounds and bruises and putrefying sores (Isaiah 1:5, 6).

Let's look at several more biblical examples:

- In Deuteronomy 28:28, the consequences of rebellion against God are that "the Lord will strike you with madness and blindness and confusion of heart."
- Jeremiah 29:26 cites a delusional state of a certain individual "who is demented and considers himself a prophet."
- Jeremiah 50:38 says the Babylonians are "insane with their idols."
- In Daniel 4:33, Nebuchadnezzar experienced a seven-year-long psychotic episode, during which he ate grass like cattle and ceased personal grooming.
- Matthew 4:24 and 17:15 speak of epilepsy. The term is translated "lunatic" in the King James Version.
- In Acts 26:11, Paul speaks of being "exceedingly mad" (KJV) in his persecution of Christians.
- In 2 Peter 2:16, Balaam's condition is spoken of as "madness."

Notice that many of these individuals harvested in their own persons the consequences of such sins as rebellion (the Israelites), idolatry (the Babylonians), egotism (Nebuchadnezzar),

DISEASES OR DEVILS? (cont.)

hostility (Saul), and materialism (Balaam). This pinpoints an important truth: In many cases, insanity can be traced to the individual's sin. The greatest mental-health liability is our choice to live in dissonance with God's plan. All departures from Him are a form of spiritual insanity, which often leads to diagnosable insanity.

How essential, though, that we recognize that innocent victims exist, people whose psychological disorders result from sin other than their own. The forces of genetic degeneration, prenatal influences, childhood abuse and neglect, failure of the parental bonds, and extreme trauma are often to blame. Such individuals can't be condemned for their condition.

But God has given even these people a free will. People with schizophrenia may not be able to fight their way out of hallucinations; but, in their lucid moments, they can choose to manage their illnesses responsibly. None of us can make our instabilities vanish, but we can all choose to build on the stable Rock, Jesus Christ. We can't change our spots, but we can choose the Savior. And choosing the Savior can only help in the battle against mental illness.

Instructions: After each entry, rate your level of participation from zero to ten (ten being the most). Follow that with an example from your own experience.

Catastrophizing. You think that past, present, and/or future events will be awful and unbearable. "If I don't get an A, it will be horrible!" _____

Mind reading. Without evidence, you assume that your intuitions never misfire and that you know what people are thinking about you. "I can tell they hated my lecture." _____

Negative filtering. You perceive only the worst of past and present events and circumstances. "Everyone I've ever known has rejected me." _____

Fortune-telling. You assume the past is entirely predictive of the future, rather than allowing for change. "I failed in that relationship, so I must not have what it takes." _____

Discounting positives. You trivialize the positive things you and others do. "Of course I take care of my children. Who wouldn't?" _____

Overgeneralizing. You apply negative traits or actions to the entire person or situation. "My husband can't do anything right!" _____

Dichotomous thinking. You regard situations and people in all-or-nothing, black-and-white terms. "Either we have fun on this campout, or we don't!" _____

Shoulds. You see people and events entirely in terms of ideals rather than reality. "People should be friendly and warm." _____

Personalizing. You take an undue amount of responsibility upon yourself. "If I looked better, my husband wouldn't be into pornography." _____

Blaming. You project personal responsibility onto other people or circumstances. "If he had been kinder, I wouldn't have cheated. He made me do it!" _____

Unfair comparisons. You view yourself in contrast to unrealistic standards. "If I'm not as smart as he is, I won't even try." _____

DISTORTED THOUGHTS (cont.)

Self-inflation. You claim personal assets, achievements, and abilities while lacking the courage to test your beliefs. "I'm a great singer. If I tried, I could be famous." _____

Regret orientation. You focus on past mishaps, assuming that they have been ruinous to your life. "If only I hadn't undergone that surgery!" _____

Emotional reasoning. You believe that because you feel something, it must be so. "I'm feeling guilty. I must be guilty!" _____

Overidentifying. You see yourself entirely in terms of one trait or event. "My shyness makes me into a complete, antisocial reject." _____

Overvaluing. You attribute to others excessive authority or worth in contrast to yourself and/or others. "She always knows what's best for me. She's never wrong! I can't take a step without her." _____

Monsterifying. You exaggerate the wrongs of others, attributing to them a global pattern of evil for which you lack evidence. "She's wholly given over to evil and can't be trusted." _____

Projecting. You see others through the lens of your own traits, assuming they share them. "Of course he was angry! I'd be angry!" _____

Supernaturalizing. You interpret events and circumstances too readily and confidently in terms of direct divine intervention. "People don't like me, so God must be judging me." _____

Singling. You place yourself in position of complete contrast to others. "God's forgiveness is for everyone, but I'm too evil." _____

Judgment focus. You view events, situations, or people completely in terms of how they measure against some arbitrary standard, rather than just seeing things for what they are. "He's too talkative and people don't like him because of it." _____

---

1. Thanks to R. L. Leahy and S. J. Holland for some of the concepts from their book *Treatment Plans and Interventions for Depression and Anxiety Disorders* (New York: Guilford Press, 2000), 299.

In November of 2005, *National Geographic* ran an article on longevity, featuring Seventh-day Adventists; Adventism was said to be "one of the nation's most convincing cultures of longevity" because "the average Adventist lived four to ten years longer than the average Californian."[1] Adventism's model of health came from author Ellen White, who said, "Pure air, sunlight, abstemiousness, rest, exercise, proper diet, the use of water, trust in divine power—these are the true remedies."[2]

Attending to these "eight doctors" will help us take charge of our own health. Below is a quick summary of each principle, along with a bibliography for further reading.

Pure air

Make sure your home and workplace are well ventilated, free of molds, dust, and other impurities. In addition, spend some time outdoors every day, preferably in a pollution-free setting. Take a few minutes each day to expand the lungs with exercise and deep breathing, slowly filling the lungs to capacity and exhaling fully.

Sunlight

Spend some time outside each day. Sunlight on the skin turns cholesterol into vitamin D. Vitamin D deficiency is pandemic because we get inadequate sun exposure. To beauty experts, sun has become the villain because it wrinkles the skin. True, care should be taken not to overexpose the face, neck, forearms, and hands. A great idea if you have privacy is nude sunbathing! In addition to vitamin D, sunlight sterilizes and cleanses our environment and also lifts the mood.

Temperance

We would do well to abstain from harmful things: alcohol, tobacco, caffeine, high sugar foods, violent or immoral mass media, sex outside of marriage, and harmful drugs. We should also avoid overuse of good things: too much sex within marriage (yes, it happens!), overeating, overworking, and overexercising. It's all about common sense and self-control.

Rest

Sleep at least seven to nine hours a day. Take vacations yearly. Finally, observe the biblical Sabbath from sundown Friday to sundown Saturday, leaving your work life behind for those twenty-four hours and focus on your Creator, Redeemer, and Friend. The weekly cycle was set in motion by God at the beginning of time. He said to take one day of seven off from work! I'm glad He told us we had to, or we'd probably work nonstop.

THE EIGHT DOCTORS (cont.)

Exercise

A sensible, sane exercise program has more benefits than can be listed here. Walking is the best exercise and also one of the most beautiful. I combine pure air, sunshine, and exercise by walking in the park (or an upscale neighborhood where I can admire the houses) a few times a week.

Proper diet

Move away from refined foods and animal-based foods toward an unrefined, plant-based diet. Volumes of scientific data are validating this one simple dietary principle as ideal for most people. Pay attention to the when of eating too. Two to three meals a day with nothing but water in between meals, plus spacing the meals five hours apart can make a huge difference in digestion.

Water

Drink about an ounce of water daily for every two pounds of body weight. This averages out to eight glasses a day. This should be drunk between meals so as not to dilute digestive juices. Water can be used externally as well, as home remedies for ailments such as the common cold. I use hot baths, finishing with a cold shower, as a remedy for colds and flu. They really help!

Trust

Worry eats away at the life forces—and it's so unnecessary. If we could make things better with worry, we could argue for its use. But typically we make things worse. Trusting in God's care for us and His divine power to strengthen us to cope with life's challenges is a skill we would do well to learn and practice.

For further reading

Health

> *Depression: The Way Out* by Neil Nedley, MD
> *Dr. Arnott's 24 Realistic Ways to Improve Your Health* by Tim Arnott, MD
> *Dynamic Living* by Hans Diehl, DrHSc, and Aileen Ludington, MD
> *Health Smart* by Walter Thompson, MD
> *The Little Book of Health for Men* by Sharon Platt-McDonald, MSc, RHV, RM, RGN
> *The Little Book of Health for Women* by Sharon Platt-McDonald, MSc, RHV, RM, RGN
> *The Little Book of Health for Seniors* by Sharon Platt-McDonald, MSc, RHV, RM, RGN
> *The Little Book of Health for Children & Teens* by Sharon Platt-McDonald, MSc, RHV, RM, RGN
> *The Ministry of Healing* by Ellen G. White

Diet

> *Counsels on Diet and Foods* by Ellen G. White
>
> *Foods for Thought: Nutrition's Link to Mood, Memory, Learning, and Behavior* by Bernell Baldwin, Vicki Griffin, and Evelyn Kissinger
>
> *Foods That Heal* by George D. Pamplona-Roger, MD
>
> *Simple Solutions: Is What You're Eating, Eating You?* by Vicki Griffin, Edwin Neblett, and Evelyn Kissinger

Natural Remedies

> *Manual of Hydrotherapy and Massage* by Fred B. Moor, MD; Stella C. Peterson, RN; Ethel M. Manwell, RN; Mary C. Noble, RN; and Gertrude Muench, RN
>
> *Plants That Heal* by George D. Pamplona-Roger, MD
>
> *Proof Positive* by Neil Nedley, MD

Cookbooks

> *Cookin' Up Good Health Recipe Collection* by Donna Green-Goodman, MPH
>
> *Cooking by the Book* by Marcella Lynch
>
> *Cooking With the Micheff Sisters* by the Micheff Sisters
>
> *Cooking Entrees With the Micheff Sisters* by the Micheff Sisters
>
> *Cooking for Two With the Micheff Sisters* by the Micheff Sisters
>
> *Cooking With Catie* by Catie Sanner
>
> *Fabulous Food for Family and Friends* by Cheryl Thomas Peters
>
> *Fast Cooking in a Slow Cooker Every Day of the Year* by JoAnn Rachor
>
> *Fun With Kids in the Kitchen Cookbook* by Judi Rogers
>
> *McDougalls' All-You-Can-Eat Vegetarian Cookbook* by John McDougall, MD, and Mary McDougall
>
> *Naturally Gourmet* by Karen Houghton, RN, BSN
>
> *Soups, Salads & Sandwiches With the Micheff Sisters* by the Micheff Sisters
>
> *Taste of Health,* volumes 1 and 2, by Barbara Kerr
>
> *Ten Talents Cookbook* by Rosalie Hurd, and Frank J. Hurd, DC, MD

---

1. Dan Buettner. "The Secrets of Long Life," *National Geographic,* November 2005.
2. Ellen G. White, *The Ministry of Healing* (Washington, D.C.: Review and Herald®, 1905), 127.

ESTABLISHING EMPATHY WITH E.A.R.

Empathy, with its sense of connectedness and shared experience, forms a basis for good communication. This exercise will help us learn the skills of developing effective, empathic bonds with one another. Often when this empathy develops in a relationship, the problems seem to solve themselves.

Meditation: Our inclination in relationships tends toward selfishness. We want to be heard and to advance our own agenda. But empathy requires focused listening.

- "So then, my beloved brethren, let every man be swift to hear, slow to speak, slow to wrath" (James 1:19).
- "In the multitude of words sin is not lacking, but he who restrains his lips is wise" (Proverbs 10:19).
- "He who answers a matter before he hears it, it is folly and shame to him" (Proverbs 18:13).

Notice the advice in James 1:19. He invites us to learn to be (1) swift to hear, (2) slow to speak, and (3) slow to wrath.

Unfortunately, most of the time, we respond in the opposite way. We are typically (1) slow to hear, (2) swift to speak, and (3) swift to wrath.

Following the counsel of James takes us in the opposite direction of our inclinations. The exercise that follows will help you learn how to show empathy.

Remember this equation: **E**mpathy = **A**sk and **R**eflect.

Two essential components to empathic listening are **asking** questions and **reflecting** what we hear.

1. **Asking questions.** The purpose of asking questions is to draw out the thoughts, feelings, and opinions of the other. Try to use What, Where, When, and How questions. Try to avoid asking Why questions because Why questions often sound accusatory. Make sure the questions aren't veiled accusations, as in, "What makes you act so mean all the time?"
2. **Reflecting.** The purpose of reflection is likewise to draw the person out. The point of reflecting is not to agree or disagree with a person but rather to understand him or her. Simply put in your own words what you heard him or her say, asking him or her to confirm or correct. Again, the point is to understand. You're not going for the objective truth, but his or her subjective truth. People don't care how much you know until they know how much you care.

ESTABLISHING EMPATHY WITH E.A.R. (cont.)

Action Step: Use the floor exercise to utilize these skills. Flip a coin. Whoever wins, goes first. This person gets "the floor" (you can use a piece of rug or a tile or simply use a book or other object). While this person has the floor, the listener must use the E.A.R. technique to draw out from the first person his or her views, feelings, and thoughts.

Here is a sample of what *not* to do.

FRED. (*Who has the floor.*) I feel lonely at times in our relationship—like you've withdrawn from me.
SARAH. I've only withdrawn because you're so pushy and demanding!

Notice that Sarah advanced her own agenda and talked from her own subjective experience, rather than drawing out Fred's subjective experience.

Here is a sample of what *to* do.

FRED. I feel lonely at times in our relationship—like you've withdrawn from me.
SARAH. How long have you felt this way? (*Asking.*)
FRED. Just since the baby was born. I feel like he took my place in your heart.
SARAH. So you feel kind of displaced by Tommy. (*Reflecting.*)
FRED. Yeah. My parents never paid much attention to me growing up, and I feel like it's happening all over again.
SARAH. Let me see if I understand you—my paying so much attention to Tommy reminds you of your childhood? (*Asking and reflecting.*)
FRED. Yeah.
SARAH. Was there a "Tommy" in your family? Someone who got all the attention?
FRED. Yeah, my little brother, Frank. He was my parents' favorite. They said so.
SARAH. It must have been really hard to have your parents play favorites.
FRED. I felt so rejected.

Notice how quickly this conversation arrived at the root of the problem—Fred's fear of rejection. Sarah's effective asking and listening got to the root of the problem. At the same time, Fred felt understood and heard. From this point on, the couple could work out some simple solutions to prevent Fred's fear of rejection. And truthfully, simply being heard and understood by his wife probably accomplished this as much as any follow-up steps.

ESTABLISHING EMPATHY WITH E.A.R. (cont.)

Meditation: Remember that the point of empathy is not to agree with people but to understand them. Once they sense that you have joined them in their subjective world, they will often begin to trust you. Once trust is in place, you will be able to correct their misconceptions. Remember that you might be the one in error too. "Brethren, if a man is overtaken in any trespass, you who are spiritual restore such a one in a spirit of gentleness, considering yourself lest you also be tempted. Bear one another's burdens, and so fulfill the law of Christ. For if anyone thinks himself to be something, when he is nothing, he deceives himself" (Galatians 6:1–3). Establishing empathy creates an environment that encourages taking responsibility.

These exercises help us learn a new skill. Eventually, this becomes second nature as we "train" in doing things God's way.

EVENT-EMOTION-THOUGHT RECORD

Date and time:	Triggering event: What happened?	Negative emotion: What did you feel? On a scale of 1–10 (10 being the most intense), how intensely did you feel?	Automatic thought: What thought accompanied these feelings?

EXERCISE PROGRAM FOR THE WILL

Keeping the will alive and active supports mood, cognition, mental health, and spirituality. Your problem may be an active addiction, a habit, simply laziness, or a lack of motivation. This exercise is designed to give a weak or broken will gradually increasing exercise over a three-week period. This would work even better if done in conjunction with a group so that members could report to one another.

Week one

Choose three things from the list below. Do them each day for one week. Don't think about the addiction or problem yet, just add these activities.

- ☐ Pray
- ☐ Eat a piece of fruit
- ☐ Style your hair
- ☐ Make your bed
- ☐ Read one full page from a book or magazine
- ☐ Clean a small area of your house
- ☐ Do something for a child
- ☐ Plan a meal
- ☐ Eat a salad
- ☐ Send a kind note or e-mail
- ☐ Smile at a stranger
- ☐ Tell a story
- ☐ Give something away
- ☐ Clean an area of your workspace
- ☐ Bake or cook something
- ☐ Wear a nice outfit

Think: How do you feel when you make small choices to engage in healthy pleasures?

Week two

Now start addressing your undesired addiction or habit. When tempted to act out, replace it with one of these behaviors at least 50 percent of the time. Have the list somewhere you can easily find it. You may want to have two or three activities underlined ahead of time.

- ☐ Take a shower
- ☐ Put on music and sing along
- ☐ Take a fast walk around the block
- ☐ Call a friend and talk for ten minutes
- ☐ Organize a drawer in your house
- ☐ Sit and do deep relaxation for ten minutes
- ☐ Play an instrument
- ☐ Drink two glasses of water

☐ Make a cup of herbal tea and drink it
☐ Play classical music and pretend to conduct
☐ Put on gentle music and dance
☐ Watch a funny video on Godtube
☐ Watch an emotionally moving video on Godtube
☐ Put together an attractive outfit
☐ Visit a pet store

Think: When you choose these pleasant behaviors over your addiction or habit, how do you feel? Is the experience better overall or worse overall? In other words, at the end of the day, which course makes you happier?

Week three

Now put the two exercises together, but choose three additional activities from the first list.

Think: This exercise is designed to give you the feel of exercising your will in small ways. Rate any improvements you feel when using your will. Use a percentage. For example, after well-being, you might put "50 percent."

Area of improvement	Percent of improvement
Well-being	_____
Energy level	_____
Self-respect	_____
Mental clarity	_____
Emotional stability	_____
Spirituality	_____

FACT, FEELING, AND FOLLOW-THROUGH

This technique facilitates good communication and sets the stage for conflict resolution.

When you have a problem with a loved one, follow these three simple steps when discussing the problem.

1. **Fact.** State the facts clearly and objectively. Make sure you stick to concrete reality versus opinion. Do not attempt to read motives: "Man looks at the outward appearance, but the Lord looks at the heart" (1 Samuel 16:7).

2. **Feeling.** This step gives an opportunity for you to own your feelings. You can use the "Feeling Words" document in the toolbox. The purpose of this is not to accuse your loved one, but to take responsibility for your own reaction.

3. **Follow-through.** In this step, you ask your loved one for a specific response. You are requesting something versus demanding it. Be specific, realistic, and fair.

Here are some examples.

Fact	Feeling	Follow-through
"We aren't communicating much. Tonight we haven't even talked . . ."	". . . and I'm feeling very lonely and sad."	"Could we please make a plan to spend at least a few minutes chatting each night?"
"You made a joke about me tonight at the dinner table . . ."	". . . and I felt humiliated."	"Could you please say some affirming things about me at dinner and avoid joking about me?"
"I found your wet towels on the floor . . ."	". . . and I became very irritated."	"Could you please hang your towels on the hook?"
"You yelled at me when you saw the credit card bill . . ."	". . . and I felt intimidated and hurt."	"Could we please discuss the bill quietly each month?"
"We're arguing every day . . ."	". . . and I feel frustrated about it."	"Could we try a couple of months of marriage counseling?"
"You told your friend about our conflict . . ."	". . . and I felt exposed and embarrassed."	"Could we please discuss what is private and what can be shared?"
"The children are fighting again, but you're sitting in your chair . . ."	". . . and I feel aggravated and overwhelmed."	"Could you please go talk to them?"

This exercise is designed to assist in thought control, which helps to stabilize mood and emotions. I've broken this process down into three main steps: find, argue, and replace, or F.A.R.

F = Find

First, find (identify) the triggering event or circumstance, such as, "My boss ignores me," or "I hate to wait in traffic jams."

Now, learn to identify your anxious or sad feelings and admit to yourself that you're feeling them. You can use the list called "Feeling Words" in the toolbox.

Next, find the thoughts that underlie the feelings. Some examples of thoughts that underlie feelings: "I will miss this deadline, lose my job, and live in poverty." Or "That person thinks he or she is better than me. I can't take being put down!" This step will take more time and energy, even prayer, because often these thoughts are unconscious or nearly so. Write them down in the space provided.

Congratulations, you've accomplished the first step!

A = Argue

Learn to argue with yourself. Use the "Distorted Thoughts" document. In doing this, you are breaking up the fallow ground of your own thinking so that the seed of truth can take root. Tell yourself what's wrong with the way you're thinking: "I'm catastrophizing missing the deadline. I'm making it much worse than it is!" Or "Where is the evidence that person thinks he or she is better than me? I am mind reading. And I am also catastrophizing how bad it is to deal with an arrogant person." In this step, you're not beating yourself up as much as confronting yourself, holding yourself accountable for the way you're treating yourself, just like you'd confront someone who said similar things to an innocent child. In other words, you're telling yourself to stop hurting yourself.

R = Replace

Learn to replace misbeliefs with truth. Truth will typically be much more nuanced, complex, and detailed than distorted thinking. If the distorted thought is, *My wife is an idiot, and I can't stand it!* then the truth would be something like, *My wife gets distracted sometimes when too much is going on. She loses her concentration. Sometimes she makes mistakes, like locking the keys in the car or leaving the stove on all night. Most of the time, the mistakes aren't catastrophic. A few times, they have caused inconvenience. But she has a PhD in microbiology, so it's not that she lacks intelligence. I get frustrated with her. But her occasional flakiness isn't horrible; it's just irritating.* Truth has shades of gray, whereas distorted thinking tends to be very black and white or extreme.

F.A.R. THOUGHT CONTROL (cont.)

Use this table to write down your answers.

Find	Argue	Replace
Event: Feeling word: Thought:		
Event: Feeling word: Thought:		
Event: Feeling word: Thought:		
Event: Feeling word: Thought:		
Event: Feeling word: Thought:		
Event: Feeling word: Thought:		
Event: Feeling word: Thought:		
Event: Feeling word: Thought:		

Anger	Anxiety	Happiness	Hurt	Sadness
aggravated	afraid	affectionate	abused	abandoned
appalled	alarmed	amused	alone	alone
annoyed	agitated	blissful	betrayed	anguished
bitter	awkward	charmed	broken	burdened
cranky	bewildered	cheerful	brokenhearted	dejected
disgusted	cornered	contented	damaged	depressed
enraged	clumsy	delighted	defeated	deserted
exasperated	disgraced	ecstatic	deflated	despondent
frustrated	embarrassed	elated	deserted	disappointed
furious	fearful	excited	desolate	discouraged
infuriated	flabbergasted	fabulous	despairing	disheartened
irritated	frightened	fortunate	devalued	downcast
offended	flustered	giddy	devastated	empty
provoked	helpless	glad	diminished	excluded
repulsed	humiliated	gratified	grief-stricken	friendless
resentful	jittery	high	grieved	gloomy
revolted	jumpy	joyous	hurt	helpless
troubled	overwhelmed	jubilant	insulted	lonely
upset	puzzled	marvelous	intimidated	inadequate
vicious	spooked	pleased	miserable	incapable
	shaken	proud	offended	incompetent
	uncomfortable	soothed	shattered	inferior
	worried	thrilled	self-conscious	isolated
		tickled	terrible	low
		wonderful	wretched	melancholy
			wounded	miserable
				moody
				powerless
				rejected
				slighted
				useless
				weary

FINDING A GOOD COUNSELOR

Jesus is the Wonderful Counselor, but a human counselor can be God's life raft to the shipwrecked. Ultimately, only He can help us, but that doesn't disallow human aid any more than the electric plant forbids the outlet in your living room. The goal of human counseling is to connect souls to the Wonderful Counselor. Through the art and science of the conversation and in the workroom of a safe, healing relationship, broken people can begin to heal.

The Scriptures contain several sketches of human counselors and their function. We find discipling, or mentoring, in these relationships and counsel.

- Jethro, a wealthy livestock owner, and his overworked son-in-law, Moses (Exodus 18).
- Deborah, judge over Israel, who coached Barak in military leadership (Judges 4:4–24).
- The prophet Elijah, who passed his mantle and his wisdom to young Elisha (2 Kings 2:1–15).
- Barnabas, who became an advocate and guide for the newly converted Saul (Acts 9:26–30).
- "In a multitude of counselors there is safety" (Proverbs 24:6).
- "The way of a fool is right in his own eyes, but he who heeds counsel is wise" (Proverbs 12:15).
- "Listen to counsel and receive instruction, that you may be wise in your latter days" (Proverbs 19:20).

As helpful as counseling can be, finding a counselor can feel a little like Russian roulette. Because counseling involves the disclosure of sensitive information, the potential for hurt is very great. Christians also worry that opening themselves up emotionally to someone not of their faith may hurt them spiritually. And, some Christians fear being a bad witness if they utilize a counselor of a different religious persuasion. For these reasons, it is ideal to find a counselor from within one's own faith group. If this isn't possible, one should select a counselor whose views of salvation are similar to his or her own.

It may be helpful for Christians to know that Christian mental health professionals hold varying views regarding the authority of Scripture. Three of the views are explained briefly.

The parallel track school. One group sees faith and science as parallel tracks. The Bible has authority over matters of salvation, and the experts in the field of psychology have authority over the matters of human psychology. These providers would respect and even encourage your faith, but may not counsel you from a biblical foundation.

The nouthetic school. From the word *noutheteo,* which means "to put into mind" and often translates into "admonish," nouthetic counseling can be found in conservative Christian groups. Counselors in this group will have a high regard for the authority of Scripture. Some of them will be excellent counselors; many will be quite "tough" on sin and oriented toward helping bring clients to repentance. They will most likely avoid the use of any techniques—and even jargon—that come from secular sources.

The cautious integrationist school. Some Christian counselors want to use the best of science, but, like nouthetic counselors, want to counsel clients according to biblical principles.

The important thing for someone who wants to live according to biblical principles is to find a counselor with a high regard for Scripture, but, at the same time, a heart for hurting people and experience in helping them.

Be sure to read the document titled "Summary of Current Counseling Models" to acquaint yourself with what modalities respective counselors may be using. Once you've done that reading, follow these few steps:

First, pray.

Second, ask around. Talk to your local pastor, any other Christian leaders whom you respect, and friends. Find out which counselors people have been going to. Contact those people and ask them about their experience with the counselor.

Third, search listings. If you don't come up with any personal referrals (which tend to be the best) you can look in the Yellow Pages, Christian business guide, or one of the referral Web sites below.

- Adventist Family Ministries has a database of counselors: Go to www .adventistfamilyministries.com and search for "counselors."
- Christian Care Network at www.aacc.net/shop/ccn/ccn_disclaimer.php.
- New Life Ministries has a comprehensive Web site with a counselor database plus inpatient counseling options. Go to http://newlife.com/.
- Focus on the Family has a one-time, free counseling offer. They also have a referral service on their Web site. Go to www.focusonthefamily.com/lifechallenges/articles/consider_counseling.aspx.

Fourth, if your finances are limited, go online and search "behavioral health" and the name of the town you live in. You should come up with some community counseling offices. If you call those offices and ask about low-fee or free counseling, they will often be able to direct you to those services.

Fifth, consider the issue of licensing. The benefit of a license is that the individual is accountable for such things as engaging in safe practices, not harming the client in any way, respecting the client's race and religion, not imposing his or her belief system on the client,

FINDING A GOOD COUNSELOR (cont.)

keeping strict confidentiality, and avoiding dual relationships with the client. However, some very good counselors are unlicensed.

Sixth, take a list of at least five options and call each one, asking for a ten-minute consultation. During the consultation, ask questions such as, What counseling model do you use? Do you use the principles of the Bible in counseling? Do you pray with clients? Are you licensed? What do you charge? Write down your answers. When finished with the consultations, look at all the information you've gathered carefully.

Finally, pray again. Decide which of the five you're most comfortable with based on much prayer. Remember, you don't have to go back if you're uncomfortable with the person!

Remember that Jesus promised, "Seek, and you will find" (Matthew 7:7).

This worksheet was designed to help those of us who recognize our need to forgive.

Failure to forgive results in bitterness. According to Hebrews 12:15, bitterness has several features: it constitutes a failure to be grace filled; it is a root, and therefore is deep within us; it springs up and causes trouble; it defiles many. Considering its high cost to our well-being and the well-being of others, we would do well to avoid unforgiveness. Yet forgiveness eludes us.

I try to approach the forgiveness issue with biblical integrity and compassion. It is my intention and prayer that through meditation and action steps, forgiveness will become simple and accessible, leading to the deep healing of long-held wounds.

Action Step: I encourage you to take a day off while working through this sheet. Go somewhere, preferably surrounded by nature, where you can be alone and quiet. If you're inside, light some candles and put on gentle music. Bring a Bible, a hymnal, and your personal calendar. You may want to fast or semifast on fruit or fruit and bread. The point is to reduce distractions and focus on the task at hand.

Meditation: Jesus taught us to pray like this: "And forgive us our debts, as we also forgive our debtors" (Matthew 6:12, NASB). The word *as* is the Greek word *hōs,* which can mean "and," "like" or "even as." Essentially, *hōs* joins two parts: God's forgiveness of our sin and our forgiveness of others' sin. The two link together like sunshine and bird song, rain and verdure. Likewise, Jesus taught, "And whenever you stand praying, if you have anything against anyone, forgive him, that your Father in heaven may also forgive you your trespasses" (Mark 11:25). Notice the bi-directional grace—receiving it from God, giving it to others.

Forgiveness Received → ♥ ← Forgiveness Bestowed

We needn't wait for people who have wronged us to repent before forgiving them. We might wait forever! In the above examples, we are commanded to forgive any and all "debtors" and "anyone" we have anything against. This forgiveness must be settled between our souls and God before we can hope for it to trickle down into the human realm.

Think of forgiveness in terms of water. God pours forgiveness into our vessels, thus washing away our sin and filling us with grace. We then spill out water on our thirsty, dirty fellow men. We share the forgiveness we receive from God. But if we hold our vessels tightly to our chests, refusing to forgive others, God won't be able to fill our vessels. Here's the point: *bestowing*

FORGIVENESS (cont.)

forgiveness expands our capacity for receiving God's forgiveness. Likewise, receiving forgiveness from God inspires us to forgive others. The giving and receiving of forgiveness exist symbiotically, in mutual sustenance of one another.

But forgiving those who have deeply wronged us presents a serious challenge. Bitter feelings cling like burrs, causing further pain. Forgiveness, in Greek the word *aphesis,* means "to release from bondage or slavery, pardon of sins." To send those bitter feelings away sounds like a good option at times, but at other times it feels as though this would leave us vulnerable to more hurt.

Wounded people need distance from their wrongdoers in order to process the pain. Without this distance, forgiveness is much more difficult. Ideally, victims of domestic violence move out; employees of a sexually harassing boss relocate; and adult children of emotionally abusive parents create appropriate boundaries. At times, victims may have difficulty creating physical distance, and emotional distance must suffice.

Action Step: Answer the following question: How can you create appropriate distance from your wrongdoer, if you haven't already?

Meditation: Many people, especially abuse victims, have a confused understanding of forgiveness. Some were trained from a young age to excuse or even approve of abuse. Perpetrators know how to find and push guilt buttons so that victims feel that imposing any accountability for wrong done is un-Christian and unkind. Others have negative feelings or memories and assume that this means they haven't yet forgiven the abusers. Distorted ideas of forgiveness prevent true forgiveness. Use this list to rout out false ideas of forgiveness:

- **Forgiveness does not equal trust.** Notice that even the great apostle Paul, who was forgiven by God and the Christians he had persecuted, had to earn the trust of the church (Acts 9). Forgiveness is not trust. Of course, forgiveness is the first step toward the restoration of trust, so trust in some cases grows out of forgiveness.
- **Forgiveness does not equal excusing.** Forgiveness is the opposite of excusing or overlooking sin. Built right into forgiveness is the fact that wrong was done. We excuse innocent mistakes; we forgive sin. If sin could be excused, why did Jesus die on the cross? Wouldn't God have found an easier way?
- **Forgiveness does not equal approval.** To forgive a person in no way indicates approval on your part. You may even choose to forgive a person who continues to do wrong, just as Jesus forgave the Roman soldiers who nailed Him to the cross; but by forgiving you're actually showing your disapproval of the act.

- **Forgiveness does not equal forgetting.** While putting people's sins out of our minds is one of the benefits of forgiveness (we don't have to think about them anymore!), it is unrealistic and unreasonable to expect that they will be completely forgotten. We must find a delicate balance of admitting what happened without dwelling upon it.
- **Forgiveness does not equal feeling.** Forgiveness is a choice—not a feeling. Often we will wrestle with negative feelings long after we have forgiven. Feelings don't constitute evidence of whether we've forgiven or not. They are just feelings. Feelings are important, but they are not conclusive evidence of reality. Typically, if we choose to forgive, then act in accordance with that choice, negative feelings will abate over time. But if an appropriate distance hasn't been made between the wrongdoer and victim, this emotional healing will be much more difficult.

Action Step: Read the above list of misconceptions carefully and answer the following question: Have I cherished any of these distorted ideas of forgiveness? If so, have they prevented me from forgiving? If so, how?

Meditation: Forgiveness is a learned skill—a science and an art. It is a conscientious, rational process of releasing the wrongdoer from the consequences of sin. Many metaphors help us understand it, but Jesus' Magna Carta on forgiveness—Matthew 18—uses debt, debt collecting, and debt forgiveness to illustrate.

In this chapter, Jesus first addresses the offender by warning against stumbling blocks—wrongs done that cause "little ones" to "stumble" (verse 6, NASB). Jesus gives very clear and shocking warning against these offenses, saying we should cut off an appendage or pluck out an eye if necessary to prevent them. Jesus leaves no room for excusing sin, particularly sin against the vulnerable, or "little ones."

Jesus doesn't require the weak and vulnerable to confront their wrongdoers. In relationships of equality, differences are ideally resolved between the two parties. In contrast, a power imbalance necessitates an advocate, a mediator.

Action Step: Read Matthew 18:1–11; then answer the following question: Were you a "little one" when a wrong was done to you? In other words, were you in some way vulnerable and unable to protect yourself? Was the wrongdoer vastly stronger than you physically, financially, mentally, or socially? Describe your situation.

FORGIVENESS (cont.)

Meditation: After advocating for the vulnerable ones of the human family, Jesus gives instruction for how to deal with offenses that occur between equals (notice the term is *brother,* indicating horizontality and equality). He counsels that we first approach the brother one-on-one. If this approach doesn't resolve the difference, we are to take one or two others with us. If this doesn't avail, we are to take it to the church. Confrontation is often part of the forgiveness process.

In order to confront and forgive the wrong done, we must have a clear idea of what was done to us. To forgive intelligently and thoroughly, we must survey the damage.

Action Step: Make sure your grievances aren't imaginary. Some things we can overlook. Did the wrongdoer cause concrete physical, emotional, mental, social, spiritual, financial, and/or relational damage? Use those categories to delineate actual damage. If possible, let a trusted person who knows the situation review the worksheet and tell you if he or she agrees with your conclusions.

Survey the Damage

Physical

Emotional

Mental

Social

Spiritual

Financial

Relational

Meditation: Some, particularly victims of family members, have a hard time admitting that others did wrong. Sometimes we want to justify them. Or sometimes we alternate back and forth between excusing them and condemning them. A close relationship with the wrongdoer, and/or having had a high degree of trust and admiration toward the person, tends to compromise our perceptions. Yet we're told to "be sober" (1 Peter 5:8), which includes a warning to be aware of the devil's tactics. "All have sinned" (Romans 3:23), and "all flesh is as grass" (1 Peter 1:24). Don't be shocked that sinners sin. With the evidence of the above worksheet, admit that you were wronged.

Another "ditch" awaiting us involves dwelling upon, ruminating on, and rehearsing the wrongs done. While our feelings of outrage show that we have a healthy sense of justice, which is well and good, forgiveness builds upon this foundation. Justice originates with God; forgiveness embraces justice with one arm and mercy with the other. Once out of denial, we must continue to grow in understanding until "mercy triumphs over judgment" (James 2:13).

Action Step: Now that you understand what forgiveness entails and you're fully aware of the damage, you can make an intelligent choice about whether to forgive or not. Below find a chart of costs and benefits of both forgiving the person and remaining in unforgiveness. This will help you recognize the nature of forgiveness and that it's a thoughtful decision as opposed to a whim or a feeling. List the effect that forgiving or not forgiving will have upon you, others, and God.

FORGIVENESS (cont.)

Chart of Forgiveness Versus Unforgiveness

Effect	Forgiveness costs	Forgiveness benefits	Unforgiveness costs	Unforgiveness benefits
On you				
On others				
On God				

Meditation: Matthew 18:21–35 relates a parable of forgiveness and debt collecting. A great landowner calls one of his staff to account, saying he owes the equivalent of ten million dollars. The landowner orders him into prison, but the employee bows before him, saying, "Have patience with me, and I'll pay you all!" (verse 26). Then the landowner does something remarkable—he forgives the employee. Tragically, the employee fails to reflect the grace of his employer. He takes one of his own debtors by the throat—even though he owes only about twenty dollars—and throws him into prison. This pushes the landowner beyond his limit. He angrily turns his employee over "to the torturers" (verse 34)! The final words of Jesus are, "So My heavenly Father also will do to you if each of you, from his heart, does not forgive his brother his trespasses" (verse 35).

These are sobering, even frightening words. A little careful thinking reveals the psychology behind unforgiveness. Notice that the employee thought he could pay God back, saying, "Have patience with me, and I will pay you all!" Denying the depth of his own sin, his hopeless debt, and his master's forgiveness, the employee has no basis from which to forgive his fellow man. Feeling righteous, he strangles and imprisons his brother.

Notice the debts in the parable. The debt between the servant and master was ten million dollars; the debt between the fellow men was about twenty dollars. While humans do indebt themselves to one another, these debts pale in comparison to the greatness of our debt to God.

Sociological research shows that those who believe they could have committed the same sins as their perpetrators are more inclined to forgive. All stand as great debtors before God. Admit that you, too, have sinned and have hurt God and others, and are, carnally speaking, capable of great sin. "Humble yourselves under the mighty hand of God, . . . casting all your care upon Him, for He cares for you" (1 Peter 5:6, 7). Choose to lay down your pride and self-righteousness.

Action Step: Using the worksheet below, recall the things you've done to others and God. This will help you face your own sinful nature and increase your inclination to forgive others.

Things for Which I've Been Forgiven

Whom did I hurt?	What did I do?	How did it affect them?

FORGIVENESS (cont.)

Whom did I hurt?	What did I do?	How did it affect them?

Action Step: Read Isaiah 53 out loud. Read with emotion, thinking carefully about each verse. Claim this promise: "If we confess our sins, He is faithful and just to forgive us our sins and to cleanse us from all unrighteousness" (1 John 1:9). Kneel down and confess your sins, then receive God's forgiveness and cleansing as a free gift, something you can't merit or earn.

Meditation: We sometimes cherish doubts of our own forgiveness. We may feel unforgiven even though we've confessed and forsaken our sin. Or we may have fallen into a habitual sin in an attempt to cope with emotional pain. Faith comes to the rescue in all such cases. We must believe the promises of God and our own prayers. If we ask for a fish, will our loving Father give us a stone (see Matthew 7:9)? When He died to forgive us, will He then withhold forgiveness when we ask? Likewise, if we ask for victory, will He not give it? To cherish doubt is to tarnish God's image. We must by faith embrace our forgiven and cleansed state. Expressing gratitude helps us accomplishes this.

Action Step: Express gratitude. Sing hymns such as "Rejoice, Ye Pure in Heart," or "My Jesus, I Love Thee." The expression of your faith deepens the impression. Read Psalm 103 aloud, thinking about how God has saved you from destruction.

Please note this: focusing on God's forgiveness of your sin does not minimize the other person's sin! It simply moves your focus from the other person to yourself, from a frustrating situation to a more productive situation. In psychology we call this an *internal locus of control* rather than an *external locus of control*.

Meditation: Now that your cup is full of forgiveness and gratitude, you are in a position to share it. You can choose to "send away" the wrong done to you and forgive the debt. This doesn't mean that you forget what was done. But you may think of it as boxing it and sending it away to a warehouse. Sin is like toxic waste. You're quarantining it by putting it away from yourself. In some cases, you will be able to tell the individual you've forgiven them. In some cases—especially where abuse is concerned—you may choose not to have any contact with the wrongdoer.

Forgiveness is a choice. You've set aside quality time to think carefully through this process. You've come to terms with what it means to forgive. You've surveyed the damage done to you; you've also acknowledged your own sin. You've received forgiveness. You've thanked God for that forgiveness. Now you're prepared to make the conscious, intelligent choice to forgive.

Action Step: Kneel down and pray, asking God to give you His Spirit as you choose to forgive. Pray for "those who spitefully use you" (Matthew 5:44). Mark the date on your calendar.

Meditation: You may have to revisit this decision. At times you may feel overwhelmed with anger or other negative feelings. Remember that forgiveness is a choice to release the wrongdoer from a debt, to send away their wrongdoing, and to separate yourself from it. Expect to return to your decision and even walk through the steps again. It may take years before your feelings catch up to your choice. Don't become discouraged. Just because you feel hurt, angry, or offended doesn't mean that you choose those things. Remind yourself that you chose to forgive. Ever so slowly, those negative feelings will disappear.

Rejoice, my friend! You're free of the root of bitterness. Your will aligns with the will of Jesus. Just like David said, "As far as the east is from the west, so far has He removed our transgressions from us" (Psalm 103:12).

GOD'S PLAN LIFE PURPOSE

Almost nothing impacts our well-being as directly as does having a life purpose. Fortunately, God meets this need. First of all, the Bible teaches that God had a special reason for creating human beings:

"So God created man in His own image, in the image of God He created him; male and female He created them" (Genesis 1:27). For the purpose of demonstrating the "image," or character, of Himself, He created us. The word *image,* from the Hebrew word *tselem,* means "likeness." God created us to be like Him.

Isaiah 43:7 expands on this idea: "Everyone who is called by My name, whom I have created for My glory; I have formed him, yes, I have made him." *Glory* can mean "honor." God created the human race to honor Him through becoming like Him.

This truth inspires and motivates, doesn't it? We want to strive for the highest state of development and effectiveness because it will reflect well on our loving Father.

But we need more than this overarching goal. We need to know what God has called us to do, specifically, individually. Differing like snowflakes, we each possess a particular calling, a life purpose tailor-made by the One who knows us better than we know ourselves. Fortunately, God has this need covered too:

- "Not more surely is the place prepared for us in the heavenly mansions than is the special place designated on earth where we are to work for God."[1]
- "For I know the thoughts that I think toward you, says the Lord, thoughts of peace and not of evil, to give you a future and a hope" (Jeremiah 29:11).
- "Who is the man that fears the Lord? Him shall He teach in the way He chooses" (Psalm 25:12).

Some people seem to hear the voice of God clearly directing them into a life mission.[2] This mission can be dictated by a direct, divinely administered call from God (Abraham, Moses, and David), a circumstance (Ruth's husband's death), an exceptional talent (the young prodigy Timothy's teaching gift), or an already developed vocation (Lydia's textile business). These fortunate ones have a clear sense of purpose, which they often pursue with blinders on, resolute to do God's will. God bless them! Most of us, however, must struggle to find our place in the world. This worksheet is designed to help gather data and then focus it so that we can use reason, logic, common sense, counsel, and creativity to identify our calling.

GOD'S PLAN

I'm using this simple acronym to structure the process of information gathering. Gifts, opportunities, doings, skills, principles, loves, activities, and needs are all factors in the quest.

Gifts

What are your spiritual gifts? What gifts have others identified? Underline three gifts in which you are the strongest (some gifts are in more than one category).

Romans 5:4, 5	Galatians 5:22, 23	Ephesians 5:9	1 Timothy 6:11	2 Timothy 3:10	2 Peter 1:5–7
perseverance character hope	love joy peace longsuffering	goodness righteousness truth	righteousness godliness faith love	purpose faith longsuffering love	faith virtue knowledge self-control

Opportunities

What opportunities have presented themselves? More broadly, what resources do you possess? In the following list, underline the entries that apply and expand on the details.

College education. Do you have an opportunity to take college classes, either through the generosity of another, scholarships, or your own savings?

College credits or degree. Do you have college training or a completed degree?

Other training. Are other training opportunities, such as an apprenticeship or short-course ministry training, available to you?

Completed training. Have you completed any training other than college?

Employment. Are there job opportunities available to you, whether skilled or unskilled?

Marriage and family life. Are you married and/or have children, or do you have that opportunity?

Mission work. Have you received a call to, or do you know of, full-time mission opportunities?

Meaningful service. Do you know of part-time or volunteer service opportunities that, although not full-time or paying work, would add to your quality of life?

Financial resources. Do you have inherited or saved money at your disposal? Do you have a vocation or business that generates money?

Good health. Do you have strength and health? Are you capable of taking on large responsibilities?

Relationships. Have you developed meaningful, deep relationships? Do you know people with whom you work well and whose companionship you enjoy?

Community. Have you connected with a particular community, such as a local church or ministry?

Other _____

Other _____

List the three most viable opportunities available to you:

1.

2.

3.

Doings

What are your doings, your life experiences so far? Answer the following:

What have you done well?

What have you done poorly?

Gleaning from your answers, list things you can do well:

1.

2.

3.

Skills

What are your particular skills and talents? Do you have a specific ability or training?

Inborn abilities:

Training expertise:

Gleaning from your answers, list your three greatest skills:
1.
2.
3.

Principles

What are your core values; what principles do you hold dear? Underline ten.

Accomplishment	Diversity	Leadership	Satisfying others
Accountability	Efficiency	Love, Romance	Security
Accuracy	Equality	Loyalty	Self-giving
Adventure	Excellence	Meaning	Self-reliance
Beauty	Fairness	Merit	Self-thinking
Calm, quietude	Faith	Money	Service to others
Challenge	Faithfulness	Openness	Simplicity
Change	Family	Patriotism	Skill
Cleanliness, orderliness	Freedom	Peace, Nonviolence	Solving
Collaboration	Friendship	Perfection	Problems
Commitment	Fun	Personal Growth	Speed
Communication	Good will	Pleasure	Stability
Community	Goodness	Power	Status
Competence	Gratitude	Practicality	Strength
Competition	Hard work	Privacy	Success
Concern for others	Harmony	Progress	Systemization
Connection	Honesty	Prosperity, Wealth	Teamwork
Continuous	Honor	Punctuality	Timeliness
improvement	Independence	Quality of work	Tolerance
Cooperation	Individuality	Regularity	Tradition
Creativity	Inner peace	Reliability	Tranquility
Decisiveness	Innovation	Resourcefulness	Trust
Delight of being, joy	Integrity	Respect for others	Truth
Democracy	Intensity	Responsiveness	Unity
Discipline	Justice	Rules	Variety
Discovery	Knowledge	Safety	Wisdom

GOD'S PLAN LIFE PURPOSE (cont.)

What would you like people to say about you at your funeral? List up to five things you'd like to hear said if you could listen in.

From the two exercises above, identify your top three principles:

1.
2.
3.

Loves

What causes light a fire in you? What do you love? What are your passions? What endeavors draw forth an intense emotional response? Check three boxes.

- ☐ Helping the needy
- ☐ Righting social injustices
- ☐ Creating beautiful art, music, and/or literature
- ☐ Delivering lifesaving messages
- ☐ Teaching, dispensing important information
- ☐ Assisting people in improving health
- ☐ Helping people in their relationships
- ☐ Helping people find emotional healing
- ☐ Ministering to a marginalized group
- ☐ Reaching out to lonely people
- ☐ Helping find cures for disease
- ☐ Fighting crime
- ☐ Working for the cause of religious liberty
- ☐ Working for the cause of civil rights
- ☐ Promoting family values
- ☐ Teaching parenting
- ☐ Helping build functional, healthy churches
- ☐ Increasing Bible literacy
- ☐ Advocating for animal rights
- ☐ Promoting education
- ☐ Scientific research
- ☐ Other _____

Activities

All of us have preferred activities, things we enjoy doing, whether vocational or recreational.

What do you enjoy doing?

What do you often find yourself doing?

What would you like to do more of?

From these questions, list your three most preferred activities:

1.
2.
3.

Needs

We all have areas that need development. For instance, we may have failed at public speaking in the past but truly desire to conquer and develop in that area. We may feel called to pastoral ministry but realize we're weak in interpersonal skills. We may not necessarily be called to pursue a life work in areas which we're already strong. God may want us to pursue something in which we're weak!

List three areas in which you need development:

1.
2.
3.

Conclusion

Now sum up your responses.

TOOLBOX

GOD'S PLAN LIFE PURPOSE (cont.)

My three strongest spiritual **gifts** are:
1.
2.
3.

Three **opportunities** available to me are:
1.
2.
3.

My three most significant **doings** are:
1.
2.
3.

My three most defined **skills** are:
1.
2.
3.

My three core **principles** are:
1.
2.
3.

My three greatest **loves** are:
1.
2.
3.

My three preferred **activities** are:
1.
2.
3.

My three areas of greatest **need** are:

1.
2.
3.

Now, underline one of the three answers in each area and plug the underlined entries into the following statement:

God has given me the spiritual **gift** of _____. He has also given me the **opportunity** of _____. My past experience (**doings**) of _____ and my **skill** of _____ may be useful in my future situation. In addition, my core **principles** of _____, my **love** for the cause of _____ and enjoyment of _____ (**activities**), are also important factors, for God cares about what makes my heart beat. Finally, I **need** to develop in _____ areas, and my future plans should provide an opportunity for this.

God has given me the spiritual **gift** of _____. He has also given me the **opportunity** of _____. My past experience (**doings**) of _____ and my **skill** of _____ may be useful in my future situation. In addition, my core **principles** of _____, my **love** for the cause of _____ and enjoyment of _____ (**activities**), are also important factors, for God cares about what makes my heart beat. Finally, I **need** to develop in _____ areas, and my future plan should provide an opportunity for this.

God has given me the spiritual **gift** of _____. He has also given me the **opportunity** of _____. My past experience (**doings**) of _____ and my **skill** of _____ may be useful in my future situation. In addition, my core **principles** of _____, my **love** for the cause of _____ and enjoyment of _____ (**activities**), are also important factors, for God cares about what makes my heart beat. Finally, I **need** to develop in _____ areas, and my future plan should provide an opportunity for this.

GOD'S PLAN LIFE PURPOSE (cont.)

Use the extra statements, using different answer responses each time. Settle on two or three statements that fit you well. The point of this exercise is to help you organize and sort through the various factors that contribute to a life purpose. God has called all His children to make His loving character known. Our individual expressions of that vary. Finding our place in this world entails knowing ourselves. Discuss your final statements with two or three trusted individuals, for "in a multitude of counselors there is safety" (Proverbs 24:6).

Next, take the matter to God in prayer. Spend at least a week, preferably a month or more, praying specifically each day for light and guidance from heaven on your personal calling. If no light comes, try fasting for a day or two, devoting the extra time to prayer. God promises that "the humble He guides in justice, and the humble He teaches His way" (Psalm 25:9).

The most important thing is that you make a contribution, however humble. God has a place for you in this world!

---

1. Ellen G. White, *Christ's Object Lessons* (Washington, D.C.: Review and Herald®, 1941), 327.

2. Abraham (Genesis 12:1–5); Moses (Exodus 3:1–12); Ruth (Ruth 1:15–18); Samuel (1 Samuel 3:1–11); David (1 Samuel 16:6–13); Esther (Esther 4:9–17); Jeremiah (Jeremiah 1:4–19); Jesus (Matthew 3:13–17); Mary Magdalene and the other Mary (Matthew 28:1–10); Mary (Luke 1:26–38); the Samaritan woman (John 4:1–30); Philip and the Ethiopian eunuch (Acts 8:26–40); Lydia (Acts 16:4, 15); Timothy (1 Timothy 4:6–16).

To successfully resolve guilt, we must submit it to the test of God's Word. Follow this simple step-by-step process to help resolve true and false guilt.

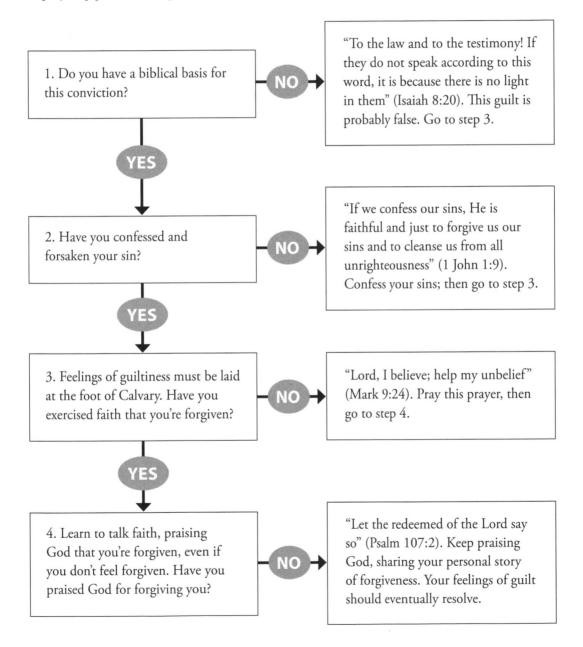

1. Do you have a biblical basis for this conviction?

NO → "To the law and to the testimony! If they do not speak according to this word, it is because there is no light in them" (Isaiah 8:20). This guilt is probably false. Go to step 3.

YES

2. Have you confessed and forsaken your sin?

NO → "If we confess our sins, He is faithful and just to forgive us our sins and to cleanse us from all unrighteousness" (1 John 1:9). Confess your sins; then go to step 3.

YES

3. Feelings of guiltiness must be laid at the foot of Calvary. Have you exercised faith that you're forgiven?

NO → "Lord, I believe; help my unbelief" (Mark 9:24). Pray this prayer, then go to step 4.

YES

4. Learn to talk faith, praising God that you're forgiven, even if you don't feel forgiven. Have you praised God for forgiving you?

NO → "Let the redeemed of the Lord say so" (Psalm 107:2). Keep praising God, sharing your personal story of forgiveness. Your feelings of guilt should eventually resolve.

A GOOD CONSCIENCE (cont.)

This feeling of guiltiness must be laid at the foot of the cross of Calvary. The sense of sinfulness has poisoned the springs of life and true happiness. Now Jesus says, "Lay it all on Me; I will take your sin, I will give you peace. Destroy no longer your self-respect, for I have bought you with the price of My own blood. You are Mine, your weakened will I will strengthen; your remorse for sin, I will remove." Then turn your grateful heart, trembling with uncertainty, and lay hold upon the hope set before you. God accepts your broken contrite heart. He offers you free pardon. He offers to adopt you into His family with His grace to help your weakness, and the dear Jesus will lead you on step by step, if you will only put your hand in His and let Him guide you.[1]

---

1. Ellen G. White, *This Day With God* (Washington, D.C.: Review and Herald®, 1979), 63.

We've been overwhelmed with evidence that a plant-based diet is preventative medicine for heart disease, diabetes, cancers, high blood pressure, obesity, and many other modern-day health scourges. What we don't often consider is the connection between food and mood. But the raw truth is that there is such a connection, and it is a rich one. Load up on whole-plant foods, and you could have a very happy brain.

Tryptophan deficiency has been linked to depression. A diet high in meat can block the flow of tryptophan to the brain.[1] The best sources of tryptophan are tofu, pumpkin seeds, gluten flour, sesame seeds, almonds, walnuts, and black-eyed peas. Time to get out the kettle, Ma, and make us some Hoppin' John.[2]

Omega-3 fatty acids are sizzling hot these days, and people are popping fish oil like breath mints at a high school reunion. But fish oil, although rich in omega-3s, is a contaminated source. A much safer alternative is flaxseed. One or two tablespoons of ground flaxseed per day (put into a bowl of cereal or blended in a smoothie) will give you all the omega-3s you need—with the added benefit of fiber. But there is also a link between those omega-3s and mood. Here's how it all cooks up: we must get both omega-3 and omega-6 fatty acids—but in the right proportions. Even vegetarian diets can be proportionately low in omega-3, which can contribute to depression.[3] Flax will boost your omega-3s and keep those fatty acids in the right proportions.

Berries are "berry" good for you, but acai berries bury the competition. Unlike other berries, they contain omega-3 fatty acids. They boast the highest antioxidant level of all berries. Uniquely delicious, they make fine health products but tend to be hard on the pocketbook. Another superfood high-antioxidant option, the blueberry, has earned the reputation of being the "brain berry." Load up on them in season! Simply rinse, dry, and freeze, for smoothies all year.

Nuts keep you from "going nuts." Packing loads of the stress-lowering amino acid arginine, they make a good nervous-system-building compliment to B vitamins and fiber-rich whole grains.

Folic acid has been linked to depression. High levels protect us from the big, bad *D*. Find abundant amounts of this in leafy greens, such as spinach, kale, or collards. The extra boost of calcium in kale and collards helps with nerve health too. Greens may also help break down high homocysteine levels, which may lead to cognitive decline. Avocado's rich supply of vitamin E has also been associated with lowering this risk.[4]

How about a breakfast of oatmeal with ground flax and almonds, topped with fresh blueberries? For lunch, baked or scrambled tofu, avocado slices on whole-grain bread, and kale in garlic sauce? Sounds like a bright idea.

---

1. A. Lucca et al., "Plasma Tryptophan Levels and Plasma Tryptophan/Neutral Amino Acids Ratio in Patients With Mood Disorder, Patients With Obsessive-Compulsive Disorder, and Normal Subjects," *Psychiatry Research* 44, no 2 (1992): 85–91.

2. A Southern dish with sautéed onions and black eyed peas.

3. P. B. Adams et al., "Arachidonic to Eicosapentaenoic Acid Ratio in Blood Correlates Positively With Clinical Symptoms of Depression," supplement, *Lipids* 31 (March 1996): S167–176.

4. "9 Foods That May Help Save Your Memory," *Shine,* accessed January 27, 2011, http://shine.yahoo.com/channel/health/9-foods-that-may-help-save-your-memory-2411607.

MENTAL HEALTH CHECKLIST

Instructions: Check the things that apply to you. The goal is to eliminate everything "fixable," to five or fewer total checked items.

PAST
- ☐ Family history of mental illness
- ☐ Early childhood trauma or abuse
- ☐ Previous episode of mental illness
- ☐ Raised by parents with mental illness
- ☐ Extreme home of origin dysfunction
- ☐ Childhood divorce or parental absence
- ☐ Recent major life stress
- ☐ Low birth weight

PRESENT—FLEXIBLE
- ☐ Lack of social support
- ☐ Irregularity in schedule (meals, etc.)
- ☐ Too little sleep (<6 hours/day)
- ☐ Too much sleep (>9 hours/day)
- ☐ Smoking
- ☐ Drug or alcohol abuse
- ☐ Heavy caffeine use
- ☐ Lack of exercise
- ☐ Lack of sunlight
- ☐ Lack of fresh air
- ☐ High fat diet
- ☐ High sugar intake
- ☐ High-protein, low-complex-carb diet
- ☐ Nutritional deficiencies*
- ☐ Low vitamin B intake, especially B_6
- ☐ Regular passive stimulation (TV, movies)
- ☐ Internet or video game addiction
- ☐ Immorality

PRESENT—FIXED
- ☐ Brain injury or defect
- ☐ Premenstrual syndrome
- ☐ Menopause or perimenopause
- ☐ Recent birth
- ☐ Single parent
- ☐ Widowed

PRESENT—POSSIBLY FLEXIBLE
- ☐ Living with an addict
- ☐ Serious marital conflict
- ☐ Raising grandchildren
- ☐ Chronic pain/ health problems
- ☐ Regular insomnia
- ☐ Poverty
- ☐ Hepatitis C
- ☐ Recent head injury
- ☐ Stroke
- ☐ Heart disease
- ☐ Terminal cancer
- ☐ Parkinson's disease
- ☐ Diabetes
- ☐ Thyroid disease
- ☐ Adrenal gland disease
- ☐ Lupus
- ☐ Infection

_____ **TOTAL**

*See the "Happy Brain Food" document or for a more comprehensive treatment of diet and other medical causes for depression; see *Depression: The Way Out* by Neil Nedley.

God, grant me the serenity to accept the things I cannot change, courage to change the things I can, and wisdom to know the difference. (Reinhold Neibuhr)

The purpose of this document is to help develop a thoughtful approach to anger management. We all have times when our tempers get the better of us. Unfortunately, when passion takes over, we say and do things we later regret. These simple steps can prevent explosions while effectively addressing the root problem.

Some anger is "righteous indignation," but most human anger is plain, old anger. The problem with simply letting off steam is that in anger, the human brain tends to become more like an animal brain, meaning that it is more impulse driven and less rational and thoughtful. Often we say things that escalate feelings and worsen the problem.

But merely suppressing anger doesn't work, either. Internalized stress causes health problems and can lead to habits and addictions. Responsible anger management involves "turning off the flame" under the pot of anger as well as appropriate release of steam through prayer and physical exercise.

The steps in this document work like a time line, beginning with prevention, moving through the anger-causing event, then on to the follow-through process. I've split the process into three phases: before the fact, during the fact, and after the fact.

Before the fact

Admit that you're angry. We gain nothing by lying to ourselves about our feelings. Increase your self-awareness by noticing your emotions, and simply admit to yourself that you're angry. Beware of excessive rumination, but do take time to process the problem, even writing it down or talking it out with a trusted friend or counselor. Pray about the situation, frankly admitting your anger to God.

Pray for the person or people who aggravate you. And pray for your own temper, believing that God wants to empower you to master your own passions rather than be mastered by them.

Resolve the problem before it escalates, if at all possible. First, talk directly to the person involved in a spirit of Christlike love. If this fails to resolve the issue, it may be necessary to bring a mediator along. Jesus laid out the reconciliation process in Matthew 18:15–20. Often being proactive and assertive in dealing with an issue prevent anger because we feel in control as opposed to frustrated.

Plan for success ahead of time. To fail to plan is to plan to fail. Envisioning a potentially escalated situation ahead of time works like a fire drill: when the forebrain shuts down and good judgment is hampered—both of which happen in anger—the previously decided upon plan of action will help you do the right thing. Memorize the next three steps—wait, breathe, leave—to ensure that you do the right thing when under stress.

MIND YOUR ANGER (cont.)

During the fact

Wait before acting. Don't view this in terms of being passive and doing nothing—which, for an angry person, feels repressive—but think in terms of delaying your response to the situation. (See, for instance, Romans 12:19.) Thomas Jefferson said, "When angry, count ten, before you speak; if very angry, an hundred." Anger is a God-given blessing when rightly directed. God doesn't expect you to be indifferent to wrong done to you, but He does ask you to wait for the wrong to be righted. Think of yourself putting the anger in a box to be opened later.

Breathe deeply and slowly. Medical research shows that deep breathing oxygenates the brain and brings about a state of calm. In addition, because you breathe slowly when calm, intentionally slowing your breathing "tricks" your mind into thinking you're calm even when you're not. Think *eight-six-eight*. Breathe in to the count of eight, hold for six, then breathe out to the count of eight. Do this ten times in a row.

Leave the immediate situation. If at all possible, physically remove yourself from the situation while the emotions are intense. A quick ten-minute walk can work miracles by oxygenating the brain, deepening your breathing, and giving you a needed break. Anger is often an attempt to control another person. By taking a break from the situation, you give yourself the important message that you can't control him or her, but only yourself.

After the fact

Move your body. Make sure to exercise after a stressful event. Stressful situations cause catecholamine to buildup in the body, and exercise metabolizes these hormones. The ideal exercise is walking outside. Walk until you feel calm. An hour at the gym or riding a bicycle works too. It helps to pray while exercising; this would give you an ideal opportunity to process the situation with God.

Analyze your thoughts. Give yourself a "checkup from the neck up" to discover if there are any imaginations or any "high thing that exalts itself against the knowledge of God," then bring "every thought into captivity to the obedience of Christ" (2 Corinthians 10:5). Are you thinking irrational things, such as *I must get even!* or *If I weren't so stupid, people wouldn't treat me that way?* Use the "Distorted Thoughts" document and the "F.A.R. Thought Control" document methods of replacing misbeliefs.

Are you afraid? Are you *pathologically* fearful? You're not alone.

Due to a cocktail of genetics, developmental problems, and/or bad choices, individuals sometimes develop serious fear-related disorders. In fact, anxiety disorders—which include panic disorder, obsessive-compulsive disorder (OCD), post-traumatic stress disorder (PTSD), generalized anxiety disorder (GAD), social phobia, agoraphobia, and specific phobia—constitute the most common mental health diagnoses.

This document can't replace professional help for serious anxiety disorders, but it can help you overcome fear.

Meditation: According to Hebrews 11:27, when confronted with Pharaoh's wrath, Moses didn't fear, but "endured as seeing Him who is invisible." "Endured," or *kartereo* only appears once in Scripture, and derives from the word *kratos,* which can mean "dominion."

God has gifted us with this marvel of faith; the fingers of faith's "hand" entwine around spiritual things and grab them as verily as our physical fingers grab a sandwich. Through faith's "eyes" we can *conceive* of what we can't *perceive*. We can envision what lies beyond our vision. And by doing this, we become powerful. We dominate. Specifically, we dominate fear.

Action Step: For at least a day, keep a record of the events that trigger your fears. A sample has been given.

Date and time:	Triggering event: What happened?	Fear: On a scale of 1–10 (10 being the most intense), how intense was it?	Automatic thought: What thought accompanied this fear?
10/23	Asked to speak to the staff about a problem.	8	"I can't talk in front of people!"

OVERCOME FEAR THROUGH FAITH (cont.)

Date and time:	Triggering event: What happened?	Fear: On a scale of 1–10 (10 being the most intense), how intense was it?	Automatic thought: What thought accompanied this fear?

Use the "F.A.R. Thought Control" document and the "Distorted Thoughts" document in the toolbox to address distorted thoughts. For instance, you might find that the thought *I can't talk in front of people!* is catastrophizing. You would learn to replace that thought with another: *I feel anxious when I talk in front of people, but with a little practice and preparation, I can learn to do it anyway.*

Meditation: Fear is an essential part of the human experience. We must admit that fear is occasionally beneficial. Dangers lurk everywhere in this sin-warped world; the human organism responds to these threats with an automatic arousal called *fight or flight.*

Let's briefly describe this state: First, a perceived threat activates the cerebral cortex. Then the brain alerts the limbic system, which arouses the autonomic nervous system. This triggers a plethora of glandular and neurochemical changes. As a result of these changes, some of which are listed below, the body prepares itself to either fight the perceived threat or run from it.

Increases strength of skeletal muscles
Decreases blood-clotting time
Increases heart rate
Increases sugar and fat levels
Reduces intestinal movement
Inhibits tears and digestive secretions
Relaxes the bladder
Dilates pupils
Increases perspiration
Increases mental activity
Inhibits erection/vaginal lubrication
Constricts most blood vessels but dilates those in the heart, leg, and arm muscles

But here's the rub: while the fear response protects us from threats, the response becomes a threat when misguided. Since the Fall, humans harbor a bent toward irrational fear. Recall Adam and Eve taking cover from the One who would ultimately cover them with His righteousness. Similarly, many of us live with our nerves on edge when we could be trusting like babies in the everlasting arms of Jesus. We fear everything from financial ruin to spiders and people's opinions, often inflating the reaction far beyond the actual potential of the threat.

Something that complicates the issue a bit is called *secondary disturbance.* When you become disturbed, you might then become disturbed about being disturbed. In the case of fear, you become afraid of being afraid. The secondary disturbance often becomes greater than the primary disturbance. As the expression goes, "We have nothing to fear but fear itself." Thank God that this is not true—because faith conquers fear, we needn't even fear *fear.*

Action Step: In the space that follows, list your primary fears. Also list if you've developed a secondary fear, and what form it takes. An example has been given.

OVERCOME FEAR THROUGH FAITH (cont.)

Primary Fear	Secondary Fear
Saying something stupid.	If I say something stupid, I'll blush and everyone will know I'm embarrassed. I shouldn't care what people think, anyway. I must be a wimp.

Meditation: In order to avoid experiencing the unpleasantness of the fear response, we often avoid what we fear. We would do well to avoid biting dogs, thugs, and burning buildings, but avoiding low-risk things—such as public speaking, house spiders, and crowds—can monopolize our lives and circumscribe our usefulness. It becomes necessary, then, to face our fears.

All of us have fear. Depending upon what we do with it, we can become either cowardly or courageous. The New Testament uses three main words for fear: *eulabia, phobos,* and *deilos. Eulabia* means reverence or godly fear. *Phobos* is simply generic fear that can be either healthy or unhealthy. *Deilos* is cowardice, which was rebuked by Jesus when He said, "Why are you fearful, O you of little faith?" (Matthew 8:26), "Why are you are so fearful? How is it that you have no faith?" (Mark 4:40), and by Paul in 2 Timothy 1:7, "God has not given us the spirit of fear." These verses point to a lifestyle of letting fear reign and displacing faith. Fear and faith can't exist side by side. It's one or the other.

In contrast, God has called us to courage. Courage is not the absence of fear, but our choice to move forward by faith in spite of fear. Don't look for your fearful emotions to go away; they won't. Go forward in obedience and faith in spite of them, and you'll find the peace of God, which passes all understanding. Your natural human fear will be subjugated to faith and trust; the fear will lose its charge.

Two simple equations illustrate this truth:

$$\text{Fear} + \text{faith} = \text{courage}$$
$$\text{Fear} - \text{faith} = \text{cowardice}$$

Avoidance increases fear. When I avoid going outside because of my fear of snakes, I increase my fear of snakes. I tell myself that snakes are everywhere, dangerous, poisonous, and must be avoided at all costs—even if my area of the country has only harmless garter snakes. If, on the other hand, I expose myself to the fear, I tell myself that the outside world is safe. Walking over my fears requires faith.

Action Step: Exposure therapy is the gold standard of treatment for anxiety disorders. There are two main types of exposure therapy: gradual, careful exposure, called *systematic desensitization;* and sudden, complete exposure, called *flooding.* For purposes of caution, I'll teach you systematic desensitization.

When you respond in fear, your mind builds an association between the feared object and your fearful reaction. The fear response becomes very automatic. Systematic desensitization breaks that reactive response and builds a new association with the feared object and a state of relaxation.

OVERCOME FEAR THROUGH FAITH (cont.)

Begin with a deep breathing and relaxation exercise. Sit comfortably, wearing loose clothing, in a chair with your head resting on the back of the chair or on a pillow. Make sure you can really sink into the chair. Breathe in to the count of eight seconds, hold for six, and breathe out to the count of eight. The idea is to slow your breathing and breathe more deeply than normal. Do this five times before incorporating tensing and relaxing.

Now use tensing and relaxing of your muscles along with the breathing. First, tense your feet while breathing in, hold the tension for the count of six, and release the tension as you breathe out to the count of eight. Continue the exercise, adding another "zone" each time:

Feet
Feet, calves
Feet, calves, thighs
Feet, calves, thighs, buttocks
Feet, calves, thighs, buttocks, stomach and lower back
Feet, calves, thighs, buttocks, stomach and lower back, chest and upper back
Feet, calves, thighs, buttocks, stomach and lower back, chest and upper back, arms
Feet, calves, thighs, buttocks, stomach and lower back, chest and upper back, arms, neck and head

This entire process should take about ten minutes. By the end, you should feel completely relaxed.

While in this state, meditate on the Word of God. Look up three or more of the following Bible verses and "chew" on them: Psalm 23:4, 5; Psalm 27:1–3; Psalm 46:1; Psalm 91:1–11; Proverbs 3:24; Proverbs 29:25; Isaiah 54:4, 14; Luke 12:32; John 14:27; Romans 8:15, 35–39. Better yet, have them written on cards ahead of time to read or memorize them.

Now, simply think about the object of your fear. In doing this, you've begun to build an association between the object of fear and a state of relaxation.

Meditation: Faith can't exist in inertia. Faith moves. In fact, it may be the motion itself. As you have received Jesus by faith, so walk in Him. The walking will strengthen you to dominate your fears. Ellen White said, "You have to talk faith, you have to live faith, you have to act faith, that you may have an increase of faith."[1]

This word of faith is "near you, in your mouth and in your heart" (Romans 10:8). God hasn't placed this faith experience legions beneath the sea or light-years above the earth. It's near you, in fact, in you, in your mouth and in your heart. This means that God has given each of us "a measure of faith" (Romans 12:3), the capacity and ability to have a vital, fear-busting, fact-filled, trust-infused, love-powered faith experience.

Action Step: It's time to take your faith into the battlefield. Continue your systematic desensitization by facing your fears *in vivo,* meaning in the real world. First, write three of your favorite Bible promises on index cards. Keep them in your purse or wallet, or, better yet, memorize them. Before you encounter the object of your fear, use the breathing and relaxation exercise mentioned above. Keep the Bible promises handy to redirect your thinking.

Now simply face the thing that you've previously avoided, whether a person, a situation, an activity, or an object. Face it in small doses, gradually increasing until you can remain relaxed with full exposure.

---

1. Ellen G. White, *Faith and Works* (Nashville, Tenn.: Southern Publishing Association, 1979), 78.

PRAYER BASICS

Jesus prayed the model prayer (Matthew 6:9–13) in response to the disciples' request, "Teach us how to pray" (Luke 11:1). Below find the basic principles that establish and enrich a strong prayer life. Use this like a checklist during your prayer time until it becomes second nature.

"Our Father in heaven"

Talk to your Father. Jesus said to pray, "Our Father." Remember, you're praying to a loved One who would do anything for you. His heart overflows with commitment, sacrifice, passion, and deep affection. Ellen White said, "Prayer is the opening of the heart to God as to a friend. Not that it is necessary in order to make known to God what we are, but in order to enable us to receive Him. Prayer does not bring God down to us, but brings us up to Him."[1] Get real with God. Be vulnerable, trusting, and open. He knows your secrets already, but you benefit in the telling.

"Hallowed be Your name"

Pray in the name. Acknowledge up front the character, or name, of God. "Hallowed" is translated from *hagiazo,* meaning "set apart, holy, or sanctified." God is different from people! We've been hurt, betrayed, and wounded by people because of their sinful, selfish ways. God's character stands in sharp contrast and therefore merits our trust. Praying "in Jesus' name" means more than reciting those words. It means asking with confidence in His goodness.

"Your kingdom come. Your will be done"

Ask according to His will. "Now this is the confidence that we have in Him, that if we ask anything according to His will, He hears us. And if we know that He hears us, whatever we ask, we know that we have the petitions that we have asked of Him" (1 John 5:14, 15). Check your list of requests. Are they things that may not be God's will? Healing, material prosperity, or a change in life circumstances—these may not be in God's plan. In contrast, the blessings of the gospel— forgiveness, grace, and a change of heart—are always in His plan. The more we pray His will, the more prayers He answers. The more prayers answered, the greater our confidence in prayer. The greater our confidence in prayer, the greater our desire to pray. Create for yourself a positive feedback loop with God by praying according to His will.

"On earth as it is in heaven"

Reach out and touch. God's will on earth is the salvation of all His children. Intercession stretches our hearts and keeps our prayers from becoming myopic and self-centered. We find hurting people everywhere. Social connections strengthen our desire to pray as we come in contact with human need. And stretching our minds to pray for others can be very therapeutic.

"Give us this day our daily bread"

Feel your need. A few days without food and our bodies start to break down; living apart from God starves our spirits. We come to God in a position of deep need and dependence. Because of our innate tendency to self-justify, to self-fix, and to live independently of God, this acknowledgment of our neediness at first feels awkward, even dangerous. But as He proves Himself over and over, we begin to relax our defenses and actually enjoy the dependent relationship.

"And forgive us our debts"

Surrender sin. "If I regard iniquity in my heart, the Lord will not hear" (Psalm 66:18). You can't ask for God's blessing while clinging to sin any more than you can ask for healing of lung cancer while smoking. While you can't promise God perfect behavior, you can acknowledge your sin before Him, accepting His gift of repentance. Prayer acts as a great catharsis, a chance to articulate and release the sins that lurk in the dark places of our hearts. Often in prayer, the Holy Spirit will point out something that needs to be addressed, a wrong that needs to be made right. Follow through on this impression with action. Prayer becomes very interactive and vital when we use it as a launching point for life changes. Prayer energizes our actions, and our actions energize our prayers.

"As we forgive our debtors"

Forgive your brother. As a tall weed blocks the sun from a seedling, cherishing bitterness against others will block the light of God from penetrating into our hearts. Often we resent people for the very things we ourselves do! As we repent, we cease to resent; accepting forgiveness naturally leads to bestowing forgiveness. Jesus said, "Whenever you stand praying, if you have anything against anyone, forgive him, that your Father in heaven may also forgive you your trespasses" (Mark 11:25).

"And do not lead us into temptation, but deliver us from the evil one"

Pray for spiritual growth. Jesus asked, "If a son asks for bread from any father among you, will he give him a stone? . . . If you then, being evil, know how to give good gifts to your children, how much more will your heavenly Father give the Holy Spirit to those who ask Him!" (Luke 11:11, 13). In other words, God wants to give His Spirit. He's more generous with His Spirit than an earthly father is with bread. Through the Spirit you're changed from glory to glory (2 Corinthians 3:18), grown into the image of God. The prayer to be like Jesus, to grow in His grace, and to resist temptation, is the safest prayer we can pray.

PRAYER BASICS (cont.)

"For Yours is the kingdom and the power and the glory forever, Amen."

Praise and thank God. "Let us not be always thinking of our wants and never of the benefits we receive. We do not pray any too much, but we are too sparing of giving thanks."[2] Gratitude has tremendous healing power. It has been scientifically linked to everything from better mood to physical health. Make sure to count your blessings after you present your needs.

"Seek and you will find"

Never give up. After praying the Lord's Prayer, Jesus told a parable of a man knocking on a friend's door at midnight asking for bread (Luke 11:5–8). "Leave me alone," the friend says, "I've already gone to bed." But as Jesus points out, the friend will get up if the man keeps knocking. Essentially, Jesus is saying, "Keep bugging Me." We need to persevere in prayer. Any trainer will tell you that muscle builds with repetition. The process is as important as product, if not more so.

"Oh you of little faith"

Believe in your own prayers. Jesus also rebuked the disciples for worrying (Luke 12:22–32). If we have fulfilled the simple, reasonable conditions for prayer and prayed according to God's will, then we can freely, joyfully believe that God will do what He has promised. This means we act in accordance with our prayers. Don't pray and then give up—instead, pray and then get going. "Whatever things you ask when you pray, believe that you receive them, and you will have them" (Mark 11:24).

---

1. White, *Steps to Christ*, 93.
2. Ibid., 103.

Read 1 Corinthians 13:4–8. Notice the descriptions of love:

- Suffers long
- Is kind
- Does not envy
- Does not parade itself
- Is not puffed up
- Does not behave rudely

- Does not seek its own
- Is not provoked
- Thinks no evil
- Does not rejoice in iniquity
- Rejoices in the truth

- Bears all things
- Believes all things
- Hopes all things
- Endures all things
- Never fails

Now, notice how many of these sixteen descriptions include negative terms: *no, not,* or *never.* Nine of the sixteen, or more than half are in the negative! I think God is telling us that we sometimes learn what love is by learning first what it isn't. Perhaps all life has taught you so far about relationships is what to avoid. Well, at least you know that much!

Think about your own relationships. I've restated the qualities of 1 Corinthians 13 as positives in the list below. In which areas did (or does) the relationship succeed? In which did (or does) it fall short of reflecting *agape*? Rate each quality from 1 to 10 for up to five relationships.

Quality	1	2	3	4	5
Longsuffering					
Kind					
Unenvious					
Modest					
Humble					
Courteous					
Unselfish					
Patient					
Affirming					
Encouraging					
Truthful					
Forbearing					
Believing					
Hopeful					
Enduring					
Unfailing					

QUALITIES OF *AGAPE* (cont.)

Answer the following questions in the space below: In what ways did you contribute to the problems in the relationships? How can you prevent repeating history in future relationships?

1.

2.

3.

4.

5.

Research shows that the failure of attachment with the primary caregiver causes attachment problems later in life. In other words, if the person who raised you didn't bond well with you, your bonding muscles are weak or even crippled. No need for despair, though. Recent neuroscience research has discovered the plasticity, or flexibility and growth potential, of the brain.

Consider constraint-induced (CI) therapy, used on people with disabled limbs. Researchers would bind the good limb so that the person was forced to use the damaged one. Unless there was irreparable damage, the individual would often regain some or all of the use of the injured limb. Why? Because, in going through the motions of using the limb, new neuropathways were developed, once more reconnecting that limb to the brain via the nervous system.

If, because of underuse, your bonding muscles are weak, exercise them. Going through the motions may make them strong. But this requires belief that you can change. You must "faith it till you make it" in relationships.

Attachment styles

Various researchers in the field of psychology have developed the *attachment theory*. Attachment theory shows how people, usually due to home influences, develop an attachment style. They are either secure, anxious, avoidant, or disorganized in relationships.

These styles are really varied ways of responding to a paradox. Relationships require a delicate balance of individuality and intimacy. We find high levels of both in

	INDIVIDUALITY	
INTIMACY	Low individuality Low intimacy — DISORGANIZED	High individuality Low intimacy — AVOIDANT
	Low individuality High intimacy — ANXIOUS	High individuality High intimacy — SECURE

healthy relationships. Sacrifice either or both and relationships tend to struggle.

People with *avoidant* attachment styles see relationships as a threat to their freedom and independence. They fear sharing their emotions. This is the classic *fear of intimacy syndrome.*

People with *anxious* attachment styles tend to experience intense insecurity in relationships. They want to be close, but fear losing the relationship if separated. The closeness takes on a fearful quality—ironically preventing true closeness.

People with *disorganized* attachment styles tend to come from abusive homes and have a kind of push-pull pattern to relationships. One minute, they seem to want closeness; the next, distance. Irresponsible, authoritarian, abusive, and neglectful parenting styles create relational chaos!

People with *secure* attachment styles have experienced balanced, healthy relationships and

RELATIONSHIP SKILLS 101 (cont.)

believe that closeness is no threat to individuality and healthy independence.

Of course, we rarely fit neatly into one category or another, but these guidelines can be helpful in identifying what needs to change in our relationship patterns.

The most important point is that good relationships and healthy bonds feature a balance between intimacy and individuality. The dependency paradox says that when people learn to be effectively *de*pendent, they become more independent. Perfect independence is an illusion. We're social beings, and we need attachments. We are ideally *inter*dependent, not independent and not co-dependent.

Here are a few steps to get you started in the relationship-building process:

1. Read about relationships. First of all, the Bible is full of teachings on how to love successfully. Second, good self-help books can open your mind to relationship principles and help build your knowledge base, not to mention making you an interesting person to talk to. (See the suggested reading section below.)

2. Choose relationships wisely. Make the best judgment call you can regarding whom you trust. Ask yourself, "Is this person humble, honest, caring, a person of integrity?" Ask yourself also, "Do we communicate well together?" Pray over the matter of relationships. Let God guide the process. Trust and intimacy always require risk, but we can minimize the risk by using our heads.

3. Be proactive. Assert yourself without being pushy. Invite the person on a hike or other activity. Express an interest in them, but wait to see if that interest is reciprocated before pushing forward. Ask them appropriate questions about themselves, and see if they reciprocate. Relationships require a back-and-forth dynamic.

4. Give a bite-sized version of your story. Learn to tell people a concise version of yourself. I recommend that people have a one-sentence version for strangers, a one-paragraph version for acquaintances, a one-page version for friends, and maybe a one-book version for the person they marry.

5. Learn to converse. For more help in this area, see the "Social Skills 101" document. Remember that conversation forms the basis of relationships. Learn to listen well, but don't lapse into tight-lipped passivity. Share yourself too. Check out the "Establishing Empathy with E.A.R." document for help with listening skills.

6. Affirm the relationship. Once the relationship is developing into a long-term bond, discover ways of affirming and celebrating it. Consider reading *The Five Love Languages* and discover which love languages communicate well to both you and your relationship partner: words of affirmation, quality time, receiving gifts, acts of service, and physical touch.

7. Relax. God is in control. He made you for love, and He'll help you form healthy relationships. If a human relationship fails, it's not the end of the world. Use cognitive behavioral exercises (see the F.A.R. Thought Control document) to correct catastrophized interpretations of bad experiences. Remember that relationship building is a high-risk, difficult business.

OK, now that you have some ideas on how to move forward, start flexing those muscles!

Suggested reading:
The Five Love Languages by Gary Chapman
Love Is a Verb by Gary Chapman
The Relationship Principles of Jesus by Tom Holladay
Loving People by Dr. John Townsend
How to Get Along With Others by Ellen G. White
Lonely? by Ruth Buntain
Many Are Cold and a Few are Frozen by A. J. Raitt

SOCIAL SKILLS 101

T O O L B O X

For various reasons, many of us are socially undeveloped. This can lead to isolation, which has been correlated with a host of problems including addictions, abuse, depression, and physical health issues. We were designed for connection, and we suffer without it. Fortunately, the principles of relationship formation are quite simple, universal, and within the reach of all.

Relationships begin with socializing, and socializing is about communication. Human beings are communicative creatures. God has given us complex systems for this purpose. For instance, we have ten groups of facial muscles that account for the multitude of expressions we make. Our voices are capable of subtle changes that reflect our many emotions. We are the only animal that has spoken and written languages. We have finely woven musculature that gives us the ability to talk in body language. You and I were made for communication!

When humans communicate, something of their inner life spills out and is taken in by another. The best communication involves reciprocity, or give and take. Think of your life as a banquet—you've been invited to an important event. You're not a nobody, or you wouldn't have received an invitation. There will be plenty of other important and interesting people there too. Get ready for the banquet by attending to etiquette, grooming, and conversation.

Etiquette

Some of us are terrified of this word because we fear a list of detailed behavioral rules that we will never be able to memorize, much less follow. Actually, true etiquette is simply based on the principles of love and respect for all human beings. Jesus conveyed the essence of true etiquette when He said, "Treat others the same way you want them to treat you" (Luke 6:31, NASB). Etiquette is simply serving others. The following are some simple practices that illustrate this:

- Opening the door for another
- Treating the elderly with extra care and tenderness
- Saying "Please" and "Thank you"
- Watching out for children
- Addressing others as "Ma'am" and "Sir"

Being courteous won't always elicit the same response, but, most of the time, polite treatment results in others treating you politely. This creates a social environment in which good communication can take place. It also builds your social confidence as you see yourself having a positive impact on people.

Grooming

We might be tempted to think that the way we present ourselves isn't really important in the grand scheme of things; but good grooming communicates positive social interest and self-respect. Part of good etiquette is giving others, in ourselves, someone who is clean and tidy. A person who doesn't attempt to look pleasant to the eye and who doesn't take care to be clean conveys a lack of self-respect and elicits pity. Ask yourself the following questions objectively:

- Do my clothes look sloppy, torn, and dirty?
- Does my hair look dirty or unkempt?
- How do I smell to other people?

Even the poorest of people can be clean and tidy, so start scrubbing! Brush your teeth regularly and use mouthwash. It's the polite thing to do. Plus, you'll feel better about yourself and more socially presentable.

Conversation

Remember the golden rule as you enter a social situation, and treat others as you would like to be treated.

The primary means of social communication is the conversation. It may seem that technology is threatening to drive the simple one-on-one, face-to-face conversation into extinction, but the person with good conversation skills is still at an advantage in all areas of life including his or her vocation, social life, spirituality, and mental and physical health.

A good conversation involves give and take, listening and speaking, flowing back and forth like a wave on the beach. It is tiring to do all of the talking, but also very tiring to do all of the listening. In contrast, good communication is energizing rather than tiring.

Conversation typically works in layers. Let's say you're meeting a person for the first time. You don't want to open the conversation with, "So, have you ever been in love? I mean really, deeply in love?" The person will run the other way! Think of a person as an onion with layers. At first the conversation is superficial, but, as trust builds, it may deepen. Here are the typical layers of conversation:

Outer layer. These are events, conditions, and situations both people share. The following are some examples:

- The weather (Don't belittle the power of talking about the weather! It's a great start!)
- Local news

SOCIAL SKILLS 101 (cont.)

- The current situation such as a delayed flight or a stalled elevator
- Recent world events, such as disasters, wars, and famines

Middle layer. These are thoughts, opinions, and observations. Here are some examples:

- Moral issues (Focus on universally agreed-upon concepts such as loyalty to family.)
- Truisms (Seeing a cute child and saying to a seatmate, "They grow up so fast.")
- Social trends ("It seems like people are increasingly tense because of terrorism.")
- Reflections on recent events

Inner layer. These are personal feelings and experiences. Here are some examples:

- Children in your life (yours or others' whom you connect with)
- Pets you love
- Monumental events such as getting married or graduating
- Spiritual beliefs
- Personal information (where you live, what you do, marital status)

Balance putting out your own thoughts with drawing out the thoughts of others. Provided that things don't get too personal too quickly, people generally like to talk about themselves. Show an interest in them, and, in most cases, they will open up.

Starting a conversation can be the hardest point. One of the most effective ways to start a conversation employs the same give-and-take principle. Typically, one gives out some bit of information or opinion and elicits a response.

Some examples of conversation starters:

- "It's a gorgeous day outside! Was it this nice last year at this time?"
- "The traffic out there is crazy. I think I'll take the subway more often."
- "Does anyone know if they caught the guy that lit the courthouse on fire?"
- "How do you like your Volkswagen? Does it get good gas mileage?"
- "Have you ever eaten at Bruno's? What did you think of it?"
- "Main Street is so full of potholes! Didn't I hear that the town voted to fix it?"

Notice that these starters generally make a statement, and then elicit a response. This way you put something out, but also show a desire to take something in. The idea is to get a flow of thoughts going back and forth. Remember that it's OK if such comments don't successfully start a conversation. You spoke up, which is an achievement in itself. With each attempt to socialize, you increase your talent for it.

Pay attention to your body language and posture. By putting yourself in a confident, relaxed stance you will tell your unconscious that you are indeed relaxed; with your shoulders back and posture erect, breathe deep (this oxygenates your brain and supports your voice), hold your chin level (this shows self-respect but not arrogance), smile slightly (seeing a smile relaxes people), and unclench your fists.

Remember to think in terms of being a guest at a banquet. You're not the star of the show, but you are an important person. God has invited you to the banquet of social life on planet Earth.

As the talk starts to flow, remember to balance between giving and receiving, sharing yourself and asking the other person to share themselves. Remember the onion. Begin more cognitively by asking their opinions, thoughts, or observations. As trust develops, you can progress to feelings, beliefs, and personal experiences.

At some point in the conversation, you will want to introduce yourself and ask the other person's name. This is generally done with a handshake but not always. It is always nice to say, "Nice to meet you," after exchanging names.

Because listening is so essential to good conversation, shy people actually have more of an edge in the art of conversation than they realize. Use reflection, or summarizing back to the person what you have heard him or her say. This will capitalize on your listening skills while still keeping you active in the conversation. It is extremely gratifying to be understood well, and it often entices the person to talk more. For instance, a conversation might go like this:

YOU: So the food was good even though the service was poor.
PERSON: Yes. The dessert made it almost worth waiting for.
YOU: Really? What did you have?
PERSON: Strawberry shortcake like I have never had before.
YOU: What was so special about it?
PERSON: It had this very light shortcake with fresh strawberries in a tangy, sweet sauce, and it was smothered with whipped cream.
YOU: I'm getting hungry just listening to you. I hate to tell you, but my aunt Betty's peach cobbler might be even better.
PERSON: Oh, yeah? Does she make it often?
YOU: Well, she lives in Georgia, so I don't see her often.
PERSON: Is that where you're from?

SOCIAL SKILLS 101 (cont.)

Notice that your summarizing and questions drew out the person and made him or her feel safe to ask questions too. The conversation flowed from food to home state in a matter of a few seconds.

Closing the conversation is another essential skill. Awkward, abrupt closes may leave someone feeling snubbed or brushed off. Some people are too passive to end a conversation, even when they have a pressing appointment. Remember that when you must move on from a conversation, a simple statement that you enjoyed speaking with the person will do much to smooth things over. If you would like to keep the relationship open, you might indicate that you'd like to talk more in the future. Here are some suggested closing lines:

- "I have an appointment, but I'm enjoying our talk. Perhaps we'll talk again some time."
- "It has been good to meet you. Hopefully, we'll bump into each other again."
- Simply extending your hand for a handshake is often a good way to end a conversation.

As you forge ahead in the development of social skills, remember that practice makes perfect. You will make mistakes, but so does everybody. In time and with consistent effort, along with the blessing of God, you will see results you never dreamed possible.

The words *soul* and *spirit* each have multiple shades of nuanced, subtle meaning. Often these meanings overlap.

Spirit

The Hebrew word *ruach* and the Greek counterpart *pneuma* each have three essential ways in which they are used. First, the spirit can simply be the life force or vital essence that animates a being.

- "God split the hollow place that is in Lehi, and water came out, and he drank; and his spirit returned, and he revived" (Judges 15:19).
- "No one has power over the spirit to retain the spirit, and no one has power in the day of death. There is no release from that war, and wickedness will not deliver those who are given to it" (Ecclesiastes 8:8).
- "Then her spirit returned, and she arose immediately. And He commanded that she be given something to eat" (Luke 8:55).

Second, the spirit can be the emotional state, disposition, or influence that governs an individual.

- "Then everyone came whose heart was stirred, and everyone whose spirit was willing, and they brought the LORD's offering for the work of the tabernacle of meeting, for all its service, and for the holy garments" (Exodus 35:21).
- "But Hannah answered and said, 'No, my lord, I am a woman of sorrowful spirit. I have drunk neither wine nor intoxicating drink, but have poured out my soul before the LORD' " (1 Samuel 1:15).
- "For God has not given us a spirit of fear, but of power and of love and of a sound mind" (2 Timothy 1:7).

Finally, the spirit can be the part of an individual that connects with the spiritual world.

- "You have granted me life and favor, and Your care has preserved my spirit" (Job 10:12).
- "Blessed is the man to whom the LORD does not impute iniquity, and in whose spirit there is no deceit" (Psalm 32:2).
- "He who has knowledge spares his words, and a man of understanding is of a calm spirit" (Proverbs 17:27).

SPIRIT AND SOUL (cont.)

- "The end of a thing is better than its beginning; the patient in spirit is better than the proud in spirit" (Ecclesiastes 7:8).
- "These also who erred in spirit shall come to understanding, and those who complained will learn doctrine" (Isaiah 29:24).
- "Then I will give them one heart, and I will put a new spirit within them, and take the stony heart out of their flesh, and give them a heart of flesh" (Ezekiel 11:19).
- "Watch and pray, lest you enter into temptation. The spirit indeed is willing, but the flesh is weak" (Matthew 26:41).
- "So the child grew and became strong in spirit, and was in the deserts till the day of his manifestation to Israel" (Luke 1:80).
- "Deliver such a one to Satan for the destruction of the flesh, that his spirit may be saved in the day of the Lord Jesus" (1 Corinthians 5:5).

Soul

The Hebrew and Greek words most often translated as "soul" are, respectively, *nephesh* and *psuche*. Like the word *spirit, soul* can refer to the life force, although this usage is rare.

- "And so it was, as her soul was departing (for she died), that she called his name Ben-Oni; but his father called him Benjamin" (Genesis 35:18).
- "He stretched himself out on the child three times, and cried out to the LORD and said, 'O LORD my God, I pray, let this child's soul come back to him' " (1 King 17:21).

There are also relatively rare times when *soul* simply means "a being."

- "The LORD God formed man of the dust of the ground, and breathed into his nostrils the breath of life; and man became a living soul" (Genesis 2:7, KJV).

Soul can refer to the inner life, personality, or character of a person.

- "Do not fear those who kill the body but cannot kill the soul. But rather fear Him who is able to destroy both soul and body in hell" (Matthew 10:28).

The majority of the times that either *nephesh* or *psuche* are used, it is in reference to this inner life. For instance, Jesus said, "My soul is exceedingly sorrowful, even to death" (Matthew 26:38); yet He promised us "rest for your souls" (Matthew 11:29), and indeed "He restores my soul" (Psalm 23:3).

W. E. Vine puts it this way: "The spirit may be recognized as the life principle bestowed on man by God, the soul as the resulting life constituted in the individual, the body being the material organism animated by soul and spirit."[1]

---

1. W. E. Vine, *Vine's Expository Dictionary of Old and New Testament Words* (Nashville, Tenn.: Thomas Nelson, 1997), 1067.

SUMMARY OF CURRENT COUNSELING MODELS

This list is designed to educate, rather than advocate. I'm not recommending a particular modality but simply helping you understand "what's out there."

Cognitive Behavioral Therapy (CBT)
- A method of thought control
- Proven to help mood regulation
- Focuses on changing irrational thoughts

Mood improves when thought life improves. The origins of CBT were humanistic, but CBT can be done biblically. It was designed as a brief therapy with quick results and may not address deep, developmentally acquired problems or relational problems.

Psychodynamic/Psychoanalytic
- Aims at revealing the unconscious
- Focuses on the dynamics of a client's family and/or childhood
- Uses transference therapeutically

Early life experience has a telling, lasting influence. People often repeat in present relationships the patterns of childhood relationships (transference). Connecting the dots between the past and present can be a first step toward change. However, psychodynamic therapy can sometimes lead people to overblame and wallow in the past.

Client-Centered Therapy
- Focuses on a warm therapeutic relationship
- Fosters a safe environment in that relationship
- Practices unconditional positive regard
- Nondirective, lets the client lead

Empathy is powerful to heal. Often the acceptance and kind listening ear of a counselor or mentor is the most therapeutic aspect of counseling. But some client-centered therapists listen passively when they could provide direction. The foundations of client-centered therapy are humanistic, based on the idea that humans possess innate goodness.

Substance Abuse Therapy
- Replaces addiction with better coping skill
- Often uses the twelve-step model

Most drug and alcohol rehab programs encourage the use of twelve-step groups. Twelve-step groups outnumber churches. The effect of the movement can't be calculated. Its effectiveness is attributable to biblical principles such as personal accountability, self-knowledge, and trust in an outside Source of power. That power tends to be subjectively defined rather than based on an authoritative revelation of God.

Motivational Interviewing (MI)
- Teaches a person to chose for himself or herself
- Aims to uncover a person's ambivalence about his or her addiction or problem
- Involves cost-benefit and pro-con evaluations

Moses used this approach when he put before the children of Israel the blessings and curses and their respective consequences, telling them to choose for themselves (Deuteronomy 30). MI emphasizes respect of the individual and his or her free will.

Feminist Therapy
- Aims to empower women
- Focuses on power disparities in relationships

Globally, women suffer from disproportionate oppression. One in three women in the world has been raped, coerced into sex, or beaten. Some feminist ideas rightly try to correct this inequity and impart to women life skills that help them rise above these setbacks. Feminist therapy focuses on helping women learn assertiveness and equality.

Creative Therapies
- Uses the arts
- Promotes self-awareness
- Processes trauma
- Helps those who have difficulty verbalizing

Creative therapies give nonverbal people a chance to express themselves and be heard and understood by another person. It can be difficult to quantify the degree of benefit from these methods.

Somatic/Body Therapies
- Works to address "bodily" memory of trauma
- Helps client to identify physical tension

The body affects the mind. All dimensions of human nature overlap and interrelate. Physical suffering and tension can affect mood. Some of the somatic therapies use pseudoscience and tend toward spiritualism.

Solution-Focused Therapy
- Focuses on client's strengths versus problems
- Uses goal statements
- Uses psychoeducation (educating client about psychology)
- Collaborative relationship with therapist

Counseling can often become too problem focused. Each person has strengths and resources that should be capitalized on. Psychoeducation involves learning principles of psychology and good self-care, and can be helpful and encouraging. But care should be taken to choose good materials.

Narrative Therapy
- Involves retelling life story
- Involves some reframing, or CBT

Narrative therapy encourages people to re-write their life story. People often benefit from seeing their life experience through a more positive lens. Unfortunately, narrative therapy uses a very relativistic model in which reality is subjective. A fictitious re-write of my life story may give me some positive feelings—but will probably lose its benefit over time.

Holistic Therapy
- Recognizes the body-mind connection
- Addresses diet, lifestyle, and physical illness

Physical health impacts mental health. In fact, humans have a three-part nature of body, soul, and spirit, in which each dimension intimately overlaps with the others. Helpers do well to address the effects of diet; exercise; and consumption of stimulants, narcotics, and alcohol on mental health. Holistic therapy may imbibe certain New Age ideas, or it may fail to address spiritual issues at all.

TEACHING CHILDREN TO CHOOSE

Often parents use ineffective means to bring about desired behaviors in their children:

- Pleading
- Bargaining
- Lashing out
- Withdrawing
- Coercing

What kids need most from their parents is help in connecting the dots between bad behavior and bad consequences. This worksheet presents a simple method that should bring about the desired clarity. It's taken from a story in the Bible. God is the ultimate Parent, and we see how He dealt with the children of Israel.

Just before Moses died, with care and compassion, he told the children of Israel that obedience would result in blessings and disobedience with curses. Then he listed the respective blessings and curses. The curses especially he listed in great detail. It's as if he wanted the people to see the complete picture of how bad things would be if they made poor choices.

Once finished with the speech, Moses said, "I have set before you life and death, blessing cursing; therefore choose life, that both you and your descendants may live" (Deuteronomy 30:19).

This is how Moses structured his speech:

- A clear identification of desired behavior
- A clear identification of undesired behavior
- The rewards of good behavior
- The punishments of bad behavior
- An appeal to do the right thing

Parents today might state Moses' simple outline this way:

- "I want you to do this . . ."
- "I don't want you to do this . . ."
- "If you obey, this will happen . . ."
- "If you disobey, this will happen . . ."
- "Now, you choose."

TEACHING CHILDREN TO CHOOSE (cont.)

Think of this process as the acronym DURPA:

- **D**esired behavior
- **U**ndesired behavior
- **R**ewards
- **P**unishments
- **A**ppeal

Parents can implement this very approach with their children. When they do, the punishment or reward is actually chosen by the child, rather than imposed by the parent. Ideally, consequences match the behavior. For instance, watching too much TV would lead to losing TV privileges, getting ready for school early would be rewarded with a quick stop at the store on the way to school, and so on.

Here are some examples: "Sammy, I've asked you to keep your rabbit outside. You've brought him in several times, and he leaves a mess on the floor. If you put him outside right now, and keep him outside, you can keep your rabbit. If you bring him inside, you'll have to vacuum the floor and clean up any excrement he leaves. If you do bring him inside three more times, I'll get rid of him. Now, what is your choice?"

"Bryan, I've asked you to get in the car. You're still sitting there in the chair. If you get in the car right now, we'll stop for a sandwich on the way home from the doctor's office. If you stay in the chair, I'll take away your television privileges for twenty-four hours. What's your choice?"

"Jenna, I've asked you to leave the Wii off until all of us have finished eating dinner. You've turned it on now. If you turn the Wii off and stay at the table with us, we'll finish dinner and then you can use it for thirty minutes. If you keep the Wii on, I'll come turn it off for you and you'll lose Wii privileges for the rest of the evening. What's your choice?"

In some cases, you'll want to offer a special reward for good behavior. Use your judgment as a parent on this. Usually, when something difficult or unpleasant is imposed on the child, such as going to the doctor, a small reward is in order. Special treats are not in order, however, when the desired behavior is simply expected, normal, or routine, such as exercising manners or simple consideration for others.

The beauty of this approach is that it leaves the child free to choose. Freedom is essential to growth. Some parents attempt to force children to obey; some don't govern them at all. Many parents go back and forth between authoritarian "bossiness" and giving up the reins completely. Children quickly learn how to bring their parents to the breaking point. The goal with DURPA is to help children learn to recognize the relationship between choice and consequence and to make good choices for themselves. This prepares them for the responsibilities of adult life.

Be prepared to back up your words with action. Make sure consequences are doable. Don't get fatigued. Once you say you'll do something, follow through. At first, the child will resist, but he or she will come to expect the consequence and will give less resistance as you exercise consistency.

This method often produces fantastic, remarkable results.

TOOLBOX

USING YOUR (AVERAGE) TALENTS

Many feel unmotivated to serve because they have no exceptional talents. "Anything I could do, someone else could do better," they say. But they forget that serving God isn't about being the best; it's about being blessed and blessing others. God's field is a vast place in which every person has a meaningful part to play. In fact, most of the positions in God's kingdom are best served by average people!

So many say, "I have no talents!" Oh, but you do. These talents are intelligence, speech, influence, time, health, strength, money, and affections. Review this list and check the points that you can use more effectively.

Intelligence

All have some intellectual abilities. Consider building your brain by teaching others what you know. You can volunteer to teach a class at the local church or library. Door-to-door Bible instruction is a fruitful and honorable service. Preparing a newsletter for the local church or another organization will be a blessing to many.

Use your **intelligence** well:

- ☐ Faithfully cultivate your mind by reading daily.
- ☐ Study the Bible every day—it's a great brain builder.
- ☐ Read one Proverb a day and put it in your own words.
- ☐ Do crossword puzzles or other puzzles.
- ☐ Limit entertainment media.
- ☐ Call people to discuss a specific topic and get their opinion.
- ☐ Teach classes when opportunities arise.
- ☐ Speak in complete sentences, clearly, and with a point.
- ☐ Converse with people about ideas rather than simply about events or people.

Speech

Conversing with people, turning the conversation toward hopeful, cheerful things, and ultimately toward God, is a ministry. Simply going about your daily tasks and choosing to converse with people in an uplifting manner can create a powerful influence for good. When given an opportunity to give a formal testimony in a church setting, do so even if you have nothing remarkable to say. You don't know who might be reached!

Use your **gift of speech** well:

☐ Speak in complete sentences, clearly, and with a point.
☐ Choose to speak most of the time about uplifting, positive things.
☐ Address negative things positively, offering solutions or hope.
☐ Eliminate curse words; limit repetitive expressions, such as "whatever," and slang words.
☐ Take opportunities to teach or preach.
☐ Engage in meaningful conversations whenever opportunities arise.
☐ Be courteous, using expressions such as Thank you and Please consistently.
☐ Address strangers as "Ma'am" and "Sir."
☐ Use a musical, happy tone in your voice.
☐ Project your voice and speak very clearly—don't make listening an effort.

Influence

Everyone has an influence. Through friendships, work relationships, relationships with loved ones, and even casual relationships with service people, neighbors, and the scores of contacts we make in a lifetime, we shed an influence. That influence can contribute to God's work in the world—or to the enemy's. Begin each day with a prayer that your influence will further God's kingdom.

Use your **influence** well:

☐ Smile—your face will brighten the room.
☐ Talk and act faith, and you'll encourage others' faith.
☐ Avoid gossip.
☐ Gently move conversations toward uplifting themes.
☐ Sing beautiful uplifting songs.
☐ Whistle beautiful songs—particularly familiar hymns.
☐ When dealing with an angry person, speak softly and kindly.
☐ Use reflective listening when conversing with people.
☐ Memorize Bible passages and repeat them when they apply to a situation.
☐ Speak a word of encouragement to the discouraged.

Time

Everyone has the exact same number of minutes in a day. It helps to have your day and week planned out in advance. While there will be exceptions and special circumstances, try to allow specific amounts of time for activities. Beware of major time drainers, such as mass media, shopping, and even long conversations.

USING YOUR (AVERAGE) TALENTS (cont.)

Use your **time** well:

☐ Begin each day with God.
☐ Buy a datebook and use it.
☐ Follow a regular schedule for routine activities, such as eating, showering, etc.
☐ Use the alarm system on your e-mail program and/or smartphone.
☐ Buy a headset for your phone so you do household tasks while talking.
☐ Learn how to delegate—get over the idea you have to do it all yourself.
☐ Watch out for time drainers, such as mass media, shopping, daydreaming, and magazines.
☐ Before accepting job positions and work assignments, pray.
☐ Learn how to say No.
☐ Avoid developing situational acquired ADD by overusing cell phones, computer, and other electronic devices.

Health

We often don't realize the blessing of health until we lose it. God created us "fearfully and wonderfully" (Psalm 139:14). If you are young, don't think you're immortal and won't have the health problems older people have. You will! Take good care of yourself starting now. Follow "The Eight Doctors" document (found in the toolbox).

Use your **health** well:

☐ Share your health practices with people you meet.
☐ Offer to give them favorite recipes using healthful foods.
☐ Share the titles of health books and even loan them out.
☐ Invite people to any nutrition and wellness classes you may know about.
☐ Join, or lead, an exercise class at your local church—even a walking club is helpful.
☐ Avoid anything that would hurt your physical health.
☐ Learn about the body; even read through anatomy and physiology books.

Strength

A healthy lifestyle includes a strong work ethic. God has given us the power to accomplish great things for Him. As Thomas Edison pointed out, genius is 1 percent inspiration and 99 percent perspiration. Good health requires that we put effort forth according to the strength God has bestowed.

Use your **strength** well:

- [ ] Plan your life, obtain a good education for the field of service you wish to enter.
- [ ] Focus your energy and bring tasks to completion.
- [ ] Balance strength of body, mind, and spirit; don't be an egghead or a meathead.
- [ ] Identify and develop natural abilities, whether writing, music, craftsmanship, and so on.
- [ ] Weave Christian principles into all your secular business.
- [ ] Share Jesus in the marketplace.
- [ ] Use wise management principles.

Money

God gives us power to get wealth. The moment we think our money is our own, it can become a barrier to our relationship with God. See your means as a gift from God even if your own blood, sweat, and tears earned it. We would have nothing and be nothing without Him. We merely exercise stewardship over the world that belongs to Him.

Use your **money** well:

- [ ] Keep track of your finances monthly; a simple ledger will do.
- [ ] Avoid debt.
- [ ] If in debt, use wise principles to pay it off.
- [ ] Money has value because it can do good—invest in God's kingdom.
- [ ] Make money with money, but don't fall prey to scams.
- [ ] Be frugal without being ridiculous.
- [ ] Tithe 10 percent of your net income.
- [ ] Give 10 percent of your net income as offering, and more as you are able.
- [ ] Spend less on self-indulgence and more on needy people.
- [ ] Pay other peoples' way sometimes.
- [ ] Give meaningful gifts to people.

Affection

Our kind and generous impulses, our ability to love and be loved, can be used for God's glory or for building our own selfish cliques. The person who allows principle to direct the affections of his or her heart reflects Jesus to a dark, lonely world.

Use your **affection** well:

- [ ] Hug people, especially elderly people.
- [ ] Be kind to grouchy people.

USING YOUR (AVERAGE) TALENTS (cont.)

☐ Give compliments.
☐ Lovingly encourage people.
☐ Smile.
☐ Say, "I love you."
☐ Invite people over for lunch after church.
☐ Be willing to entertain strangers; house out-of-town guests.
☐ Sit in a different place in church every week and mingle with your "neighbors."
☐ Sit with strangers at potlucks and other gatherings.

Here are a few practical suggestions for volunteer opportunities in which you can use your God-given talents:

Church ministries. Church is an excellent environment for the use of talents. Often churches offer multiple ministry opportunities, such as food and clothing banks, Bible study programs, door-to-door programs, various classes, and other events.

Community organizations. Homeless shelters, food banks, state parks, hospitals, nursing homes, and animal shelters often welcome volunteers.

National volunteer programs. Organizations such as Big Brothers and Big Sisters line up volunteer tutors with students. There are a number of organizations that work in disaster relief, crisis hotlines, and so on. Try going to http://www.volunteermatch.org to find a suitable place to volunteer.

Short-term mission trips. Maranatha Volunteers International takes groups to build churches and schools in developing countries. ShareHim organizes worldwide evangelism. Often speaking or singing in a developing country is less frightening than doing it at home! These are two examples of numerous options.

WHAT ARE YOUR FAVORITE FIG LEAVES?

As soon as Adam and Eve fell, they felt guilty and ashamed and "knew that they were naked." Quickly, they "sewed fig leaves together and made themselves coverings" (Genesis 3:7). This provided a temporary relief from their disturbed feelings.

Meditation: In a sense, self-justification is the original sin. Yes, in their innocence, the pair partook of the fruit—the first sin ever committed by humans. But self-justification was humanity's first sinful response to the sin problem and is therefore the first sin committed by fallen humans. It was inconceivable that they should eat the fruit, but it's entirely conceivable that we try to cover our nakedness. In other words, since the Fall, self-righteousness comes to us naturally. But our fig leaves compound the sin problem. Perhaps they provide temporary relief from the dissonance of sin, but they are sinful in and of themselves. And most of all, they minimize the problem by minimizing the solution. Sin is a God-sized problem, and only a God-sized solution will fix it.

Self-justification comes in many forms. We use countless kinds of fig leaves to cover our souls. They all come from our desire to fix ourselves, to right what's wrong, to make ourselves worthy. And they all fail. Here is a list of common fig leaves, reprinted from chapter 2:

- Legalism—trying to save ourselves by obedience and works of the law.
- Rationalism—making excuses for sin through argument and false reasoning.
- Hedonism—pursuing pleasure to avoid pain and drown the conscience.
- Materialism—acquiring riches as a means of feeling worthy and building pride.
- Narcissism—exhibiting vanity and pride; exaltation over others as a means of feeling worthy.
- Emotionalism—seeking the ultimate relationship or emotional state.
- Achievism—setting and fulfilling goals as a means of achieving worthiness.
- Egotism—replacing the desire for God's approval with the approval of others.
- Perfectionism—doing things precisely and perfectly to alleviate a sense of dissonance.
- Nihilism—obsession with death and self-destruction; atonement through self-punishment.
- Other _____
- Other _____
- Other _____

Action Step: Underline your personal favorite fig leaves (there will probably be several) from this list. Add your own if you can think of others. Then number them in order of preference, putting the most central ones first. The purpose is to become aware of the ways in which we defend against God's goodness and prevent the successful assimilation of the righteousness of Christ.

WHAT ARE YOUR FAVORITE FIG LEAVES? (cont.)

List your fig leaves here, with specific examples of how you use them. Then try to explain the consequences of them. For example:

Fig leaf: *Materialism. I feel compelled to become wealthy. Money makes me feel good about myself. I put the pursuit of money before God. As a result, my spirituality suffers and I feel as if I'm going through the motions.*

Fig leaf 1:

Fig leaf 2:

Fig leaf 3:

Fig leaf 4:

Fig leaf 5:

Fig leaf 6:

Fig leaf 7:

WHAT ARE YOUR FAVORITE FIG LEAVES? (cont.)

Meditation: Read the following Bible verses and Ellen G. White quotations, out loud if possible. After reading, use the blank space below to restate what you read, putting it in your own words. Also, make it personal by inserting your own name. An example is given.

- "For they being ignorant of God's righteousness, and seeking to establish their own righteousness, have not submitted to the righteousness of God" (Romans 10:3).

  When I, Jennifer, am ignorant of God's way of fixing me, I run around trying to fix myself.

- "Most men will proclaim each his own goodness, but who can find a faithful man?" (Proverbs 20:6).

- "There is a generation that is pure in its own eyes, yet is not washed from its filthiness" (Proverbs 30:12).

- "We are all like an unclean thing, and all our righteousnesses are like filthy rags; we all fade as a leaf, and our iniquities, like the wind, have taken us away" (Isaiah 64:6).

- "And He said to them, 'You are those who justify yourselves before men, but God knows your hearts. For what is highly esteemed among men is an abomination in the sight of God' " (Luke 16:15).

WHAT ARE YOUR FAVORITE FIG LEAVES? (cont.)

- "Because you say, 'I am rich, have become wealthy, and have need of nothing'—and do not know that you are wretched, miserable, poor, blind, and naked—I counsel you to buy from Me gold refined in the fire, that you may be rich; and white garments, that you may be clothed, that the shame of your nakedness may not be revealed; and anoint your eyes with eye salve, that you may see" (Revelation 3:17, 18).

- "Nothing but the righteousness of Christ can entitle us to one of the blessings of the covenant of grace. There are many who have long desired and tried to obtain these blessings, but have not received them, because they have cherished the idea that they could do something to make themselves worthy of them. . . . Christ is our only hope of salvation."[1]

- "Rest is found when all self-justification, all reasoning from a selfish standpoint, is put away. Entire self-surrender, an acceptance of His ways, is the secret of perfect rest in His love. . . . Do just what He has told you to do and be assured that God will do all that He has said He would do. . . . Have you come to Him, renouncing all your makeshifts, all your unbelief, all your self-righteousness? Come just as you are, weak, helpless, and ready to die."[2]

Action Step: Now take these fig leaves you have personalized one by one and renounce them before God in prayer.

---

1. Ellen G. White, *Patriarchs and Prophets* (Mountain View, Calif.: Pacific Press®, 1958), 431.
2. White, *Mind, Character, and Personality*, 2:802.

IF YOU'RE SEARCHING FOR PEACE, THESE BOOKS CAN HELP!

Blessings
by Jerry D. Thomas

Ellen G. White's timeless classic *Thoughts From the Mount of Blessing* is now available in this contemporary adaptation, bringing the powerful yet simple truths of the original to the world of the twenty-first century. Christ's teachings amazed the humble and confused the proud back then. They still do today. Allow the stories and teachings that thrilled the simple country folk of Galilee to bless your life and awaken hope and love in your heart as well.

Hardcover with dust jacket, 144 Pages
ISBN 13: 978-0-8163-2284-8
ISBN 10: 0-8163-2284-8

Hooked on Unhappiness
by Carol Cannon, MA, CADC

Do you find yourself in a bad mood more often than not? Are you critical of everyone and everything around you? Do you dwell on painful memories? When someone says, "Good morning," do you think, *What's good about it?* If so, this book could change your life by breaking the cycle of discontent.

Paperback, 192 pages
ISBN 13: 978-0-8163-2260-2
ISBN 10: 0-8163-2260-0

Pacific Press®
Publishing Association
"Where the Word Is Life"

Three ways to order:

1	Local	Adventist Book Center®
2	Call	1-800-765-6955
3	Shop	AdventistBookCenter.com